ITALY IN CRISIS
1494

THE EUROPEAN HUMANITIES RESEARCH CENTRE

UNIVERSITY OF OXFORD

The European Humanities Research Centre of the University of Oxford organizes a range of academic activities, including conferences and workshops, and publishes scholarly works under its own imprint, LEGENDA. Within Oxford, the EHRC bridges, at the research level, the main humanities faculties: Modern Languages, English, Modern History, Literae Humaniores, Music and Theology. The Centre stimulates interdisciplinary research collaboration throughout these subject areas and provides an Oxford base for advanced researchers in the humanities.

The Centre's publications programme focuses on making available the results of advanced research in medieval and modern languages and related interdisciplinary areas. An Editorial Board, whose members are drawn from across the British university system, covers the principal European languages. Titles include works on French, German, Italian, Portuguese, Russian and Spanish literature. In addition, the EHRC co-publishes with the Society for French Studies, the British Comparative Literature Association and the Modern Humanities Research Association. The Centre also publishes *Oxford German Studies* and *Film Studies*, and has launched a Special Lecture Series under the LEGENDA imprint.

Enquiries about the Centre's publishing activities should be addressed to:
Professor Malcolm Bowie, Director

Further information:
Kareni Bannister, Senior Publications Officer
European Humanities Research Centre
University of Oxford
47 Wellington Square, Oxford OX1 2JF
enquiries@ehrc.ox.ac.uk
www.ehrc.ox.ac.uk

LEGENDA

EUROPEAN HUMANITIES RESEARCH CENTRE
MODERN HUMANITIES RESEARCH ASSOCIATION

Italy in Crisis
1494

EDITED BY

JANE EVERSON AND DIEGO ZANCANI

LEGENDA

European Humanities Research Centre, University of Oxford
Modern Humanities Research Association
2000

Published by the
European Humanities Research Centre
of the University of Oxford
47 Wellington Square
Oxford OX1 2JF
in conjunction with the Modern Humanities Research Association

LEGENDA is the publications imprint of the
European Humanities Research Centre

ISBN 1 900755 13 0

First published 2000

British Library Cataloguing in Publication Data
A CIP catalogue record for this book is available from the British Library

© 2000 European Humanities Research Centre of the University of Oxford
and the Modern Humanities Research Association

LEGENDA series designed by Cox Design Partnership, Witney, Oxon
Printed in Great Britain by
Information Press
Eynsham
Oxford OX8 1JJ

Copy-Editor: Dr Bonnie Blackburn

CONTENTS

ACKNOWLEDGEMENTS

We would like to thank the Institute of Romance Studies, University of London, for hosting the original conference, organized in the context of international celebrations for the quincentenary of Boiardo's death, at which some of the papers were presented, and in particular Simona Cain for her efficient support. The Comune of Reggio-Emilia also gave its moral support in the form of a welcoming telegram to the participants. Our sincere thanks go to all those who have contributed with their expertise to the publication of this volume; in particular we thank Dr Valentina Olivastri for her joyful and effective support and her computer skills. We also wish to express our gratitude to the Modern Humanities Research Association and the Department of Italian, Royal Holloway University of London for financial support towards the publication of this volume.

LIST OF CONTRIBUTORS

Peter Brand is Emeritus Professor of Italian, University of Edinburgh

Alison Brown is Honorary Research Fellow, Royal Holloway University of London

Remo Catani is Senior Lecturer in Italian, University College of Cardiff, University of Wales

Mark Davie is Senior Lecturer in Italian, University of Exeter

Marco Dorigatti is College Lecturer, St Peter's College, Oxford

Jane Everson is Senior Lecturer in Italian, Royal Holloway University of London

Martin McLaughlin is University Lecturer, University of Oxford, and Student of Christ Church, Oxford

Letizia Panizza is Honorary Research Fellow, Royal Holloway University of London

Denis V. Reidy is Head of the Italian and Modern Greek Section, British Library, London

Diego Zancani is Reader in Italian and Fellow of Balliol College, Oxford

INTRODUCTION

Jane Everson and Diego Zancani

1494 18 ottobre, ha fato intrata in Piacentia de note el Re de Franza [Charles VIII] con gran baldoria et tapeti et populo che cridava viva. Se crede che farà giustitia, se sarà patrono perché ha fato bone promissioni, ma za sarà lo steso gloria se ghe sarà mutatione de Stato, et me recordo de tute le promissioni del duca de Milano et poi le cose andarono pezo de prima et el popolo ge crede sempre.[1]

The words of the anonymous Piacentine writer neatly encapsulate the twin poles on which the essays of this volume focus, crisis and continuity. Like his more famous compatriots, Machiavelli and Guicciardini, the anonymous writer clearly considered the year 1494 to be both significant, marking change and crisis, and yet at the same time part of a well-established pattern of historical and political events in Italy in the later fifteenth century. This latter point, coming from an ordinary contemporary observer, also provides a nice justification for the commemoration of the whole decade rather than a single year. Unlike the anonymous diarist, however, the scope of this volume extends to a consideration of crisis and continuity not only from a historical perspective, but especially from a cultural one, and seeks to provide answers to questions such as how we define crisis and continuity, and how these phenomena manifest themselves in particular in the realm of culture. Some of the essays are devoted to an examination of the political and economic history of Florence at the end of the fifteenth century and to a discussion of currents of intellectual debate and fashionable ideas in the same period. These essays set the broader cultural context for those essays which are devoted to an examination of the work of individual authors, especially Pulci and Poliziano in Florence, and Boiardo in Ferrara. The long-term effects of some consequences of the year 1494 on one of these authors, Boiardo, is the subject of the last essay.

From the beginning of the sixteenth century the year 1494 and the invasion of Charles VIII were perceived by Italians as a watershed in their history. The point is made strongly by Francesco Guicciardini in the opening chapters of the *Storia d'Italia*:

> Ma le calamità d'Italia [. . .] cominciorono con tanto maggiore dispiacere e spavento negli animi degli uomini quanto le cose universali erano allora più liete e più felici [. . .] non aveva giammai sentito Italia tanta prosperità, né provato stato tanto desiderabile quanto era quello nel quale sicuramente si riposava l'anno della salute cristiana mille quattrocento novanta, e gli anni che a quello e prima e poi furono congiunti [. . .] (*Storia d'Italia* I, 1)

but it is echoed by other political observers, and equally strongly from within the world of literature and humanist culture. Matteo Maria Boiardo attributes the interruption of his major work, the *Orlando innamorato*, to the events of 1494, the beginning of the wars of Italy, in lines that are frequently quoted as emblematic of reactions to those events:

> Mentre che io canto, o Iddio redentore,
> Vedo la Italia tutta a fiamma e a foco
> Per questi Galli, che con gran valore
> Vengon per disertar non so che loco [. . .] (*O.I.* III, ix, 26)

but a similar trauma is evident in the works of other writers who, unlike Boiardo, who died in December 1494, struggled to continue their cultural activities against a background of warfare and depredations:

> Tanto n'offende la gallica nebbia
> ch'è scesa giù dell'Alpi aspre e maligne
> che il Tanaro, il Tesin, l'Adda e la Trebbia
> mostrano l'acque lor tutte sanguigne
> e ognor detto mi vien che cantar debbia
> d'arme e d'amore, cose vaghe e benigne
> ma la stagione è sì contraria al canto
> che ogni mio verso si risolve in pianto.[2]

Although the deaths in the autumn of 1494 of a number of important cultural figures cannot be causally linked to the French invasions, the sense of psychological trauma, of crisis—personal, political, and cultural—should not be underplayed. One of the chief reasons for the depth of reactions (especially by non-combatants) must surely be the fact that Charles's invasion occurred after many decades in which the Italian peninsula had been effectively free from foreign invasions and aggression, while, internally, endemic conflicts between states had been kept under control by the maintenance of the agreements of the Peace of Lodi. Indeed as Guicciardini's words stress, to Italians of his generation the period before 1494 seemed like a Golden Age when viewed from the perspective of the 1530s, after thirty years of warfare and increasing loss of autonomy.

The impact of the invasion on the political regimes of certain Italian states, including Florence, is well attested, but it was not a universal phenomenon. Ferrara, in contrast, suffered no such political revolution in 1494. From the purely political point of view, the notion of crisis is scarcely applicable to Ferrara in this decade, and it is significant that it was political writers based in or connected to Florence who promulgated the idea of crisis most vigorously. Nevertheless, not even in Florence can the political crisis of 1494 be attributed solely to the French invasion. The death of Lorenzo in 1492, the loss from Florentine and Italian politics of a consummate politician and diplomatist, and the succession of Piero, his much less gifted son, had already begun to provoke anxiety and unease in Florence well before the negotiations with Charles and rumours of his invasion. This same sense of anxiety lent itself to Savonarola's moral crusade, which in turn provoked a sense of trauma, of soul-searching among leading players in the Medici cultural elite, evident in the changing opinions and attitudes of scholars and artists, and monitored especially in their reactions to Savonarola himself. On the political front, as Alison Brown demonstrates, opposition to the Medici had been building up slowly but inexorably through the last years of Lorenzo's regime, and can, for certain aspects, be traced back even to 1478 and the aftermath of the Pazzi conspiracy. The coincidence of the first French invasion with the political and economic crisis in Florence thus is precisely that—a coincidence, an instance of *fortuna*— since, as Brown suggests, political crisis, rooted in opposition to the Medici, and Lorenzo especially, was coming to a head quite independently of international events. Moreover, the cultural changes in Florence in the 1490s had similarly been growing through the later years of Lorenzo's regime and indeed had been stimulated by Lorenzo himself, not least through his invitation to Savonarola to settle in Florence. Thus the idea of a watershed year, 1494, even for Florence, is better replaced by that of a watershed decade, the 1490s, or better still, by the concept of *fin de siècle*, expressive of a deeply felt, but as yet not fully articulated, sense of conflicting pressures in culture and society, of culmination and conclusion, of a vague desire for change and innovation provoked by the ending of one century and the beginning of another, a mixture of celebration of the present and anxiety about the future, and the need to face new challenges, not least in the form of new discoveries and technologies.

And yet we should be wary of denying altogether the contemporary perception of this year as a year of crisis and its terrible events as liminal, dividing before from after. As early as the summer of 1495 and the immediate aftermath of the battle of Fornovo, the invasion of Charles VIII, and the subsequent campaign against him culminating in the 'victory' of Fornovo and the withdrawal of Charles were seen as decisive, a moment of crisis overcome, as is evident in the medal struck for Francesco Gonzaga and proclaiming him as the restorer of Italian liberty: Universae Italiae Liberatori.[3] And yet though a sense of change, of a welcome of change, is evident in the quotation with which we began, the anonymous Piacentine writer, pragmatically and rather world-wearily, suggests that for most people continuity has a far greater influence in their lives, and is far more powerful than any idea of political crisis, and certainly more so than the cultural crisis provoked by the deaths of poets and philosophers.

The interpretation and presentation of an event such as the invasion of 1494 and of the culture surrounding it can, as has been suggested, be observed from many perspectives. Since the aim here is to focus on the interaction of history and culture, we might draw attention to just four of the major sources of evidence for assessing the validity of the concept of crisis, which are: eyewitness accounts and those composed at the time and as those events occurred, where we shall, when dealing with Renaissance Italy, find divergent views according to the state in which the writer lived; accounts by 'laudatores temporis acti', harking back to the good old days, in this case of Italian liberty, freedom from foreign domination; the comparisons and contrasts between history and culture, or crisis and continuity; and fourthly the distant mirror, the perspective backwards from the future. Each of these has source materials that are particularly useful and appropriate to its method: chronicles, diaries, and letters, political archives, and diplomatic correspondence for the first; contemporary historians, political thinkers and writers of the next generation reflecting the first historical reactions; the activities and products of artists of all kinds in the period under review; and finally modern studies of the same phenomena, the possibly sympathetic and objective overview.

In the sphere of culture, as in politics, there is some logic for the celebration of a single year, 1494, and yet it is impossible to do so without paying attention to the activities of individual writers before this date. Where 1494 is concerned, the links existing between major writers and their mutual influences on each other must also be part of the discussion. Thus while the deaths between September and December of 1494 provide the immediate justification for the selection of Pico, Poliziano, and Boiardo as the authors chiefly commemorated here, as the various contributions repeatedly demonstrate, the life and work of each of these authors has not only a 'before' involving other cultural figures, but also and perhaps more importantly an 'after'. In the world of culture, as in life, no man is an island, and here too therefore the perspective needs to be extended backwards not just to the death of Lorenzo in 1492, but to the 1480s and the intense cultural activities of that decade which saw the formation and flowering of so much of the literary talent celebrated here, of Poliziano, Pulci, Pico della Mirandola, and Ficino, as well as the arrival in Florence of the controversial Savonarola. Similarly, as Catani and Panizza show for Pico, and Dorigatti and Brand for Boiardo, these authors continued to 'live' in their works, for their immediate associates and rivals, Pico for Ficino and Savonarola, Boiardo for Degli Agostini and Ariosto, in a way which suggests that their death did not immediately spell definitive ending, but rather that their 'life' continued, in the case of Pico until the subsequent deaths of Savonarola in 1498 and Ficino in 1499, and in Boiardo's case, for much longer.

Thus far we have suggested that the twin impetus behind this volume of essays—the invasion, or cataclysm, of 1494, and the deaths of Pico, Poliziano, and Boiardo—run along parallel lines, in that both require a wider perspective than just that of a single year. But it will be abundantly apparent that there is another pairing to be considered at this juncture, one much more suggestive of dichotomy, namely the twin poles of Florence and Ferrara.[4] From the political point of view these two states could be taken as representative of the two opposing systems of Renaissance Italy, united in one thing only, their traditional alliance with France. The apparent stability of Este rule in Ferrara, celebrated so warmly by Boiardo, is a marked contrast with the complexities of Medici control of Florence, explored here by Alison Brown, and currently the subject of a considerable body of research. The skill of Duke Ercole and his successor Alfonso in riding out the storms of the French invasions and retaining the independence of Ferrara contrasts with the fall of the Medici on the arrival of Charles

VIII and their dependence on outside powers to restore them eventually to power in 1512, while the republican traditions and passions of Florence find no counterpart in the culture of Ferrara, even if the court was frequently seen in a critical light. Culturally too there is a tendency to see the environment and productions of these two states as distinct and complementary rather than closely comparable. And yet, such a facile differentiation does not stand up even to a first scrutiny, much less to close analysis. The chivalric epic, claimed as typically belonging to the northern courts, and especially Ferrara, had its first Renaissance flowering in Florence in the work of Pulci, and arose out of the well-established Tuscan tradition of the *cantari* and the work of Andrea da Barberino. Indeed as Davie points out, it was perhaps this Florentine success in a literary domain perceived as Ferrarese that first prompted Boiardo to take up his pen on *Orlando innamorato*. The study of Greek, and consequently of Greek philosophy, had linked Ferrara and Florence from the time of the Council of 1438–9, and if under Borso the humanist culture of Ferrara took a back seat to the 'volgare', Ercole's interests in both classical literature and theatre, and especially in matters of religion, re-established Ferrara's place alongside Florence in the humanist debates of the end of the century. Before he was called to Florence, Savonarola was a friar in Ferrara, where his grandfather Ser Michele was court physician to Niccolò III d'Este and his successors.[5] Pulci's influence on Boiardo, the subject of very recent research, reminds us that the genre of the narrative poem, even before the mass circulation of printed versions, was always mobile; far-reaching in its influence, it travelled easily, like good wines. The *Trecento novelle* of Sacchetti, for example, record numerous travellers between Florence and Ferrara in the late fourteenth century. Good ideas, inspirational stories are not bound by geographical limits, but neither is the world of philosophy and intellectual enquiry. Pico's correspondence with his Venetian counterpart, Barbaro, explored here by Panizza, is testimony to the internationalism of these figures, their sense of being at home wherever like minds were gathered together. Culturally therefore there are good reasons for associating these two states, for examining the reactions, on the cultural plane in each of them, to the events of the 1490s.

In considering this period, contributors started from the perspective already outlined, namely that of crisis, watershed, fundamental change, but all with the aim of asking how accurate this view was of the history, politics, and culture of the 1490s. The deaths of important political figures, rulers of major Italian states, Lorenzo de' Medici, Ferrante of Naples, Innocent VIII, and Gian Galeazzo Sforza, together with the invasion of 1494, are undeniable aspects of change, but whether they were perceived also as crisis by contemporaries is more questionable. Guicciardini's concept of the watershed of 1494, the year in which Italy lost her liberty, dates from some thirty years after the event, and inevitably reflects all that happened subsequently. Boiardo's final stanza seems to confirm Guicciardini's idea, but as Neil Harris has shown,[6] and as Dorigatti reminds us here, Boiardo had interrupted each of his previous books at a moment of political and military crisis, but no claim is made on that basis for either 1478 or 1482 as watershed years. We have alluded above to the fact that political and cultural change may not go hand in hand, but both are affected by economic factors and change in the economic climate. War is undoubtedly a costly business, and thus a potent economic force on culture. Predatory troops of invading, and even allied, armies laying waste the countryside may depress the poetic 'inspiration', but the expanding world consequent upon the discoveries of Columbus and his successors, also dating from 1492, the diary accounts and maps that made their way rapidly precisely to Florence, home of Amerigo Vespucci, and Ferrara, on account of Ercole's personal interests, excited the imagination of writer and reader alike and provided welcome distraction from events closer to home. Indeed Francesco Cieco in his narrative poem, *Il Mambriano*, written during the decade of the 1490s, repeatedly refers to pressure on him to write, to provide entertainment and escape from the depressing environment nearer home. But even this superficial tendency, when talking of cultural crisis, of seeing such an environment as negative and gloomy, productive only of 'serious' writing, may be misplaced, as both Brand and Panizza remind us, since the humanist idea of 'serio ludere', the outrageous humour of Lucian, does not lose its element of play, comedy, and humour just because it also transmits a serious message.

Above all the notion of crisis is susceptible of many meanings, not just political and cultural, but equally between the individual and society, and may concern financial matters and intellectual inspiration, ideas, and fashions. So, as Catani suggests, the fashionable enquiry into astrology of the 1490s may be both a symptom and a cause of crisis in one sphere of intellectual engagement, a transference of external elements of crisis into the inner forum of the psyche, revealing itself in turn in the shifting and ambiguous emphases of prominent thinkers like Ficino. Crisis may relate to what the Renaissance might have termed *fortuna*, simple, coincidental facts such as the failure of a work, or an author's whole oeuvre, to reach the medium of print, which constituted for Piero della Francesca a crisis which lasted for almost 500 years.

But as these comments begin to suggest and as the essays collected here repeatedly confirm, out of this double perspective, of cultural and political history, comes the revelation of a paradox, that of simultaneous continuity and crisis in both history and culture, and in both of the states principally under consideration here, Florence and Ferrara. Continuity and crisis, as Dorigatti shows, are frequently linked to precise historical, but also personal, experiences; crisis, as McLaughlin argues, may reside in the very structure and aims of the text, fragile and fragmented, but which in the skilful hands of Poliziano turns not only into a virtue, echoing his linguistic eclecticism, but in its open-endness, its multiple links to other genres and texts, also testifies to a continuity in literary culture that stretches almost to infinity—crisis then in one area which is supported and complemented by continuity in the other.

Numerous individuals could have figured in this examination of the cross-currents of culture and history in the 1490s in Italy, for the decade was notable for the deaths of many eminent figures and the birth of others whose life and works touched both their own times and significantly coloured later perceptions of the Renaissance in Italy. Among the deaths, on the political front we have referred already to those of Lorenzo de' Medici, Ferrante of Naples, and Gian Galeazzo Sforza; upon writers and artists the 'flagellum' of Savonarola's apocalyptic vision fell with a terrifying force, significantly influencing some of the most gifted intellects of the day, whom death would carry off, in some cases while still young: Poliziano, Pico, Boiardo, Piero della Francesca, Ghirlandaio, Ermolao Barbaro, Cristoforo Landino, Carlo Crivelli, Cosmè Tura, Ercole de' Roberti, and Melozzo da Forlì, and in the last few years, from 1497 Benozzo Gozzoli, Antonio Pollaiuolo, Savonarola, and Ficino, together with the principal patron of the arts in Milan, Beatrice d'Este. So many deaths, and especially, as Brown shows, those of 1494, cannot but seem like a cultural watershed, a definitive ending, a closure.

More interesting, however, especially for the thesis that in this decade culture provided at least as much an element of continuity as a sharing in the sense of crisis, is the examination of the activities and achievements of those who reached maturity in the 1490s, who lived through the 'annus horribilis' and its aftermath. The voyages of Columbus were followed by those of Vespucci almost yearly from 1497, radically altering the contemporary world view and spelling the end of Italy's central position in the 'Middle Sea'. 1495 marks the real start of Aldus Manutius' printing press in Venice, the date of the full launch of his business and of his innovative Greek type, the result of experiments with founts begun probably in about 1490 and culminating in the series of octavo editions of the classics which began in 1501.[7] In this decade too Venice became the dominant centre of printing, with all the concomitant changes produced by the shift to a reading culture (so that we might perhaps be tempted to call this an aspect of crisis in culture), while the 1490s also saw the printing of the first books by the Florentine dynasty of the Giunti. But the element of continuity is most striking if one turns to examine the careers in this period of those who came to political and cultural maturity in the 1490s. In the case of both Michelangelo and Leonardo da Vinci, though they were frequently on the move, Leonardo in particular, these years saw the production of Leonardo's most famous works, for Lodovico Sforza in Milan, and the first Roman period of Michelangelo. This is the decade in which Isabella d'Este began her patronage of the arts in Mantua, which was to continue until her death in 1539, and in which Ariosto first entered Este service in Ferrara. For all these, crisis brought development and innovation, and in the long term cultural domination if not continuity.

What these essays reveal is precisely the strange mixture of continuity and crisis that characterized the culture of the 1490s in Italy. As Alison Brown points out, this paradox of crisis and continuity is present in the conflict evident between the language used to describe events, which is suggestive of crisis, and the actions and reactions of those involved, which are indicative much more of a sense of continuity. The culture of the early 1490s can be seen, on many fronts, as vibrant, forging ahead, typified by a lively interplay of humanist ideas and texts and the explorations and developments of vernacular literature, evident already in Boiardo's *Timone* (1490), and sustained by a strong and dynamic sense of continuity with the immediate cultural past, which Davie reveals in Pulci's sense of handing on the torch to Poliziano, and which clearly underpins Boiardo's engagement with the romance epic. Continuity in this area, the romance epic, seems broken by the death of Boiardo, yet from the point of view of the genre 1494 is no more than a hiccough almost completely obscured by the simple continuity represented by Niccolò degli Agostini and the complex continuity of Ariosto, and most significantly of all, in a consideration focusing on the 1490s, by the tenacity and individualism of Francesco Cieco evident in *Il Mambriano*, revealing within its forty-five canti both a strong sense of continuity with the cultural past of the genre and the historical past in which the composition was initiated and a repeated sense of crisis to be faced and overcome. And if crisis is often the term more appropriate when speaking of individuals, represented by changes of emphasis (Ficino), death (Boiardo and Pico), or definitive loss of a homeland (Sannazaro in Naples), in the realm of literature and thought continuity is triumphantly demonstrated by the incessant production of printed books in all genres and for a suddenly much wider public, a point from which the Renaissance never looked back.

The anniversary conference on Italy in the 1490s, from which these essays originate, formed one in a whole series of international celebrations and commemorations of particular events and individuals connected with this decade in Italy. These celebrations included those commemorating the death of Lorenzo il Magnifico in 1492, the 'discovery' of the New World by Columbus—perhaps the most extensive exercise in revisionism in the recent history of such commemorations—the beginning of the Wars of Italy, and the deaths of Poliziano, Boiardo, Pico della Mirandola, Piero della Francesca, and most recently Savonarola and Ficino, a rash of commemorations which cannot be divorced from the preoccupations of the 1990s and the impending millennium. These preoccupations have created a climate of revisionism downwards, of a loss of confidence in the 'great achievements' of Western culture, a calling into question of what constitutes greatness in culture, producing paradoxically but usefully the re-examination of the works both of major figures like Poliziano and of previously neglected or unfashionable artists, and of the narrow focus which too often in the past has lead to a facile division of events into before and after, cause and effect, the allocation of authors to the status of major or minor, or to certain genres and not others.

Some of the figures of Italian culture commemorated here could be seen, and in some cases until fairly recently were seen, as 'the defeated', those wiped off the stage, often quite literally by the events of 1494, those who became as a result the subject of neglect, dead both historically and culturally. The most significant case is surely that of Boiardo, removed by death in 1494 from controlling the 'fortuna' of his great poem, traduced and disfigured by the efforts, more or less well meaning, of continuators, editors, printers, and revisers, as Harris has memorably shown on several occasions.[8] Only centuries later, in the nineteenth century, in the movement towards Italian unification and the related (though again paradoxical) treasuring of local heroes, cultural as much as anything, were they brought back to full critical attention and a new revisionism, upwards, as Reidy brings out in the examination of the role played by the political exile and cultural giant Antonio Panizzi. Through Panizzi's work and his own sense of cultural and geographical association with his fellow Emilian, Boiardo became a key figure of Italian culture for British Italianists, since, as Reidy shows, it was largely as a result of Sir Anthony Panizzi's interest in Boiardo and the romance epic that the British Library acquired its outstanding collection of early editions of the genre, and it is fitting therefore that Boiardo should also have his English centenary volume.

Pico, Poliziano, and Boiardo, whose deaths coincided with the watershed year, are the central focus of the volume and throughout the concentration is on literature and thought rather than the other arts, and the interaction of such artists with the events of history. Moreover, since no individual functions in a vacuum, cultural or political, the creation of a *Zeitgeist* through the concatenation of events and the development of fashionable ideas and practices, such as the pursuit of irrational solutions in the realms of astrology and the attractions of millenarianism, serve to set a context, through Catani's study, for a troubled decade dealing with issues which affect not just a famous few but the generality of the populace, and forming a potent link with our own *fin de siècle* and its fashions of thought.

Again and again as contributors grappled with the notion of crisis, whether historical or cultural or both, they found themselves independently and inexorably driven to admit the force of continuity in this decade; in the survival of states, political systems, and rulers, or in the clear evidence that the crisis had been so long in preparation that it could only be seen as a continuation of an existing trend; in the determination of surviving friends and relatives to ensure the publication and dissemination of a writer's work, however inadequately, and in the recognition that ideas, concepts, narrative structures, and poetic inspiration, in this period perhaps more than any other, have roots buried deep in the past and thus belong to a tradition of continuity that spans not just the years of a decade but centuries and even millennia. The final conclusion of the discussions here was that the 1490s in Italy demonstrated as much culture in continuity as in crisis, a sense of renewal, dynamism, and determination, which is confirmed by the monuments of culture, literary and artistic, of the new century.

Notes to the Introduction

1. The quotation is cited in A. Bonora, *Il conte Bernardo Pallastrelli: studio biografico* (Piacenza: Tipografia Favari, 1877), 14–15.
2. Francesco Cieco da Ferrara, *Il Mambriano*, XXXII, 1; see also cc. XXXIII, 1, XXXVI, 1–2, XXXVIII, 1–3. Quoted from Francesco Cieco da Ferrara, *Libro d'arme e d'amore nomato Mambriano*, ed. G. Rua, 3 vols. (Turin: UTET, 1926). The first edition is Ferrara: Mazzochio del Bondeno, 1509.
3. The medal is by Sperandio. See also S. Brinton, *The Gonzaga Lords of Mantua* (London: Methuen, 1927), 114.
4. It is worth noting, as we go to press, the recent major exhibition in Venice which focuses on the impact that northern artists had in shaping the trends of much Italian art in the early 16th century. Cf. *Il Rinascimento a Venezia e la pittura del Nord ai tempi di Bellini, Dürer, Tiziano*, ed. Bernard Aikema and Beverly L. Brown (Milan: Bompiani, 1999).
5. See Michele Savonarola, *Libreto de tutte le cosse che se magnano; un'opera di dietetica del sec. XV*, ed. Jane Nystedt (Stockholm: Almqvist & Wiskell, 1988).
6. N. Harris, *Bibliografia dell' 'Orlando Innamorato'*, 2 vols. (Modena: Panini, 1988–91), ii. 19–28.
7. See M. Lowry, *The World of Aldus Manutius* (Oxford: Blackwell, 1979), 82 ff.
8. Harris, *Bibliografia*, and id., 'L'avventura editoriale dell'*Orlando Innamorato*', in *I Libri di Orlando Innamorato* (Istituto di Studi Rinascimentali di Ferrara; Modena: Panini, 1987).

CHAPTER 1

The Revolution of 1494 in Florence and its Aftermath: A Reassessment

Alison Brown

In March 1494, conversing with the Florentine ambassador resident in Milan, Lodovico il Moro described Italy reductively as a duck pond, everyone busy with his own concerns and ignoring the impending disaster. '"The Venetians, who are old and wise, are busy concealing themselves with those hoods of theirs"—saying this [the ambassador reported] with some derision—"You [in Florence] spend your time jousting, here [in Milan] they devote themselves to falconry and hunting, the Pope devotes himself to creating cardinals and the king [Ferrante] to making counts." And in this disaster (*ruina*) that was about to befall them, the Florentines were particularly guilty of self-deception, persuading themselves of the opposite for greater effect.'[1] *Ruina* is also the word used more famously by Francesco Guicciardini in his *History of Florence* to describe the events that followed Lorenzo's death in 1492 and the subsequent invasion of Italy by the French, who, by overturning 'not only Florence but the whole of Italy', led 'to Italy's ruin'.[2]

This view of Italy's general indifference to the forthcoming invasion seems to confirm the current revisionism of historians who minimalize its significance. Far from being the cataclysm that Lodovico il Moro had predicted and Francesco Guicciardini later described, they argue that from a wider perspective the events of 1494 were predictable and unsurprising. Italy was a constant prey to fear of outside invasion, especially after the Turkish slaughter of Christians on the Italian mainland at Otranto in 1480. Milan was the regular instigator of foreign invasions throughout the 1470s and 1480s.[3] Nor was Florence as destabilized by the overthrow of the Medici as Guicciardini suggests. Instead of being responsible for creating the panic that empowered Savonarola, the prophet of doom, the religious revival was evidently in full swing before Savonarola's prophecies had had time to make their effect.[4] And Savonarola's political reforms in turn were more conservative than they might appear, since instead of opening and expanding the citizen class through the creation of the Great Council, they in fact closed it by limiting membership to citizens who were already office-holders.[5] All this speaks of continuity, not change, suggesting that 1494 was much less of a crisis than we have been led to believe.

It is, of course, difficult to pinpoint change, particularly the deep sea changes that affect cultural as well as political outlooks and attitudes before they are visible to the surface eye. There is another difficulty for us as historians, in that governments—the official 'voice' in our records—naturally overplayed the stability of their regimes, and this was particularly true of the Medici regime after Lorenzo's death, as Lodovico il Moro suggests. Both when writing to outsiders and when flattering Piero himself, the regime devoted much time and effort to promoting the notion of continuity and stability. Criticism was *not* allowed, so in accepting the official version of events we are playing the regime's game, even to the extent of blaming the hapless Piero and the invasion itself for its own collapse. This means we must rely on a variety of evidence—hints in letters between intimates, as well as the less intimate evidence afforded by financial and other post-revolutionary records—to understand fully the domestic context of the 1494 revolution in Florence.[6]

Without returning to Guicciardini's 'crisis' interpretation of these years, I shall re-examine the evidence for seeing 1494, if not as a *tournant*, at least as a more important moment of change than is currently argued. Neither the sudden catastrophe that Guicciardini describes, nor the non-event of recent history, the revolution in Florence was planned and anticipated well before the French invasion, which served simply as the means and occasion for bringing it about. That Piero's second cousins (once removed), Lorenzo and Giovanni di Pierfrancesco de' Medici, headed opposition to the Medici has long been acknowledged, but the extent of their involvement with the French and the Francophile party in Florence needs re-examining as a first probe into these events. More surprising than the cousins' involvement was that of families like the Capponi, whose opposition to Piero stemmed less from traditional political factionalism than from conflicting banking and financial interests, a second area for investigation. A third, and even less familiar one, is the role of the people in the revolution. The elite alone are unlikely to have overthrown the regime, even with French backing, without popular support. This was forthcoming as an incensed assault on the corrupt practices, or *tangentopolism*, of the post-1478 Medici regime. Both elite and people were necessary to make a revolution; together, their hostility provides convincing evidence of the strength of opposition to this regime before 1494 which the French knew about and exploited. Going beyond the revolution to its aftermath demonstrates the extent of change in Florence. For the new, harsh climate in Florence provoked not only the social radicalism of Savonarola and his followers, but also an overturning of the cultural consensus of the Laurentian period. The apocalypticism and primitive naturalism that replaced the golden-age *tems <qui> revient* serve to confirm, in conclusion, the depth of the sea change in post-1494 Florence.

Plotting the Revolution

Although there was no open rebellion against the Medici regime between the Pazzi Conspiracy in 1478 and Lorenzo's death fourteen years later, a series of non-judicial executions and exiles showed that fear of an uprising was endemic. Nothing betrays this better than the charged atmosphere in the days after Lorenzo died on 8 April 1492, when his friends hastened to reassure each other that there would be a smooth handover of power. 'The city and people, great and small, are united with the greatest union and contentment to preserve Piero [. . .] who responds to everyone like a Solomon', one supporter wrote; a week later 'things go better every day for Piero'; and three weeks later 'things go from good to better for Piero';[7] while another spoke enthusiastically about 'Piero's way of doing things and his excellent conduct in these ceremonies and in everything he does'.[8] Yet within a month of Lorenzo's death, there were rumours abroad of the carryings-on of his cousins, Lorenzo and Giovanni di Pierfrancesco de' Medici. In a sequence that is all too familiar today, these were initially denied; then partially admitted: 'as to the other gossip that you say you have heard down there about the behaviour of

Lorenzo and Giovanni di Pierfrancesco, there is some little affair, though little or nothing shows itself. It began before Lorenzo's death as a result, it seems, of some adolescent tiff or love affair—powerful enough but at the same time, since it doesn't affect their otherwise extremely wise behaviour, somewhat farouche.' And finally acknowledged: 'whether true or not, it is being said that Lorenzo di Pierfrancesco is entering into conclave with our own cardinal'.[9]

That Cardinal Giovanni de' Medici should have been conspiring with his cousin against his brother Piero during the papal conclave in July–August 1492 perhaps seems improbable, but we know that Giovanni was very angry with his brother from a letter in which he complained bitterly of Piero's attempt not just to nanny him but to boss him about as Lodovico il Moro bossed Ascanio Sforza.[10] Giovanni particularly resented the 'imperious' and threatening letters to him from his brother's secretary, ser Piero Bibbiena, in favour of Michele Marullo, the soldier-poet, which he said were counterproductive, since he didn't 'go for threats'.[11] We know that in April 1492 Lorenzo di Pierfrancesco was already considered a friend of the prince of Salerno, Antonello Sanseverino, the Neapolitan exile and invasion activist then living in France.[12] Both men were patrons of 'that beast, Michele Marullo' who in the following year joined Salerno at the French court, where he was thought to be acting as a spy for Lorenzo di Pierfrancesco.[13] Cardinal Giovanni's letter suggests that some scheming may already have been afoot in Rome and Florence, as well as in France, in 1492.

The first overt evidence that a revolution was being planned was nine months later, in April 1493. On 29 April 1493 the Florentine ambassador in France, Piero Capponi, wrote in cypher to Piero de' Medici about his conversation with the cardinal of San Malo, Guillaume Briçonnet, earlier that day:

This morning, San Malo asked me who was willing to *mutare lo stato* and who would give the king of France money, troops and support from the lords of Italy [. . .] and before going off to hunt, he entered into the strangest details in the world. [. . .] On his return, thinking it would be no bad thing, I entered into a bit of a discussion for the good of the city and my merchants, without staining your reputation, [by suggesting] that they should be more enthusiastic about the business; and—to play him along—that I needed to know, before I answered him, which the king would prefer, revolution (*mutatione dello stato* [that is, the overthrow of Piero's regime]) or support (*il favore*); he replied, 'revolution would be more certain, but considering present needs [. . .] to get the government to serve him would be better and I would acquire favour with the king'.

And Capponi concluded this extraordinary letter with the mention of a large reward he might be offered and the threats being made that the Florentines would hand over Florence and that the people were French.[14]

From then on, the danger of revolution and Florence's Francophilia are recurrent themes of diplomatic letters from France. In late October 1493, following a veiled allusion to Lorenzo di Pierfrancesco as 'the serpent [which] has its tail there in Florence',[15] news reached Florence that Charles VIII had ennobled Lorenzo di Pierfrancesco de' Medici and his brother and given them positions in his household— doubtless encouraged not only by the *douceurs* Lorenzo di Pierfrancesco had given the French ambassador and the prince of Salerno's secretary in Florence in July 1493 but by his reported promise of the large sum of 500,000 ducats to Salerno himself, then masterminding the forthcoming invasion in France.[16] Then in January 1493 Gentile Becchi warned Piero that unless he declared his support for the king in his forthcoming expedition, the king would believe all the bad things he'd been told about Piero and would 'ensure that there was a revolution there' (in Florence) and that this was the only reason he had summoned Giovanni di Pierfrancesco to France.[17] In March Becchi reiterated his warnings that a revolution was being planned in Florence, telling Piero that unless he confirmed the oath of loyalty to France taken by every Signoria on assuming office, 'we'll be certain you're Aragonese and you can despatch to the young Lorenzo's house all the lilies you have in your own palace'.[18] At the same time, Lodovico il Moro in Milan urged Piero to remember 'liberty, the people, and all the city' and said he would willingly 'leap into a pulpit in Florence and preach this to all the people'.[19]

Because Piero wanted to minimalize the threat to his regime, the imprisonment and exile of Lorenzo and Giovanni di Pierfrancesco in late April 1494 have also been minimalized by historians.[20] But as Mario Martelli has argued, these events on the anniversary of the Pazzi Conspiracy had much more serious implications and were doubtless intended to forestall the predicted revolution in the city.[21] Faced with the difficult task of justifying the cousins' imprisonment and at the same time playing down its seriousness, ambassadors and Medici apologists like Poliziano praised Piero's clemency in pardoning his cousins while explaining the gravity of the initial charges against them. Thus, as Vespucci and Capponi explained to the French court, the fact that the Council of Seventy initially wanted to execute them and then condemned them, as well as a third conspirator, Cosimo Rucellai, to life imprisonment and confiscation of goods meant 'they must certainly have plotted against the state and its leading citizens'.[22] Other chroniclers suggest a different scenario, however, in which it was Piero and his henchmen who needed to be restrained from destroying the conspirators, Piero only pardoning his cousins in response to their evident popularity in Florence.[23] Although the initial excuse for their capture was their slight to the Signoria in entertaining the French ambassadors in their villa instead of in the official hostelry arranged for them, it emerged from their later confession that many other people were involved.[24] In addition to Cosimo Rucellai, who had attempted to win over Gabriele Malaspina, Marquis of Fosdinovo, when on his way to the French court in January 1494,[25] there were four other leading Florentines, as well as the king of France, Lodovico il Moro, and the Marquis of Mantua.[26] 'I'm only surprised the Pazzi aren't among the herbs in this salad', Piero's emissary in Rome commented sardonically.[27]

This reference to the Pazzi betrays the regime's underlying fears about these events. When reporting Lorenzo and Giovanni di Pierfrancesco's appointments in the royal household, Francesco della Casa had already suggested that they had been promoted by the same men who 'had on another occasion, with the same malignity, discussed favouring the Pazzi family',[28] and Becchi had also drawn a parallel between the embassy of 'Ubigny' (Bérault Stuart, lord of Aubigny) to Florence in May 1494 and that of the papal ambassador, Giovanbattista da Montesecco, before the Pazzi Conspiracy.[29] Even so it is as difficult for us as it was for the regime to know how much importance to attribute to 'the youths', as they were dismissively called. Lorenzo and Giovanni di Pierfrancesco were in fact then aged nearly 31 and 26, compared with the 22-year-old Piero.[30] Was Lorenzo's appointment as chamberlain to the king really 'so tiny an affair?' Lodovico il Moro asked the Florentine ambassador, 'knowing the people are pro-French and Lorenzo is of the standing he is?'[31] And when the pope asked Piero's emissary in Rome about the brothers, he was told that 'they had always been useless citizens to the city, and for this reason enjoyed no favour, as their situation demonstrates'.[32] Ascanio Sforza received the same reply when he asked, 'Who is this

Giovanni? I don't know him [. . .] Lorenzo I saw when he came here and spoke to him once, and he seemed to me to be a gentleman', for he, too, was told that they were mere youths and would be treated as such, and that their qualities and behaviour in the city had brought them hatred and ill-will rather than credit.[33] Nevertheless the cousins' evident popularity and their standing in France was serious enough to suggest—at least to the pope—that Piero's life was in danger and that he must stop his night-time sorties in search of pleasure, for there had already been 'bad designs' on them.[34] Were the cousins as irresponsible and unpopular as the ambassador suggested, or did they seriously threaten Piero's regime in Florence?

Money and the Medici

The cousins' power—and the source of their discontent—was money. Since money provided one of the principal sources of popular grievance against the Medici regime when it fell, it offers a means of understanding how their 'youthful love affairs' had repercussions far outside the immediate circles involved. Lorenzo and Giovanni di Pierfrancesco were not only richer than Lorenzo il Magnifico and his son Piero, but for the second generation in succession, they resented their treatment as minors at the hands of the elder branch of the family. Just like their father in 1465–6, they had been forced to hand over money to the elder branch at a time of political crisis. But whereas Lorenzo il Magnifico used special legislation to avoid political disqualification for his large debts at the end of the Pazzi War—thereby also acquiring a means of accessing the public-funded debt, he apparently denied his cousins the benefit of the same legislation, to which they were entitled.[35] As a result, Lorenzo di Pierfrancesco found himself disqualified from office in 1484 through debt and was only able to recover the money owed him when he came of age the following year.[36] Thus it was perhaps no coincidence that in late August 1492, when Piero was already concerned about 'the conclave' between his brother and Lorenzo di Pierfrancesco in Rome, he approved a law making citizens restore to the state-funded debt money that they had illegally 'usurped' from it;[37] nor that he transferred to his cousins nearly 22,000 florins in Monte credits in November that year.[38] For both must have been in some way responses to the perceived injustice of the earlier situation.

An early sign of Lorenzo di Pierfrancesco's political standing was the privilege he was granted when he came of age—hitherto unique to il Magnifico—of a personal bodyguard.[39] An even earlier sign was his success in getting himself elected, though under age, as one of the three ambassadors to congratulate Charles VIII on his accession in 1483—a decision his cousins had good cause to rue, since it must have established the basis of his later close relationship with the French king.[40] In the event, however, it was his money that proved to be his most provocative asset in the run-up to the invasion, especially when used, together with Lodovico il Moro's money, to bribe the war party.[41]

In financial terms, the rivalry between the two branches of the Medici family mirrored the contrasting, though interwoven, financial interests of the French lobby and the Curial–Neapolitan lobby. The latter consisted of the four Florentine banking firms who shared with other firms the farm of papal revenues. Since they included the elder Medici, who in 1489 had made a huge loan to the College of Cardinals in return for the Papal tiara as surety, there was understandably deep concern about its fate during the August 1492 conclave and about cardinal Giovanni's untimely dealings with Lorenzo di Pierfrancesco.[42] This lobby was also contributing secretly to the *condotta* of the pope's son; it was involved in negotiations to re-establish the Medici bank in Naples;[43] and, using the Spinelli, it was planning to bribe the French with money provided by both Florence and Naples.[44]

By contrast, the French lobby consisted of the numerous Florentine banking and commercial firms in France—including both branches of the Medici family—with some 300,000 ducats invested in France in 1494.[45] Their unwillingness to lend the king the money he demanded without referring to Florence, followed by their expulsion from the kingdom in June 1494, explains why, as Becchi put it, the merchants, as well as the *popolo minuto*, were 'enemies of the government'.[46] It also explains why a banker like Piero Capponi was prepared—as we saw—'to play along' with the idea of revolution from his concern for 'the city and my merchants'. As banker to French cardinals like San Malo and Lyons, his *grande maestro*, he lost an important patron when the Cardinal of Lyons was prevented by Charles VIII from claiming his benefices in Rome, and prayed God (and Piero de' Medici) that 'we get another occasion to win similar types'.[47] The Capponi were undoubtedly one of 'the four leading Florentine families in Lyons' who Piero was warned were in cahoots with Charles VIII after the expulsion of Florentine bankers and merchants from Lyons in June 1494, with orders to reveal themselves when the king approached Florence in the expectation of an uprising in late October.[48]

And this is in effect what happened. On 20 October the flight of cardinal Giovanni and Giuliano de' Medici from Florence was 'known to everyone in Rome, where it is firmly believed that there's going to be some uprising in Florence'.[49] And two days later the alarming news was despatched to Piero that, following the death of Gian Galeazzo Sforza, Lodovico had plans to become king of Lombardy, and worse, that Piero's belated offer of 300,000 francs to Charles VIII had been rejected with contumely.[50] Encountering his banker, Filippo da Gagliano, in the Duomo on the morning of the 26th, Piero called to him and asked him to do 'that business'. This he did after lunch and Piero rode off at once: 'he was almost alone, his friends following behind, one by one. And [he asked for] safe-boxes, clothes, and other things as though he was going to the king [. . .] and this is the route he's clearly taken.' As Gagliano described it to Michelozzi, the decision was taken 'quite straightforwardly by Piero alone, without consulting anyone, least of all the leading citizens, yet it was thought there must have been some contact with the other side' and there was speculation that the trip was planned by Spinelli. Hoping that all was for the best, he predicted that 'tomorrow we should have a letter from him like the one his father wrote from San Miniato'.[51] The following day Piero did send a letter to Florence, not from San Miniato al Tedesco—from where his father had announced to the government his peace mission to the enemy in December 1479, during the Pazzi War—but from Empoli.[52] Nor did Piero's mission have the happy outcome of his father's. For despite appealing in his letter to the citizens' loyalty to 'the bones of your Lorenzo, my father',[53] this last-minute attempt to treat with the king came too late to save Florence's fortresses or the Medici regime.

The city was already in a state of 'great *mutazione*' and 'entirely French' when Bernardo Dovizi returned there on 30 October, before Piero had agreed to surrender the Florentine fortresses at Serezzano (recently built at huge expense), Pietrasanta, Pisa, and Livorno.[54] The offer of money on which it seemed Piero was relying to avert French wrath, 'knowing the avarice of the French and their cupidity', was in vain.[55] On 6 November, gabelles were halved on all food and drink coming into the city; and on the 9th, a day after he returned to Florence, Piero was refused an audience with the Signoria and later, after a popular uprising, fled the city.[56] So the surrender of the castles was not the cause of the revolution, merely the event that precipitated what had been predicted and planned long before. In order to understand the full extent of the popular alienation against Piero, however, we have to look at the events which followed as well as preceded this domestic revolution.

The Events and Aftermath of the Revolution

The accepted version of events is that Piero's overthrow initially represents merely an attempt by the factious *ottimati* to restore electoral power to themselves, which they did by appointing themselves as the twenty *accoppiatori* approved by the *parlamento* on 2 December, and that it was only Savonarola's preaching that radicalized the situation by the creation of the popular Great Council on 24 December.[57] However, what is most striking and novel about the revolution is the animus immediately shown against the wealth and corrupt practices of the Medici and their intimates. This is not the occasion to recite the details of this 'clean hands' campaign,[58] but its seriousness is apparent from the initial attack on Medici possessions and from the unprecedented vetting of the accounts of all public offices since 1478.

Despite the fact that no official charge of rebellion was brought against Piero or his brothers until 20 November, the government issued a bann on 10 November that Piero's and Giuliano's possessions, as well as those of their associates, were to be confiscated and 'must be revealed to them' that day.[59] Thus stimulated, trunks of pearls, silver, vases, and carpets were retrieved from monasteries and hospitals in Florence and others were dug up from the hillside above Careggi.[60] Moreover, despite the fact that the decree of rebellion (with its corollary, confiscation of goods) was rescinded on 2 December—as one of the conditions of the treaty with Charles VIII—the new popular government nevertheless appointed five syndics on 28 December to recover Medici property. The seriousness of their operations is indicated by the fact that they met on average every two to three days—half of every working week—throughout the whole of the following year, 1495.[61]

Two weeks later, in an even more surprising move, another five syndics were appointed to audit all the accounts of the government and its financial magistracies since 1478.[62] These syndics were well into their stride by March, and from then until the end of August a stream of past financial officials flowed to the Palace, to be confined there until their accounts were cleared, exceptions being made only for a few individuals who were granted exeats, or weekend breaks, on condition that they promised to return 'on Monday morning'.[63] Although prudently disbanded for six weeks during the king of France's return from Rome, the syndics nevertheless worked remorselessly on through this period and through the heat of July and August to bring Lorenzo de' Medici's financiers to book.[64] Although they claimed that Filippo da Gagliano owed the commune 17,700 florins, the Signoria finally cleared him of debts owed as treasurer of the Dieci di Balìa from 1482 to 1485 over and above the sum of 13,752 florins, but declared that the latter sum, which on his own admission he gave Lorenzo and could now claim back from the Medici, was owed to the state and must be repaid by him within the next four years. Incensed by his being let off so lightly, the waiting crowds shouted 'hang him, hang him' as the officials laboured into the night on this difficult case, and when he finally emerged, he was attacked and seriously wounded on the head by two unknown assailants.[65] The passions aroused by this case can serve to illustrate popular hostility to the Medici regime, and although the syndics' office did not last for more than a year, the work of auditing the regime's accounts nevertheless went steadily on, as we can see from the deliberations of the Signoria.[66]

On 16 August 1495 Charles VIII signed a new treaty with Florence for the restitution of territory and payment of the last 30,000 ducats owed to him, with lengthy arrangements for levying another 70,000 ducats from Florence as a loan to be repaid in Lyons.[67] The high war taxes and famine caused by the soaring price of grain ensured that before too long the old semblance of continuity returned to Florentine politics. However, the events I have described, combined with the deaths of almost an entire literary generation, transformed the cultural as well as the political climate. In this context, I offer as a conclusion one example of how these changes may have influenced writers as well as painters in late fifteenth-century Florence.

Conclusion: Cultural Change

Lorenzo's death in 1492 was followed by Ermolao Barbaro's in July 1493, and by Giorgio Merula's in March 1494. And then, in a tightly-packed and ill-boding sequence of Medici intimates, Matteo Franco died on 6 September 1494, Baccio Ugolini on 27 September, Angelo

Poliziano the following day, and Giovanni Pico della Mirandola on 17 November: a conjunction that Parenti thought indicated 'impending disaster to Italy'.[68] Savonarola's sermons and the popular prophecies associated with the French invasion only served to confirm these apocalyptic fears, to which the discovery of the New World —equally publicized in popular ballads and print runs—also contributed.[69] After the invasion, the increasing economic hardship in Florence and the regime introduced by Savonarola played their own part in introducing change.[70] The consistently high war taxes and soaring price of grain in 1496–7 created widespread famine and hardship.[71] There were bread-riots in March 1497, following which the government took measures to provide food and lodgings for the homeless, as well as commandeering the Medici palace for the storage of grain.[72] In this situation, we are told, Lorenzo di Pierfrancesco and his brother Giovanni earned the gratitude of the populace by bringing from Forlì 'a vast amount of grain': well behaved and gentlemanly, like their father, who never got involved in politics, they too acted in the public interest as good citizens should and 'never sullied themselves with communal money'.[73]

This situation not only radicalized the Savonarolan movement, as Lorenzo Polizzotto has described.[74] It also transformed the cultural consensus of Lorenzo's Florence, as we can see from my example of cultural change, the 800-line poem 'On trees' written by the chancellor of Florence, Bartolomeo Scala, in exactly these years, 1496–7, and dedicated to Lorenzo di Pierfrancesco.[75] As former secretary to Lorenzo's father and future father-in-law of 'the beast Michele Marullo', Scala was well placed to act as a bridge not only between generations but also between cultures. He was also, with Marsilio Ficino and Cristoforo Landino, one of the very few politicians and humanists of the old regime to survive the revolution. Although this has suggested to Martelli that Scala was already alienated from Lorenzo il Magnifico's circle before Lorenzo died, he was in fact still close to many of its members and participated fully in Laurentian culture.[76] He dedicated all his writings to Lorenzo, as well as writing two fables for Piero in 1492; he employed the same architect, Giuliano di San Gallo, and the same sculptor, Bertoldo, whose friezes for both patrons' palaces reflect a shared culture. Not only do many of Scala's fables illustrate the same deterministic cycle of '*tems qui revient*' as Lorenzo's frieze at Poggio a Caiano, but they contain the same allusive references as the Poggio frieze to Lorenzo's cosmic role as Apollo and the source of Delphic wisdom.[77] Scala was also a 'great friend' of Pico della Mirandola, for whom he wrote a fable about Pico's *Heptaplus* called *Mundus* and whom he entertained in his garden in Borgo Pinti. It was there, we are told, that he hosted 'those discussions that our Pico held on friendship a few days before he left us', which were attended by Poliziano and Ficino—though not by Piero Ridolfi and Jacopo Salviati (two leading Florentines married to Lorenzo's daughters), who evidently also formed part of this literary circle.[78]

All the more striking, then, is the contrast between the evolutionary primitivism of Scala's late poem and the cyclical determinism of his earlier writings, which participated in the platonizing, synthesizing culture of Lorenzo's circle.[79] It is true that even before Lorenzo il Magnifico's death, his cousins had encouraged an alternative or counter-culture in Florence, as patrons of Marullo's paganizing *Hymni naturales* and Botticelli's *Primavera* and *Pallas and the Centaur*, and as heirs to the pro-French Charlemagne tradition from which the elder branch had had to disassociate itself.[80] Now these strange new worlds become integrated into the harsh realities of post-1494 Florence to form a new cultural idiom, as we can see from the poem 'On trees'.

It opens topically with a description of boys and girls skating together on the Arno, which froze over in December 1494,[81] and of a world governed by the orders of Jupiter and the changing seasons. But soon this develops into an account of difference: the two solstices turning the land, sea, and sky into contrary parts, and the different effect of the heavens on different regions. Its pastoralism is replaced by an account of man's cruelty to animals and plants: 'eating unwarlike cows and placid sheep [. . .] slaying everything and devouring whatever inhabits the earth, sky, and sea', while boys (as he knows from his own experience) 'wound pregnant mother trees with dangerous stones and steal the nuts'. The comforting repetition of nature's cycle is replaced by protean change—laurels that bear lemons, apples pears and vice versa—and, thanks to the discovery of fire from a chance thunderbolt, by civilization as we know it.[82] This included not only cheap and more abundant printed books in Greek made from palms, but also famine, which was savaging people throughout Italy as he wrote, forcing them to seek nourishment from herbs: 'and on the roads and in empty buildings their dying bodies collapse', moving

Lorenzo Popolano [di Pierfrancesco] to supply food from outside with his own money.[83] The poem ends disturbingly by describing a fantastical encounter with a soothsayer, who after revealing a circle of fifty marble agriculturalist heroes in Elysium (including Aristotle, Theophrastus, Cato, Varro, Pliny, Virgil, Columella, and Palladius) refers to Bacchus' shipwreck while sailing to Naxos, while an owl hoots and black nocturnal birds fly in the breezes, hissing reminders of former vain frenzies.

The obvious influence of Lucretius and of new texts like Palladius and Theophrastus might suggest that the poem's novelty has more to do with patronal tastes than with cultural change. However, its topicality roots it firmly in the context of famine-stricken Florence and in the apocalyptic fears of this post-1494 world, showing how closely the new culture was related to the social context in which it developed. Its anthropomorphism and hard primitivism heralded new artistic and literary tastes, such as the strange animals and anthropomorphic trees in Filippino Lippi's and Piero di Cosimo's paintings. Or the prophecies and fables of Leonardo da Vinci, in which men are 'suddenly transferred into opposite hemispheres', unable to understand each other's speech, sheep, cows, and goats are 'ripped open and flayed and most barbarously quartered', asses 'sold into slavery' and beaten, screech-owls dashed to pieces, walnut trees beaten, their 'children taken and flayed [. . .] their bones broken and crushed'.[84]

Scala died in July 1497 before the death of Savonarola the following year. So he usefully documents the influence of the revolution before the reaction that followed Savonarola's death. The creation of a Life Gonfalonier in 1502 and the Medici restoration in 1512 revived the themes of the Laurentian Golden Age and among them the idea of continuity, making it difficult for us in retrospect to gauge the disjunctive effect of 1494. By investigating the context of the revolution, its immediate impact, and the new thinking that it stimulated, however, we are perhaps able to see that it marked a greater change in outlook and thinking than the later evidence suggests.

Notes to Chapter 1

This chapter is based on work currently in progress and is intended to raise questions as much as to provide answers to the problems discussed. I am especially grateful to Jane Everson and Diego Zancani as editors of this book and organizers of the conference 'Culture in Crisis' at which it was originally presented. In 1995 I also discussed differing aspects of this topic at the

Renaissance Society conference on the French Invasion at Gonville and Caius College, Cambridge and at The Johns Hopkins Renaissance seminar at the Villa Spelman, Florence. I would like to thank the participants for their comments and questions and especially, as organizers, David Abulafia, Antony Antonovics, and Richard Goldthwaite.

Abbreviations:
ASF   Archivio di Stato, Florence
BNF   Florence, Biblioteca Nazionale
GC   Fondo Ginori Conti
MAP   Mediceo avanti il Principato
SS. Delib.   SS. Deliberazioni ord. aut.

1. Piero Alamanni to Piero Medici, Vigevano, 19 Mar. 1494 (ASF, MAP 50,254): 'un guazo d'anitre, perché Venitiani attendono a 'scursi con quelli loro chappucci & sono vecchi & savi, dicendo questo con qualche irrisione, voi costì attendete a giostrare, loro qui attendono a falchoni et chaccia; el Papa a fare Cardinali, et il re a ffare conti & in tanto questa ruina certissimamente ne viene adosso et voi maxime attendete a inghannarvene persuadendovi el contrario a più potere.'

2. Guicciardini, *Storie fiorentine,* ed. R. Palmarocchi (Bari: Laterza, 1931), 72 ('con scompiglio non solo della città ma di tutta Italia'); 88 ('Questi furono e' principi e le origine della ruina di Italia e particularmente di Piero de' Medici').

3. R. Fubini, 'I rapporti diplomatici tra Milano e Borgogna con particolare riguardo all'alleanza del 1475–76', in *Italia quattrocentesca: politica e diplomazia nell'età di Lorenzo il Magnifico* (Milan: F. Angeli, 1994), 327–50. See now D. Abulafia (ed.), *The French Descent into Renaissance Italy, 1494–5* (Aldershot: Variorum Press, 1995).

4. On the increase in masses and concern about salvation, see Sharon Strocchia, *Death and Ritual in Renaissance Florence* (Baltimore: Johns Hopkins University, 1992), 204–91; and on Savonarola's influence before 1494, Mario Martelli, 'La politica culturale dell'ultimo Lorenzo', *Il Ponte*, 36 (1980), 923–50, esp. 934–8.

5. R. Pesman Cooper, 'The Florentine Ruling Group under the "Governo popolare", 1494–1512', *Studies in Medieval and Renaissance History*, 7 (1985), 73–9 on the conditions of membership, limited to major office-holders over four generations, law of 23 Dec. 1494 (ed. G. Cadoni, *Provvisioni concernenti l'ordinamento della repubblica fiorentina, 1494–1512* (Rome: Istituto Storico Italiano per il Medio Evo, 1994), 41), cf. 78: out of 700 possible new entries to the Great Council from 1494 to 1497, only thirty-nine were admitted, twenty-eight from major guilds and just under half of these from magnate houses; Humphrey Butters, *Governors and Government in Early Sixteenth-Century Florence, 1502–1519* (Oxford: Clarendon Press, 1985), 22, 36: between 1500 and 1512, there was only one new man in the Signoria; cf. N. Rubinstein, 'Oligarchy and Democracy in Fifteenth-Century Florence', in *Florence and Venice: Comparisons and Relations*, ed. S. Bertelli *et al.*, vol. i (Florence: La nuova Italia, 1979), 108–10. On Savonarola's conservatism, D. Weinstein, *Savonarola and Florence: Prophecy and Patriotism in the Renaissance* (Princeton: Princeton University Press, 1970), ch. 1, and now L. Polizzotto, *The Elect Nation: The Savonarolan Movement in Florence, 1494–1545* (Oxford: Clarendon Press, 1994), 22 (though with different emphasis; see below).

6. See particularly M. Bullard, *Lorenzo il Magnifico: Image and Anxiety, Politics and Finance* (Florence: Olschki, 1994), esp. chs. 2 and 3; and on the publicity role of chanceries, G. Ianziti, *Humanistic Historiography under the Sforzas: Politics and Propaganda in Fifteenth-Century Milan* (Oxford: Oxford University Press, 1988).

7. Ser Francesco di ser Barone to Piero Guicciardini in Pisa, 10 Apr. 1492, Florence, Archivio Guicciardini, Leg. Comm. I, 113: 'tucta questa cicta et popolo et grandi & piccoli con grandissima unione et contenteza si monstrano uniti alla conservatione di Piero et che e succeda pariter a Lorenzo [. . .] risponde a ognuno chome uno Salamone'; 18 Apr. (I, 122): 'Le cose qui et per tucto si monstrano tucti dì in meglio in favore et beneficio di Piero'; 9 May (I, 125): 'Le cose qui procedono tucto dì a mio iudicio di bene in meglio a confermatione dello stato et a riputatione di Piero.'

8. Filippo da Gagliano to Niccolò Michelozzi in Naples, 27 Apr. 1492, BNF, GC XXIX, 69 (3421560): 'Ser Niccolò, voi non potresti stimare il modo e la buona maniera che usa il Magnifico Piero e in queste ceremonie e in ogni suo atto dello ingiegnio e giudizio suo.'

9. Filippo da Gagliano to Niccolò Michelozzi in Naples, 15 May 1492, GC, 3421563: 'Di quell'altre achalerie che dite avere udite costì circha il prociedere de L<orenz>o e Giovanni di Pierfrancesco non n'è nulla se non tutto bene & non si potrebono essere portati ne portar meglio che ffanno in ogni cosa'; 21–4 May, GC 3421564: 'E mi pare pure intendere che di quella coxa mi dimandasti di L<oren>zo e Giovanni di Pierfrancesco sia qualche cosetta ancora che poco o nulla si dimosti. Era coxa cominciata inanz'ala morte di L<orenz>o dipendente da qualche sdegnio per quanto intenda di coxa di giovani o d'amore, che sogliono avere forza assai e più presto si può dire qualche salvaticeza, perché in altro non si dimost[ri], portandosi l'uno e l'altro savissimamente, pure che questo sia é oppinione di qualchuno.'; 1 Aug. 1492, GC 3421569: 'Quello che mi dispiace, o sia o non sia, è che qui s'è detto accirchio che Lorenzo di Pierfrancesco entra in conchlavi col cardinale nostro.' Cf. MAP 75,38, Guidantonio Vespucci and Piero Capponi in Lyons to Piero de' Medici, 9 May 1494, that they had told Charles VIII 'li modi haveano [Lorenzo and Giovanni di Pierfrancesco] servati con voi dal dì che morì vostro padre in qua'. Other chroniclers refer to Giovanni's marriage to Piero's sister Luisa (d. 1488) as a cause of their early differences (B. Cerretani, *Storia fiorentina*, ed. G. Berti (Florence: Olschki, 1994), 191), or to this and an incident in a game of *calcio* (Filippo Nerli, *Commentari* (Trieste: Coen, 1859), i. 96–7, 191, and Jacopo Nardi, *Istorie della città di Firenze*, ed. A. Gelli (Florence: Le Monnier, 1858), i. 23); whereas Scipione Ammirato, *Istorie fiorentine*, bk. xxvi (Turin: Pomba, 1853), vi. 121–2, followed by G. Pieraccini, *La stirpe de' Medici di Cafaggiolo*, i (Florence: Vallecchi, 1924), 345, refer to a love affair.

10. MAP 14,296: Giovanni to Piero de' Medici, 21 Aug. 1492, headed 'Stracciatelo', ed. Picotti, *La giovinezza di Leone X* (Milan: Hoepli, 1927), app. I, no. 20, 626–8; cf. 439–40.

11. Ibid. 628: 'perché io non vo per minaccie'.

12. See Cosimo Sassetti's letter to Piero de' Medici on Lorenzo's death, 15 Apr. 1492 (MAP 14,270): 'Et perché e' [the prince of Salerno] tiene qualche poco d'amicizia con Lorenzo di Pierfrancesco, trovandosi presente quando el siniscalco et io ordinamo le lettere del re, disse che gl'era bene che si scrivessi ancora una

lettera a detto di Pierfrancesco a fine che ancora lui consigliassi di quello poteva
[. . .]'. Salerno had been in France since the Barons' War, where he was also
joined by Giuliano della Rovere, 'San Vincula'; see C. Shaw, *Julius II, the Warrior
Pope* (Oxford: Blackwell, 1993), 93–6.

13. Francesco della Casa to Piero de' Medici, Lyons, 21 May 1494 (MAP 75,87):
'Marullo bestia et un frate Lorenzo Tristo, che qui sollecitono per Lorenzo et
Giovanni di Pierfrancesco, dicono che il re l'ha scripto di costì in loro favore et
manda per loro' (ed. G. Canestrini and A. Desjardins, in *Négociations diplomatiques
de la France avec la Toscane*, i (Paris: Impr. Impériale, 1859), 303 (but omitting
'bestia')). On 7 Apr. 1494 Gentile Becchi had reported to Piero de' Medici his
conversation in France with Marullo, who told him that 'per fare capitare male
vostro padre, ci are' messo la vita: con voi non ha né bene né male', MAP 75,151
(7 Apr. 1494), cit. Martelli, 'Il libro delle Epistole di Angelo Poliziano', *Interpres*, 1
(1978), 214. On Marullo's role in France, ibid. 213–15, and id., 'La cultura
letteraria nell'età di Lorenzo', in *Lorenzo il Magnifico e il suo tempo*, ed. G. C.
Garfagnini (Florence: Olschki, 1992), 69–70.

14. Piero Capponi to Piero de' Medici (MAP 35,47, deciphered from a letter dated
29 Apr. 1493), partly ed. Canestrini-Desjardins [Can], *Négociations*, i. 393, with
no date: 'Stamani Sa' Malo mi fè richiedere chi [*che* Can] fussi contento [*operare
di* Can; s.l.add.?] mutare lo stato e da pensare io chi dessi al Re di Francia danari
gente e favore di Signorie d'Italia e tutto entròmmi ne' più strani particulari del
mondo e in su questo n'andò a caccia col Re & tornato rientrò su questa pratica,
io, con consiglio di messer Guido e parere mio, stimando non fussi male entrai
in uno poco di pratica pel bene della città et mercatanti mia in modo non si
maculassi la vostra reputatione, che chostoro pigliassino più animo a la impresa;
e fecili entrare così che innanzi io diciesi al bisogno volere saper da lasciare [om.
Can] quale il [il *ante* quale *del.*] Re di Francia harebbe più caro, o la mutatione
dello stato o il favore: rispose la mutatione sarebbe più sicura ma, considerato el
bisogno presente, quando mi rinchorassi fare che lo stato servisse sarebbe il
meglio et che io n'acquistarei grado col Re [...].'

15. Becchi to Piero de' Medici, Amboise–Tours, 28 Sept. 1494, ed. Canestrini-
Desjardins, *Négociations*, i. 329: 'Piero Soderini teme questa serpe abbi la coda
costì in Firenze e che non sia per dare a voi'; cf. his letter to Piero of 22–3 Jan.
1494 (MAP 75,127, ibid. 359: 'insino nel proprio sangue vi trovate insidiatori').
On Lorenzo di Pierfrancesco's emblem of a snake with its tail in its mouth, see
E. H. Gombrich, 'Botticelli's Mythologies', in id., *Symbolic Images* (Oxford:
Phaidon, 1978), 66, and Jonathan Nelson's discussion of Filippino Lippi's Uffizi
Allegory, with its inscribed message 'Nulla deterioris pestis quam familiaris
inimicus', to be published; cf. id., 'The Later Works of Filippino Lippi' (Ph.D.
diss., Institute of Fine Arts, New York University, 1992).

16. Francesco della Casa to Piero de' Medici, Tours, 21 Oct. 1493 (MAP 18,151):
'che il principe di Salerno et Perone 6 dì sono havevono facto expedire lettere
et patenti per le quali questo Re fa suo Ciamberlano e Consigliere Lorenzo di
Piero Francesco [. . .] Et per quanto intenda quando Perone fu costì Lorenzo li
dette qualche cosa, et così servì questo homo del principe che allhora era con
Perone di danari, et chi m'ha detto primamente tal cosa anchora mi dice che
Lorenzo ha promesso servire il principe di 500 mila ducati. [. . .] Emmi suto
accenato che con Lorenzo è anchora nominato Giovanni.' In fact 5 million was

written, but the extra zero, clearly visible from the verso of the letter, seems to have been deleted to produce this large but more realistic figure. This account is verified not only by della Casa (ibid.: 'Intesi tutto questo come vi dicho davanti hieri da uno amicho nostro degni di fede et di poi sono ito copertamente investigando se è vero, et in effecto per altri buoni riscontri trovo così essere apunto') but by ser Bernardo Dovizi's letter to Piero de' Medici [*c*.21 July 1493] (MAP 18,306, ed. G. L. Moncallero, *Epistolario di Bernardo Dovizi da Bibbiena*, i (Florence: Olschki, 1955), 25: 'El parente et vicino vostro fa un grande stare con questo franzese et col secretario che ha seco del Salerno, insieme tucti e tre spesso e spesso con ciaschuno di per se. A quel secretario ha mandati cento ducati d'oro in oro'). According to B. Corio, *Storia di Milano* (Padua: Paolo Frambotto, 1646), 906, the bribe was 100,000 gold florins. See also below, n. 24.

17. G. Becchi to Piero de' Medici, 23–6 Jan. 1494 (MAP 75,130), cit. Martelli, 'Il *Libro*', 200: 'et provederà chostì si faccia mutatione, ché per altro non hanno chiamato qui Giovanni di Pierfrancesco se non per havere, etc.'

18. Letters of 30 Mar. 1494 (MAP 18,371, ibid.), 194: 'Il dì di Pasqua habiamo da uno che sa le cose che s'atende al mutare costì lo stato'; 8 Mar. (MAP 75,139; Martelli, 196) and 12 Mar.: 'le minacci sono hor sul mutare dello stato' (MAP 75,144; Martelli, 195).

19. P. Alamanni to Piero, 19 Mar. 1494 (MAP 50,254): 'che ci raccomandava la libertà el populo e tucta la Citta, & volentieri vorrebbe potere salire in su uno pergamo costì et predicare queste cose a tucto el populo'. In an earlier bracketed and underlined passage (i.e. deleted from his account of this interview), Lodovico reported the news from France that the king had told the Florentine ambassadors there 'che quando e' suoi exerciti fussino in Italia, la città nostra si schoprirebbe, etc.' at which Lodovico interjected, before returning to the letter, 'et di questo non mi havete voi però conferito niente'.

20. Beginning with Francesco Guicciardini, *Storie fiorentine*, 90: 'benché Piero fussi malissimo disposto con loro, nondimeno non concorrendo a insanguinarsi e' cittadini dello stato, furono liberati e confinati fuori di Firenze [. . .] e Cosimo Rucellai assente ebbe bando di rubello', and id., *Dialogo del Reggimento*, ed. R. Palmarocchi (Bari: Laterza, 1932), 79: 'che furono machinazioni contra lo stato e contra Piero, e pure furono governate piacevolmente'. Nardi gives one of the fullest accounts of this event, though admitting 'né si seppe mai che di ciò [their imprisonment] fusse la cagione' (*Istorie di Firenze*, i. 23–240).

21. 'Il *Libro*', 190–1, citing Landucci, who says the cousins were imprisoned on 26 Apr. (*Diario fiorentino*, ed. I. del Badia (Florence: Sansoni, 1883, repr. 1985), 67), like Piero Parenti ('giorno infelice: passati già anni XVI', *Storia fiorentina*, ed. A. Matucci, i (Florence: Olschki, 1994), 70). Tribaldo de' Rossi (*Ricordanze, Delizie degli eruditi toscani*, xxiii (Florence: Cambiagi, 1786), 291) dates it 24 Apr., 'the Feast of S. Mark', in fact on 25 Apr., which is the date given by Tommaso Ginori (Libro di debitori e creditori e ricordanze in J. Schnitzer, *Quellen und Forschungen zur Geschichte Savonarolas* (Munich: Lentner, 1902), i. 94), according to whom the 70 met on the 23rd, imprisoned them on the 25th, condemned them on 28th and accepted Piero's pardon on 29th; this is the date recorded in SS. Deliberazioni ord. aut. [= SS. Delib] 96, fo. 25^r, of their 'relegatio [. . .] eorum vita durante extra civitate Florentiae et utrum unum miliare circum'; neither imprisonment nor exile is recorded in Otto di Guardia 97.

22. Guidantonio Vespucci and Piero Capponi to Piero Medici, 9 May 1494 (MAP 75,38, ed. Canestrini-Desjardins, *Négociations*, i. 390): 'che tutti li 70 li havevan condemnati in perpetuo carcere et confiscati li loro beni, noi tenevamo per certo volessino machinare contro lo stato et principali citadini di quelle [. . .] et dicemo come la clementia vostra era stata tanta che haveva mitighato la pena', concluding that although their information came only from 'questi mercatanti', 'erano cose di mala natura' (391). Cf. Puccio Pucci, Florentine ambassador in Rome, to Piero Medici, 16 June 1494, ibid. 90: 'consigliorono e giudicarono gli errori loro essere mortali e meritare supplizio della vita'. Poliziano, too, stressed Piero's clemency, 'divinus hic iuvenis, decus praesidiumque nostrum', letter to Pico della Mirandola of 20 May, ed. Martelli, 'Il *Libro*', 191–2; cf. Guicciardini, n. 20 above.

23. e.g. Parenti, *Storia fiorentina*, i. 69, who describes in detail the various procedures used by Piero to control his cousins, both constitutional and non-constitutional (such as having them examined by three private citizens 'fuori dello uficio delli Otto della Balìa', ibid. 67–71); and Bartolomeo Cerretani, *Storia fiorentina*, 191, according to whom Piero 'tenttò [. . .] per mezzo di chancellieri, tre ghonfalonieri a la fila di fare tagliare la testa a cimque di loro et de' primi de la ciptà' but the gonfaloniers refused to execute these five conspirators 'sanza intendere Piero proprio et gl'huomini de lo stato'.

24. Parenti, *Storia fiorentina*, i. 67–8; C. Delaborde, *L'Expédition de Charles VIII en Italie* (Paris: Firmin-Didot, 1888), 362–3; according to Parenti, the cousins produced 'autentica scrittura' showing they were the king's men and that they each received from him an annual pension of 2,000 écus (ibid. 68; cf. Jacopo Pitti, '2,000 florins' (*Istoria fiorentina*, ed. F. L. Polidori, *Archivio storico italiano*, 1 (1842), 28). See also Vespucci's and Capponi's letter of 9 May in n. 22 above: 'che vi era altro che volere onorare li oratori del Christianissimo Re'.

25. Pietro Tornabuoni to Piero de' Medici, 5 Jan. 1494 (MAP 56,84): Marchese Gabriele Malaspina 'mi disse che Cosimo Rucellai era a Fosdenuovo [. . .] e haveva detto al Marchese che la venuta sua era per far doglenza di que' danari che la Magnificenza Vostra fece dare a messer Galeotto, e che la domenica Cosimo haveva hauto um fante aposta di costì con lettere di Bernardo e d'altri e che gli haveva mostro quella di Bernardo e narròmi il tenore d'epsa' and he asked Tornabuoni what to do. On 28 Apr. 1494 Francesco della Casa reported to Piero Bibbiena from Lyons: 'Cosimo Rucellai partì hieri di qui dove è stato 6 dì, ne si è visto darvi alchuna mala dimostratione' (MAP 72,72); Cosimo was summonsed by the Signoria on 29 Apr. 1494, 'Qualiter ipse tentavit et plura fecit contra [. . .] pacificum statum populi Flor', and on 30 June, wanting to proceed 'non secundum delictorum et inobedientie merita sed cum humanitate', he was exiled for life to the territory of Prato; SS. Delib. 96, fos. 25^v, 47^v–49^r; on the machinations of Cosimo 'e forse di Bernardo', see Guicciardini, *Dialogo*, 79.

26. According to Parenti (*Storia fiorentina*, i. 68–70), the Florentines were Francesco Soderini, their secretary Zanobi Acciaiuoli (and his uncle Jacopo Acciaiuoli, Lorenzo and Giovanni's cousin, then living in Ferrara), Piero di Jacopo Ridolfi, and Giannozzo Manetti, as well as three members of their household.

27. Antonio [Guidotti] da Colle to Piero de' Medici, 3 May 1494 (MAP 55,177): 'et maravigliomi che in questa insalata non sia dell'erba di questi Pazi, practicando il veschovo assiduamente come fa con As<canio>'. On Charles's role as

'catalyseur des Oppositions' in effecting the return of exiles like the Pazzi, see A. Denis, *Charles VIII et les italiens: histoire et mythe* (Geneva: Droz, 1979), 96–7 and n. 11.

28. Letter to Piero de' Medici from Tours, 21 Oct. 1493 (MAP 18,151; see above, n. 16): 'Et questi medesimi autori et motori di tal cosa hanno anchora con la medesima malignità altra volta ragionato di fare favore alla casa de' Pazzi.'

29. Letter to Piero of 30 Mar. 1494 (MAP 18,371): 'Il primo aviso vi de' fare aprire l'ochio che Ubigny non venga uno Montesecco' (on being sent to Florence with an excuse, to plot the conspiracy); on these embassies, see Parenti, *Storie fiorentine*, i. 14–16, 73.

30. Lorenzo was born on 4 Aug. 1463, Giovanni on 21 Oct. 1467, Piero di Lorenzo on 15 Feb. 1472.

31. Piero Alamanni to Piero de' Medici from Vigevano, 4 Mar. 1494 (MAP 50,242): '[Lodovico] mi domandò se io sapevo che Lorenzo di Pierfranceso fussi facto Ciamberlano del re di Francia. Risposi che noi n'havamo havuto qualche sentore. Dixemi "vedete che voi non mi comunicate cosa alchuna". Risposili che eravamo per confereli le cose degne di stima & che d'una sì piccola cosa ci verghogneremo a tenere conto. Dixemi "parvella però sì piccola, sappiendo ch'el populo è inclinato a Francia et Lorenzo è della qualità che è?"' to which the ambassador replied 'quanto alle qualità di Lorenzo [. . .] non era da pensarvi puncto'; and when asked about Giovanni's visit to France summoned by the king, he feigned ignorance, 'et domandai S. Excellentia se sapeva di che qualità era Giovanni, di che cervello & di che experientia. Et di poi feci molto bene la chiosa a questo testo con dire che noi sapavamo che questa era una favola mendicata o dal principe di Salerno o da altri.' In Jean Matharon's instruction dated 11 June 1494, the brothers are described as 'Regis officiales [. . .] ordinarii' (Canestrini-Desjardins, *Négociations*, i. 416).

32. Antonio da Colle to Piero de' Medici, letter of 3 May cit.: 'et discorrendo le nature di Lorenzo & di Giovanni mostrai ad sua Santità che erano sempre stati inutili cittadini alla città & per questo non havere gra<tia> come s'è dimostro in questi lor casi'.

33. The same, 7 May 1494 (MAP 14,408): after telling Ascanio 'che Lorenzo et Giovanni erano stati distenuti et poi puniti per li loro mali portamenti et per havere errato gravissimamente', Ascanio 'sanza domandarmi d'altro dixe "che ho<mo> è quello Giovanni? Io non lo conoscho. Lorenzo vidi quando venne qui et parla<i>le una volta che mi parve homo da bene." Risposi che l'uno & l'altro erano giovani et come giovani s'erano ghovernati, monstrandoli dextramente che per le qualità & modi loro nella città havevano più odio et malivolenza che credito.'

34. The same, 3 May cit.: after being told by Ascanio Sforza 'come Lorenzo & Giovanni erano stati liberati et da gran numero di cittadini erano stati acompagnati a casa con dimostratione d'havere dispiacere del caso loro', the pope professed to be pleased by Piero's measures and wanted Antonio to caution him 'che viva con cura della persona et guardisi dal andare di notte a' suoi piaceri, perché sopra questo suo andare di notte s'è facti già di mali disegni.'

35. A. Brown, 'Lorenzo, the Monte and the Seventeen Reformers', in ead., *The Medici in Florence: The Exercise and Language of Power* (Florence: Olschki, 1992),

170, 190–1 (where the tax debt of both cousins is described as 3,000 florins); ead., 'Pierfrancesco de' Medici, 1430–1476', ibid., 96–7 (on the 33,600 florins borrowed from them during the war, which with other loans to the Magnifico totalled 53,643 florins).

36. Ibid. 97–8.

37. Cento 3, fos. 13^v–14^r (28 Aug. 1492); cf. Parenti, *Storia fiorentina*, i. 35.

38. See Brown, 'Lorenzo, the Monte and the Seventeen Reformers', 175 n. 68, quoting from Notarile antecos. 10200, fos. 362^v–363^r (6 Nov. 1492).

39. ASF Otto di Guardia rep. 74, fo. 2^v (2 July 1486); the list to be drawn up by one of the Otto, Francesco di Matteo di Nero Orafo, a Medici land agent (see my edition of *The Political and Humanistic Writings of Bartolomeo Scala* (MRTS; New York, 1996), 152, letter 186, note a). Whereas Lorenzo il Magnifico was allowed *balistarii* as well as *staffieri*, the cousins only enjoyed the latter, however.

40. A. Brown, *Bartolomeo Scala, 1430–1497* (Princeton: Princeton University Press, 1979), 120; their mandate is edited by Canestrini-Desjardins, *Négociations*, i. 200–4.

41. See Lorenzo Spinelli to Piero de' Medici, 24 Aug. 1493 (MAP 19,194): 'Avisendovi che per ghuadangnare di questi signori che ssono intorno al re in qualche alturità il Signore Lodovico à donato di molti danari. Noi ne paghamo d<ucati> ii mila a Mons. di Molans e altanti a mons. d'Albingni [. . .] e Coximo [Sassetti] comprendo ne paghassi altri ii mila a ii altri. O inteso che mons. d'Albingni n'à avuti degli altri. Et ò inteso paghò a madama di Borbone et che le disse che il signore Lodovico era contento dare allei xii mila ducati l'anno di pensione et ella lo servissi a questo chaso, hofferendone dare altri xii mila a più altri ghovernatori.' Although she refused to be bribed, Spinelli reported that his friend thought that Lodovico's money 'sia chagone da fare che alchuni, in chui il re, à fede [. . .].' The money received by Charles VIII for the expedition is listed by Y. Labande-Mailfert, *Charles VIII et son milieu (1470–1498)* (Paris: Klincksieck, 1975), 237–8. Cf. also G. B. Ridolfi's letters to Piero de' Medici of 25 Sept. and 7 Oct. 1494 listing loans to the king from Lodovico and others (MAP 74,104 and 107).

42. M. Bullard, 'Financing the Pope's Debt' and 'Banking on Reputation' in ead., *Lorenzo il Magnifico*, 155–214, esp. 199, 207, 179. Concern for the fate of the *regnio* is reflected in Filippo da Gagliano's correspondence with Niccolò Michelozzi, then in Rome, e.g. GC 3421570 (4 Aug. 1492); cf. MAP 14,293 (Niccolò Michelozzi to Piero de' Medici, 14 Aug. 1492, reporting favourably on Cardinal Giovanni's behaviour despite 'tanta iniquità' 'tentato da altri contra di noi').

43. At Alfonso's request, Florence agreed to contribute 15,000 ducats to the condotta of the Duke of Candia provided it was 'segretissimo' (Bernardo Dovizi to Piero de' Medici, 8 Mar. 1494, ed. G. L. Moncallero in *Il Cardinale Bernardo Dovizi da Bibbiena* (Florence: Olschki, 1953), 96). Cf. Dionigi Pucci's letter to Piero from Naples of 28 Apr. 1494 (MAP 19,557), describing the king's gift to Piero of an estate at Ostone for olives and for the recreation of the bank officials, into which the king would put 20,000 ducats and Piero the same. Piero, however, replied on 6 May that although the citizens would agree to the Duke of Candia's condotta if 'si potessi fare infra pochi e sanza molto publica deliberatione', he politely

rejected the estate at Ostone, since his family had always lived 'civilmente [. . .] delle loro traffichi et possessioni né mai hanno cerco havere altro che privato', and hoped the king would show his favour to the bank in Naples instead; ed. in *Archivio storico italiano*, 1 (1842), 346–7 (appendix, for the reference to which I am indebted to Jonathan Nelson). On the Medici bank in Naples, cf. M. Jacoviello, 'Affari di Medici e Strozzi nel regno di Napoli nella 2a. metà del Quattrocento', ibid., 144 (1986), 196.

44. See J. de la Pilorgerie, *Campagne et bulletins de la Grande Armée d'Italie commandée par Charles VIII, 1494–5* (Nantes and Paris: V. Forest et E. Grimaud, 1866), 91: that Spinelli had offered the king on behalf of Alfonso 150,000 ducats every six months, that is an annual tribute of 300,000 ducats; cf. below, n. 50, and Filippo Valori's letter to Piero de' Medici dated 13 Oct. 1494 on payments and tips to be paid to the French by Spinelli (and Piero) on Ferrante's behalf (ed. Canestrini-Desjardins, *Négociations*, i. 461–2).

45. Parenti, *Storia fiorentina*, i. 64: 'più di ducati CCC mila si reputava'. According to Marcel Vigne (*La Banque à Lyon du xve au xviiie siècle* (Lyons and Paris: A. Rey, 1903), 87), there were *c*.33 Florentine banks in Lyons in 1469. Lorenzo Spinelli and Cosimo Sassetti, who ran the Medici bank in Lyons (R. de Roover, *Il Banco Medici dalle origini al suo declino, 1397–1494* (Florence: La Nuova Italia, 1970), 447–9), were also involved in lending money to the French, see above, n. 41 and below, n. 46.

46. Letter to Piero de' Medici, Amboise–Tours, 28 Sept. 1493, ed. Canestrini-Desjardins, *Négociations*, i. 329: 'La mercanzia è nimica dello stato.' According to Parenti (*Storia fiorentina*, i. 67), the Florentine bankers in France refused Charles VIII's demand for a loan of 60,000 scudi before receiving consent from Florence, only to find that the Medici bank had agreed to it, 'la qual nuova assai dette da pensare a' mercatanti qui nostri'; cf. Philippe de Commines to Lorenzo Spinelli (Vienne, 6 Aug. 1494, ed. Canestrini-Desjardins, 418), describing Piero's un-willingness to lend the king money when 'autreffois Florentins ont presté deux cens mille ducas contans au Roy Ferrand et payé cinquante mille ducas tous les ans comme par tribut', to which Spinelli responded, as he told Piero, 'qu'en particulier je croys qu'on eust trouvé avecques vous [Piero] quelque somme raisonnable'. At the end of Dec. 1493 Becchi reported San Malo's opinion that 'L'universale di Firenze sappiamo che è per Francia' (MAP 72,49; see Martelli, 'll *Libro*', 199–4); cf. above, n. 14.

47. See Piero Capponi in Lyons to Piero de' Medici, 8 June 1494 (MAP 75,52): beginning 'non è cosa alchuna che sia da extimare tanto quanto è ad mantenere ad uno suo amico l'amicitia de uno grande maestro', he reminded Piero of the known 'servitù' of him and his brothers towards the cardinal of Lyons [André d'Espinay, also cardinal bishop of Bordeaux; Canestrini-Desjardins, *Négociations*, i. 249 n. 2; Labande-Mailfert, *Charles VIII*, 222] and asked Piero with money or with his influence with Virginio Orsini to help him, since 'sarebbe da preghare Idio che desse alle volte occasione di potere guadagnare simili personagi'. On Capponi banking interests, see R. A. Goldthwaite, *Private Wealth in Renaissance Florence* (Princeton: Princeton University Press, 1968), 199–213. On San Malo's discussion with Capponi's agent in France and threat to direct his son to Lorenzo di Pierfrancesco instead of Piero, see Becchi's letter of 30 Dec. 1493–3 Jan. 1494 (MAP 72,49; Martelli, 'Il *Libro*', 199).

48. Angelo Niccolini to Piero de' Medici, Milan, 20 July 1494 (MAP 74,97, decoded), reporting a discussion with a secret messenger in Piacenza that 'egl'hanno quattro famigle delle prime della Città, le quali tengono questa praticha in Lione col Re di Francia et che hanno ordinato scoprirsi come il Re avvicina'. On Piero's Francophilism, see Becchi's undated note possibly referring to his election as Gonfalonier of Justice in Nov.–Dec. 1493 (to Piero de' Medici, MAP 75,103: 'O voi havete facto il figluolo d'Orlando gonfaloniere, chome può dire alcuno che non siete per Carlo re di Francia?'). Another Francophile optimate was Pagolantonio Soderini, who was sent an anonymous *ricordo* when ambassador in Venice that declared the 'corona di Francia [. . .] è il naturale instituto nostro et in spetie della servità di casa mia' (11 Oct. 1494, MAP 75,24).

49. Antonio da Colle to Piero de' Medici, 20 Oct. 1494 (MAP 18,344): 'La fugha de' parenti vostro qua s'è publicata per tutto et credesi certo che habbi a parturire qualche novità nella città.' His letter was received in Florence on 22 Oct. Giovanbattista Ridolfi had earlier reported from Milan that 'e' siano in grande speranza che [decoded] *nella città sopravenendo loro habbi ad essere novità, faciendo opinione che voi confidiate pocho ne' cittadini et converso che e' non vi sieno affectionati*' (MAP 74,110).

50. Giovanbattista Ridolfi to Piero de' Medici, 22 Oct. 1494 (Canestrini-Desjardins, *Négociations*, i. 584–6): 'Messer, tale e passerà pochi giorni, che voi harete un altro nuovo Duca' from which they inferred 'che gl'habbi in animo di farsi re di Lombardia'; and that Charles VIII had told Lodovico il Moro 'che voi [Piero de' Medici] li havete mandato a offerire 300,000 franchi et che e' si ritragghi dall'impresa. Et lui dice, che non ha bisogno di danari.' In fact, Florence's indemnity to Charles was 120,000 florins, slightly less than a half-share of the tribute Alfonso and Piero were said to have offered him before the invasion; see above, n. 44.

51. Filippo da Gagliano to Niccolò Michelozzi, 26 Oct. 1494 (GC 3421514): 'Io avevo caro di darvi stamani [. . .] come P<iero> schontrandomi stamani in Santa Maria del Fiore mi chiamò e dimandòmi quella faccenda. E andando dopo mangiare per ordinarla fec<[......]> chavalchato subito. E' quasi solo e la brighata li andava drieto a uno a uno E da <[......]> di mandare forzaretti e veste e altro come si avessi andare a trovare il re [. . .] in effetto chiaramente si dicie à preso il camino per là [. . .] Diciemi uno amico mio che questo partito è tutto schietto [. . .] è preso da Piero e che non à conferito con <niuna ?> maxime di questi principali. Stimasi pure debba essere con qualche intelligenzia dala banda di là e qualchuno dicie essere questa praticha dello Spinello. Come si sia, Iddio li dia buona fine [. . .] Domattina ci doverà essere sua lettera come quella che ffè il padre a Sa' Miniato.' He ends by urging Michelozzi to return, 'anchora che io ò visto andare tanto lieto e ridente ser Piero [Bibbiena], che pare che sia andato fino al Poggio'. On Gagliano's relationship with Piero and his father, and the charges subsequently made against him, see below, n. 65.

52. Piero's two letters of 26 Oct. from Empoli, one to ser Piero Dovizi, the other to [the Otto di Pratica], 'cotesti ciptadini, che alla Signoria mi parebbe arrogantia la mia a scrivere' as he wrote to ser Piero (MAP 72,79 and MAP 124,346) are edited by Canestrini-Desjardins, *Négociations*, i. 587–9. Lorenzo's letter to the Signoria of Florence dated 7 Dec. 1479 (with two letters to the Dieci di Balìa), is in *Lettere*, ed. N. Rubinstein, iv (Florence: Giunti-Barbera, 1981), 265–70.

Parenti reports that in September only Piero resisted ceding to the king, 'usando dire [. . .] che sempre sarebbe a tempo a gittarsi nelle braccia al signor re di Francia' (*Storia fiorentina*, i. 97).

53. Letter to the Otto di Pratica of 26 Oct. cit: 'per la fede et affectione debbono alle ossa del vostro Lorenzo, mio padre'.

54. Ser Bernardo Dovizi to the duke of Calabria, 31 Oct. 1494 (MAP 72,85, in *Epistolario*, ed. Moncallero, i. 235): 'Io arrivai qui hyeri et ho trovato, Signore mio, questa città in tanta mutatione [*s.l.ex.* tribulatione] et tanto diversa da quello che la lasciai [. . .] Come io ho dicto più volte ad la Ex. V. questa città è franzese tucta [. . .].' Piero was summoned to meet the king on 30 Oct. 1494, when he wrote to inform ser Piero, 'perché meco rallegriate di tanto honore', asking him to inform the Otto di Pratica, his wife and brothers, though only adding his reference to the 'Signori Octo' above the line, as an afterthought (MAP 72,82, cf. 72,83, both dated 30 Oct., Canestrini-Desjardins, *Négociations*, i. 592–3). On the cost of the fortresses, see A. Brown, 'Lorenzo, the Monte and the Seventeen Reformers', 176 n. 71, and Cerretani (*Storia fiorentina*, 197) that the city had spent more than 50,000 gold florins on Sarzana, 'ed era cosa fortissima'. They were ceded to the king on 31 Oct.; Labande-Mailfort, *Charles VIII*, 288; Parenti, *Storia fiorentina*, i. 112–14.

55. See above, n. 44; on French greed, Cerretani, *Storia fiorentina*, 199, quoting Piero Capponi's reported speech in the Seventy on what to do after Piero had handed over the fortresses: 'et chognosciuto l'avaritia de' franzesi et loro chupidità no si manchi per danari in chontentarlli'.

56. SS. Delib. 96, fos. 86^r (6 Nov.); Cerretani, *Storia fiorentina*, 205–7; Parenti, *Storia fiorentina*, 122–6. Technically, Piero was in contempt of the Signoria for failing to appear when later that day he was summonsed by them; on the same day, the Signoria opened the Stinche, and 'attenta humanitatis & bonis moribus Laurentii & Ioannis Pierfrancesci de Medici', recalled them and Cosimo Rucellai from exile and Pagolantonio Soderini from his embassy in Venice; SS. Delib. 96, fos. 86^v–87^r (9 Nov.).

57. See N. Rubinstein, 'Politics and Constitution in Florence at the End of the Fifteenth Century', in E. F. Jacob (ed.), *Italian Renaissance Studies* (London: Faber & Faber, 1960), 152; Pesman-Cooper, 'The Florentine Ruling Group', 71–2; Butters, *Governors and Government*, 21.

58. I shall return to it in my study of the ruling elite from 1480 to 1502.

59. SS. Delib. 96, fo. 87$^{r–v}$: 'et eisdem dominis manifestari debeant [. . .] per totam presentem diem'.

60. Ibid., fos. 87^r–91^v, 94^v, 114^v; SS. Delib. 97, 5^v–6^r, 7^r, 8^v, 19^r, 28^v–29^r, etc. Despite this, many possessions escaped detection, as we know from the evidence of the Medici factor Francesco Cegia; see G. Pampaloni, 'I ricordi segreti del mediceo Francesco di Agostino Cegia (1495–97)', *Archivio storico italiano*, 115 (1957), 188–234. The first person to be declared a rebel on 12 Nov. was Piero's *staffiere*, Giuliano Rossi of Pistoia, al. Salvalaglio, Piero himself being declared a rebel 'propter inobbedientiam et indignationem' on 20 Nov. (ibid., fos. 90^r, 96^r).

61. SS. Delib. 96, fo. 102$^{r–v}$ (2 Dec. 1494); Provvisioni 185, fos. 19^v–21^v (29 Dec. 1494), fo. 124$^{r–v}$; Strozz. ser. I, no. 4 (Bastardello: Deliberazioni degli officiali sopra i fatti e negotii di Piero de Medici). The treaty is published in *Archivio*

storico italiano, 1 (1842), app., 372 (clause 17), summarized in Canestrini-Desjardins, *Négociations,* i. 605.

62. Provvisioni 185, fo. 26ʳ (13 Jan. 1495). They had authority to vet the accounts and payments made by the following magistracies since 1478: the Ufficiali del Monte, Otto di Pratica, Dieci di Balìa, Capitani della Parte Guelfa, Otto di Guardia, Camera delle Arme, Zecca, Dogana, Cinque del Contado, the Sea Consuls, as well as those of all tax officials, treasurers, and accountants of communal monies.

63. Listed, with the appeals of officials charged, in SS. Delib. 97. The first permission to leave the palace for the night was granted to Simone Niccolini on 12 Apr. 1495, and again on 14 and 25 Apr., fos. 39ᵛ, 43ᵛ.

64. The officials were officially disbanded on 12 May and reconstituted on 20 June; SS. Delib. 97, fos. 51ᵛ, 68ᵛ.

65. SS. Delib. 97, fos. 88ᵛ–89ʳ (18 Aug. 1495): 'Ma in quanto a detta somma et quantita di f. 13,752 s. 7 d. 9 havuti Lorenzo [. . .] de Medici dal detto Filippo [. . .] da Gagliano, come nel ricorso di detto Filippo si narra, dichiarorono decto Filippo [. . .] havere male ricorso [. . .] contro al quale Lorenzo de Medici et suoi heredi et beni per la presente si da et concede al detto Filippo [. . .] pieno rigresso per decti somma [. . .] el quale pagamento s'abbia a ffare per detto Filippo [. . .] in termine d'anni quattro proximi futuri da oggi, pagandone ogn'anno la quarta parte.' cf. Parenti, *Storia fiorentina,* i. 260, according to whom the Colleges wanted him to repay the full amount, prolonging the case until 'ore 5 di notte [. . .] Ridussesi tale iudizio in tanta contenzione che, mentre si discuteva la materia in Piazza [. . .] gridato fu "impicca, impicca".' On Filippo da Gagliano's role in providing Lorenzo with money through the Monte, see A. Brown, 'Lorenzo, the Monte and the Seventeen Reformers', esp. 172–5, and my forthcoming study.

66. SS. Delib. 97–9. The appointment of five syndics in 1527 to review all government spending since 1512 shows the importance this review played in the ideology of the last republic, which revived not only the religious but also the political programme of the 1494–1512 republic; see Polizzotto, *Elect Nation,* ch. 7, esp. 353; cf. J. Stephens, *The Fall of the Florentine Republic, 1512–1530* (Oxford: Clarendon Press, 1983), 220–41, who seems unaware however (220) that syndics were appointed in 1494–5 to pursue public officials as well as the Medici.

67. SS. Delib. 97, fos. 149ʳ–154ᵛ at 151ᵛ–153ᵛ (Turin, 16 Aug. 1495, summarized in Canestrini-Desjardins, *Négociations,* i. 630–2, and dated 26 Aug.; the final 30,000 florins were paid on 15 Aug. 1495; ibid. 605 n. 1).

68. Parenti, *Storia fiorentina,* i. 135: 'Così in brevissimo tempo tre singulari uomini mancorono. Un quarto s'aggiungneva, Giorgio Merula [. . .] per la qual cosa coniettura si fece, che alla Italia gravissimi mali soprastavano [. . .]'.

69. On Savonarola's prophecies and his *Compendio di rivelazioni,* printed in 1495, see Weinstein, *Savonarola and Florence,* ch. 2; on popular verse, and printed prophecies, O. Niccoli, *Prophecy and People in Renaissance Italy* (Princeton: Princeton University Press, 1990), ch. 1, 'Prophecies and the Italian Wars'; and on the New World, A. Grafton, *New World, Ancient Texts: The Power of Tradition and the Shock of Discovery* (Cambridge, Mass.: Belknap Press of Harvard University Press, 1992), ch. 2.

70. See Parenti, *Storia fiorentina*, i. 103, 106, 245–6, and on the charitable programme of Savonarola and his followers, Polizzotto, *The Elect Nation*, 30–7. As evidence of economic hardship, fifty Benedectine nuns in S. Piero a Monticelli complained they were unable to earn any money spinning thread and embroidering cloth since the invasion (G. A. Brucker, 'Monasteries, Friaries, Nunneries in Quattrocento Florence', repr. in id., *Renaissance Florence: Society, Culture and Religion* (Goldbach: Keip, 1994), 295).

71. See Goldthwaite, 'I prezzi del grano a Firenze dal XIV al XVI sec.', *Quaderni storici*, 28 (1975), 34: the average price in the preceding decade of *c.* £23 per staio doubled and tripled to reach £40 per staio in 1496 and £64 in 1497; cf. G. Pampaloni, 'La crisi annonaria fiorentina degli anni 1496–1497 e le importazioni di grano dalla Romagna', *Atti e memorie d. Deput. St. Pat. per le province di Romagna*, NS 15–17 (1963–4), 277–303; Tribaldo de' Rossi, *Ricordanze*, 299–302: 'O quante ansietà e afanni e miserie erono nelle persone se ben vi richorda in questo tempo.'

72. C. Carnesecchi, 'Un tumulto di donne', in I. Del Badia (ed.), *Miscellanea fiorentina di erudizione e storia* (Florence: Landi, 1902), ii. 45–7; Polizzotto, *Elect Nation*, 49; cf. Tribaldo, *Ricordanze*, 300–1; on the government measures, SS. Delib. 99, fo. 41ʳ (21 May 1497: that the Buonuomini of S. Martino be given empty accommodation 'ut in eis amore dei hospitentur et receptentur existentes in civitate Florentiae non habentes domicilium vel hospitium in quo possint hospitari'); fo. 69ᵛ (3 Aug. 1497: 'volentes abundantie frugum favere', they granted full powers to the Grain Officials 'super puniendo et mulchtando fornarios et sue molendinarios vel alios tractantes frumente'); fo. 81ʳ (5 Sept.: these Officials to give the poor every day for eight days '6 frumenti eorum officii [. . .] pro distribuendo dictis pauperibus'); fo. 84ʳ (19 Sept.: they can 'habere et eligere quascunque mansiones voluerint in domo habitationis olim Piero Laurentii de Medici pro tenendo ibidem frumentum et alia opportuna dicti eorum officii', etc.).

73. P. Vaglienti, *Storia dei suoi tempi, 1492–1514*, ed. G. Berti, M. Luzzati, and E. Tongiorgi (Pisa: Nistri-Lischi e Pacini, 1982), 50: 'l'uno e l'altro sempre sono stati uomini da bene e costumati in ogni loro affare e così fu Piero Francesco loro padre, che mai si curò di stato né di governo [. . .] né mai s'imbrattonno della pecunia del Comune ma sempre per esso popolo cerconno ogni bene e ogni onore che per esso Comune s'appartenesse.' Cf. Tribaldo de' Rossi, *Ricordanze*, 302, and above, n. 71.

74. *The Elect Nation*, esp. ch. 1. On the transformation of art under the influence of Savonarola, see R. M. Steinberg, *Fra Girolamo Savonarola, Florentine Art and Renaissance Historiography* (Athens: Ohio University Press, 1977), ch. 12; M. B. Hall, 'Savonarola's Preaching and the Patronage of Art', in T. Verdon and J. Henderson (eds.), *Christianity and the Renaissance* (Syracuse: Syracuse University Press, 1990), 494–522.

75. BNF Magl. VII, 1195, fos. 102ʳ–117ᵛ; ed. A. Brown, Bartolomeo Scala, *Humanistic and Political Writings*, VI, 5.

76. On Marullo, see above, n. 13. An undated and placatory reply from Scala to Marullo rejecting innuendos against Marullo suggests that Scala was then a mediator rather than a partisan in Marullo's affairs (see below, n. 77). Moreover,

as late as 1493 Scala was suggested to Piero as the person best able to provide the
king of France with information, not just about Florence but about the Medici
family, 'come sono i privilegi che havete et quanto altro è occorso che sia
notabile'; Francesco della Casa to Piero de' Medici, 21 May 1494 (MAP 18, 117).
Martelli shows as evidence of his alienation that he had already replaced Lorenzo
de' Medici as the dedicatee of Alessandro Braccesi's third book of *Carmina*, 'La
cultura letteraria', 70–1.

77. On Scala's *Centum Apologi* as a source for the frieze in his own courtyard, see A.
Parronchi, 'The Language of Humanism and the Language of Sculpture', *Journal
of the Warburg and Courtauld Institutes*, 27 (1964), 108–36, now published in
Italian, 'Il latino di B.S. e quello di Bertoldo', in his *Lorenzo e dintorni* (Florence:
Polistampa, 1992), 63–105, with an appendix, 'Anno Aureo', 113–27;
on references in Scala's frieze to Lorenzo, see J. Draper, *Bertoldo di Giovanni*
(Columbia, Mo. and London: University of Missouri Press, 1992), 224. The first
hundred fables, published by C. Müllner (Vienna, 1897), the recently discovered
second hundred, the fable *Mundus* below, and the letter to Marullo referred
to in note 76 above, are in A. Brown (ed.), Bartolomeo Scala, *Humanistic and
Political Writings*. Five fables titled *Day* as well as at least seven others (I, 49, 53,
90; II, 25, 26, 37, 39) discuss Nature's determinism, while two fables, *Tempus* (I,
41) and *Felicitas* (II, 97) allude more overtly to Lorenzo as Apollo and Pan,
divinities whose will must be obeyed. On the Poggio frieze, see P. H. Foster, *A
Study of Lorenzo de' Medici's Villa at Poggio a Caiano*, 2 vols. (New York: Garland
Pub., 1978); J. Cox-Rearick, 'Themes of Time and Rule at Poggio a Caiano',
Mitteilungen des Kunsthistorischen Institutes in Florenz, 26 (1982), 167–210, and
ead., *Dynasty and Destiny in Medici Art* (Princeton: Princeton University Press,
1984), 65–86; F. Landi, *Le temps revient: il fregio di Poggio a Caiano* (S. Giovanni
Val d'Arno: Landi, 1986), and Draper, above.

78. Lionardo Salviati, 'Dialogo d'Amicizia', *Opere*, i (Milan: Società tipografica de'
Classici italiani, 1809), 27: 'm'avete rinfrescata nell'animo ricordanza di quei
ragionamenti che ebbe il Pico nostro sopra dell'amicizia nel giardino dello Scala
suo e nostro amicissimo di pochi giorni avanti che e' partisse da noi, a' qual' né
Piero [Ridolfi] qui ned' io [Jacopo Salviati], che allora in Bologna per alcuni
nostri comuni affari eravamo, potemmo ritrovare. Ma dal Ficino nostro e dal
Poliziano altresì [. . .]'. Pico left Florence *c*.13 Apr. (Filippo da Gagliano to N.
Michelozzi, 16 Apr. 1492 (GC 3421553): '3 dì sono'); on 27 Apr. he wrote again:
'Io non so se vi schrissi che il conte della Mirandola se n'andò insalutato ospite,
fra 6 in 8 dì della morte di Lorenzo. Dicono è andato a fferara, non s'intende la
cagione. E al magnifico Piero nonn è molto piaciuto [. . .] e il conte nollo doveva
fare sendo suto tanto favorito e onorato da Lorenzo' (GC 3421560); Pico died
on 17 Nov. 1494.

79. Typified by its cult of the ruler as wise man above the stars in semi-public, semi-
private plays and debates on the nature of sin and grace; see Martelli, 'La cultura
letteraria', 78–9; C. Vasoli, *Profezia e ragione* (Naples: Morano, 1974), 17–21; A.
Brown, 'Platonism in Fifteenth-Century Florence', repr. in ead., *Medici in
Florence*, 229–34, etc. On Scala's other new writing in this late period, his
Apologia contra vituperatores civitatis Florentiae (Florence, [Antonio di Bartolommeo
Miscomini], 1496), see A. Brown, *Bartolomeo Scala*, 307–9.

80. See A. Brown, 'Pierfrancesco de' Medici', 100–1; Lorenzo was also the dedicatee of Amerigo Vespucci's later *Mundus novus*. The pro-French tradition was represented by Luigi Pulci, whose *Morgante* was also interested in new worlds and antipodean culture (Constance Jordan, *Pulci's Morgante* (Washington and London: Associated University Presses, 1986), 20–7, 148–51). It was continued by Ugolino Verino, who pressed his *Carliados* into the hands of the Florentine ambassadors to France in 1493, with a letter to Francesco della Casa, already at the royal court, 'et intercedat ut liber legatur etiam discutiatur iudicio doctissimorum', Ugolino Verino to ser Piero Dovizi in Milan, 2 Aug. 1493 (MAP 72,66).
81. Tribaldo de' Rossi, *Ricordanze*, 296, referring to Christmas night, 1494, 'ch'era un sì gran fredo che [. . .] era ghiacciato Arno'.
82. Whereas Pliny and Vitruvius ascribe the discovery of fire to the rubbing together of branches, Diodorus Siculus attributes it to lightning, Lucretius to both; E. Panofsky, 'The Early History of Man in Two Cycles of Paintings by Piero di Cosimo', in *Studies in Iconology* (New York and Evanston: Harper & Row, 1962), 41.
83. *De arboribus*, lines 235–9.
84. See Leonardo da Vinci, *Literary Works*, ed. J. P. Richter (London: Phaidon, 1970), ii. 292, 293, 296, 299, 305, 306 ('Prophetie', nos. 1293, 1300, 1303). I have benefited from conversations with Jonathan Nelson about Filippino Lippi's later paintings; see his dissertation (above, n. 15); on Piero di Cosimo, S. Fermor, *Piero di Cosimo, Invention and Fantasia* (London: Reaktion Books, 1993).

CHAPTER 2

Astrological Polemics in the Crisis of the 1490s

Remo Catani

Once regarded as a fascinating feature of middling importance, the Renaissance debate on astrological belief has in a generation or two come to hold a modest but firm place in the front rank of scholarship. The range of interest has widened to embrace the greater part of Western Europe and a variety of intellectual and social levels, while the focus of individual studies has become markedly sharper. The polemics which were fought, often bitterly, during the closing years of the fifteenth and the opening decades of the sixteenth centuries have received particular attention. In the Italy of the 1490s they are at their most intense and most significant. While in some respects they can be considered the culmination of a long line of disputes dating from late classical and early medieval times, or, on a narrower time scale, can be linked to the attacks at the end of the previous century by Nicole Oresme and Heinrich von Langenstein, more specifically they are part of a cathartic moment proper to late fifteenth-century Italy.[1] In this chapter it is my intention to consider those three major figures whose paths, certainly in this respect, are so inextricably intertwined, Ficino, Pico, and Savonarola.[2] The uncertainty and soul-searching, the longing for renewal and reform that underlie their personal and public involvement in the astrological question are among the best indications we have of the importance of that question in understanding the wider spiritual travail of their age. In large measure, I shall adopt a contextualist approach, undertaking, where circumstance requires it, conjectural biographical and bibliographical reconstruction.[3]

I shall be referring to both astral magic and judicial astrology, and should perhaps briefly explain the distinction. Astral magic involved drawing beneficial influences from the planets through the use of talismans, music, plants, and the like. This was permitted, if done by an allegedly 'natural' process that used the *spiritus*, a corporeal vapour that is a halfway house between body and soul. But the practice of invoking planetary demons was strictly forbidden by the Church. Demonic magic was uncommon and esoteric, whereas the use of 'natural', spiritual magic was firmly established in medieval medicine. Much less suspect was judicial or divinatory or genethliac or apotelesmatic astrology, which involved studying the stars and their movements, either as causes or signs, in order to make predictions or draw up horoscopes. This was widely practised at every level of society and tolerated by the Church if it kept within certain limits. We could agree with D. P. Walker that 'it is [. . .] generally true that astrology was accepted or rejected in so far as it safeguarded or infringed human responsibility and divine providence'.[4] I would add that, reading the popular prognostications of the day, one would think that this yardstick had been fashioned by the astrologers themselves, who are at pains to uphold human freedom in pious declarations of orthodoxy, and that Christian thought had in large measure come to an accommodation with the astrologers by accepting causalistic forms of astrology that appeared to protect free will.

Marsilio Ficino's *De vita coelitus comparanda* in twenty-five chapters, essentially medical in scope and ostensibly based on Plotinus, appeared in 1489 as the third book of his *De triplici vita*, dedicated to Lorenzo de' Medici. In it he dwells at great length and with particular insistence on astrological images or talismans, but is careful to protect himself by telling his reader that, if he is not happy about the use of talismans to benefit his health, then he can discount them, because the writer is not so much giving them his approval as simply describing them.[5] Despite this, Marsilio was accused of illicit magic and a complaint was made to Innocent VIII. Nine busy, anxious months had to pass before Ficino could feel that he had cleared his name sufficiently to be free from censure. On 15 September he addressed a letter, his well-known *Apologia*, to three friends in which he asked them to seek the help of Landino, Poliziano, and Pico, and drew a careful distinction between demonic magic and that which consists in an investigation of latent, natural forces.[6] His correspondence remains as a striking testimony to the trouble taken to give the *De vita coelitus comparanda* and the *Apologia* the widest possible publicity.[7] Copies were sent to friends and acquaintances in a position to plead his case with the Pope and influential churchmen, and on each occasion he made a point of stressing his orthodoxy and Christian piety.[8]

It must have been with considerable relief that he finally received a letter in June 1490 in which Ermolao Barbaro informed him that he had been successful in persuading the Pope in Marsilio's favour.[9] With the help of his friends Ficino had managed to silence his accusers, but indelible suspicion had been cast on him. It is for this reason that later, when he knew Pico was devoting most of his time to his confutation of astrology, awaited so eagerly by some and so apprehensively by others, he felt obliged to make his own standpoint clear. On 20 August 1494 he sent Poliziano a letter to this effect. In it he allied himself with Pico and Poliziano and nervously reminded them of his own role as an anti-astrological polemicist in his commentary on Plotinus. This could not of course erase the memory of the *De vita coelitus comparanda* with its suspect talismans. He had to defend himself once more by stressing the medical scope of his work and claiming that he was not necessarily giving his own approval but gathering together everything that might possibly be beneficial. He did, however, end by admitting that perhaps here, and later in the *De sole* and *De lumine* (1492), he had overstepped the mark after all. His uneasiness is unmistakable.[10] While welcoming Ficino's support, Poliziano remained unconvinced by the explanation.[11] What mattered, though, was Marsilio's public image, and here Pico, not forgetting the interests of his own campaign, gave him the fullest backing. When the *Disputationes* finally appeared, Ficino was presented in the first book as an enemy of astrologers and his explanation was fully accepted. This was supported by an intimate picture of Pico, Ficino, and Poliziano making fun of astrology together in their friendly conversations.[12] Such a pretence, far from concealing the prevailing climate of ecclesiastical hostility, which had already been seen in the altogether more serious condemnation of Pico's thirteen theses, only serves to draw attention to the cultural ambiguity and fragile acceptance of Ficino's ideas at the start of the 1490s. Even today, in the cold light of modern analysis, Marsilio's magic is scarcely less equivocal.[13] Is it truly a 'comparatively harmless attempt at astral medical therapy', as described by Frances Yates?[14] Experts are unable to agree, and Paola Zambelli has not only found that a close reading of the *De vita coelitus comparanda* fails to dispel doubts on its use of demon-evocation, but maintains that the concept of natural magic is itself utopian.[15]

Although the problem of Ficino's apparent vacillation and hesitancy with regard to the commoner type of astrological belief has received considerable critical attention, it has never been satisfactorily resolved.[16] In its simplest expression it can be perceived as the paradox of his conscious, if sporadic, stance as an anti-astrological campaigner, seen against a background of deep-rooted, lifelong conviction.

We can confidently suppose that this conviction was in no small way the legacy of the medieval medical tradition absorbed by a doctor's son who himself occasionally practised medicine. Be that as it may, Ficino's letters in particular reveal a firm acceptance of the usefulness of astrology on a day-to-day basis. They are peppered with talk of horoscopes and auspicious days and quips about the stars.[17] This social, at times even lighthearted, manifestation finds supportive counterpoint in letters that show a more serious Marsilio, obsessed by a fear of his star Saturn who condemns him to melancholy, letters in which we detect an uncertain and despondent note in his voice.[18]

Despite this, on a number of occasions, he echoed the theologians' wrath against the impieties of astrologers, without ever totally negating planetary influence: in the De Christiana religione (1474);[19] in his unpublished Disputatio against astrologers and its proemium in the form of a letter to Francesco Ippolito Gazolti (1477–8);[20] in a long letter to Federico, duke of Urbino (January 1481);[21] in his commentary on Plotinus' Enneads, II, 3 (1486–90);[22] and in the letter to Poliziano, already mentioned, of August 1494. Each of these corresponds to either a period of adjustment in his intellectual and spiritual development, or a tactical expediency.

In examining this development, it is hard to overemphasize the importance of what has come to be described as his Platonic mission, and of his translation and propagation of Hermetic and Neoplatonic texts that were often highly suspect (Psellus, Proclus, Iamblicus) and which exerted almost impossible demands on his self-imposed task of philosophico-religious reconciliation. The established biographical pattern is of an early penchant for Hermetic Platonism preceding a more orthodox period during which he entered the priesthood (1473) and completed the Theologia platonica (1482), followed in turn by a sudden and clearer re-emergence in the second half of the 1480s of a pantheist vision that resulted in public suspicion. This pattern can be fairly accurately calibrated with the pattern of the contrasting stances taken towards astrology, so long as one takes into account, where necessary, the tactical requirements dictated by circumstance. Seen in this perspective, Ficino's anti-astrological attacks before the commentary on Plotinus emerge as apologetic works.[23] In contrast, the commentary, levelled against plebeian, fatalistic astrologers, and his anxious letter to Poliziano can both be related to the composition of the *De vita coelitus comparanda* and the subsequent threat of condemnation.

Sebastiano Gentile argues convincingly that Ficino was consciously influenced by George Gemistos Plethon's proposed vast reform, of many years before, which included a return to the worship of the ancient gods as a last defence of spiritualism.[24] The similarity which Gentile draws between Plethon's warning and Ficino's famous call in the preface to Plotinus of 1490 for a return to a *pia philosophia*, purged of its impious elements, is both striking and enlightening. It is clear that, despite the threatened censure, Ficino entered the 1490s in confident mood, convinced of his role as Platonic *renovator*, which he saw clearly written in the stars. He wrote to Janus Pannonius in Hungary, just a few years before the Plotinus edition, confirming that his horoscope did indeed indicate the birth of a 'rerum antiquarum innovator'.[25] But his vision of renewal, unlike Plethon's, enjoys the vantage point of the Christian tradition, and his *Apologia*, while certainly defending his own orthodoxy, also lays claim to a place for astrology within that Christian tradition.[26] The early 1490s are in some ways Ficino's most buoyant years. In 1492 we find him reasserting the syncretic thrust behind the *De vita coelitus comparanda*, when he attempts to show the Christian religion's affinity with Neoplatonic demonic theory in a letter to Braccio Martelli.[27] In the same year, writing to Paul of Middelburg, he proclaims the arrival of the golden age, the *Saturnia regna* celebrated by the Sybil and prophets and announced by Plato.[28]

But Ficino was swimming against a powerful tide that was returning to sweep away the fragile dreams of that closing decade of the century. The events of those years did not allow him to continue in the same spirit of elation and expectancy. The fateful year 1494 saw an end to any hope he may have had of a Medicean reign of Saturn. The years 1493 and 1494 also witnessed the conjunction of two forces against astrology over which he had little power, those of Giovanni Pico and Savonarola, whom I shall very shortly come to consider. A new tone of anxiety entered with the letter to Poliziano of August 1494. He would appear to have given Savonarola his support into the next year, but no sooner had the friar fallen from power and been executed than Ficino wrote his sad, vindictive Apology to the College of Cardinals against Savonarola, adducing astrological and Platonic arguments to show Girolamo had been possessed of evil demons.[29] Gone for ever was the lofty friendship that characterized an earlier, happier Florence when Ficino offered Pico, who had exhorted him to translate Plotinus, peace and protection by the banks of the Arno, and Pico in his turn asked Lorenzo to have Savonarola recalled to San Marco.

Pico's position in the 1490s is considerably clearer.[30] The negation of judicial astrology in the *Disputationes adversus astrologiam divinatricem* is total. He confutes the apotelesmatic art on several tactical levels which show an uncommon awareness of his adversaries' standpoint. His fundamental arguments are contained in the third and fourth books, and are based on an almost entirely Aristotelian order.[31] Modern scholarship has tended to perceive a modernity in other parts of the work, such as the sensitive insights of Book XII,[32] or the clear separation, in the first book, of the scientific from the superstitious elements of astrology.[33] Eugenio Garin in particular sees the *Disputationes* as the continued vindication of human freedom and dignity, as an attempt to clarify every field of knowledge and action, as a work of notable cultural importance ('un gran fatto culturale'), which is both a call to reason and human dignity and an act of faith in the possibility of critical and historical inquiry.[34] Garin's overall view of Pico as the champion of free human initiative has been comprehensively attacked by William Craven in his attempt to destroy the myth of Pico who, in his eyes, has become 'the mirror-image of the historians' expectations', and whom he somewhat harshly relegates to the banal orthodoxy of his time.[35] Craven's volume, as Louis Valcke puts it, had to be written sooner or later.[36] Nonetheless, Craven puts the extreme view, and in the particular case of the *Disputationes* fails to accept as significant that Giovanni's argumentation is for the most part intended to be tactical rather than logically succinct. The work proceeds through a succession of easily identifiable layers or levels in which Pico never exhausts his case, but produces primary, secondary, and tertiary arguments, mostly of a technical nature, that seem to deal a succession of new blows aimed at the dyed-in-the-wool opponent.[37] It is Craven's failure to take this into account that leads him to consider Pico's attack too comprehensive and too complex to support the case for religious motivation, and to view the defence of free will as an irrelevance to Pico since he was not specifically attacking fatalistic astrology but astrology in general. This fails to grasp not only the tactical nature of his layered attack, but also its totality, which refuses to accept Thomistic concessions. Such a totality implies Pico's abhorrence of human servility to the stars, which underpins all of his twelve books. As we have seen, in the opening book human servility stands alongside irrationality and impiety as one of the fundamental evils inherent in stellar divination.[38] Even if the *Disputationes* are not all Garin makes them out to be, they contain much that saves them from banality, including their methodological contribution[39] and the constructive challenge to authority in the attack on Galen and the theory of critical days, which paved the way for medical progress.[40] Many of Craven's excesses have, however, more recently been redressed, and the modernity of the *Disputationes* in large part restored, by Anthony Grafton's analysis of Pico's achievement at the philological and historiological level.[41]

It is part of the Pico myth that he nurtured a dream even grander than Ficino's, that he dwarfed Marsilio's mission with his ambition to reconcile all philosophies and all religions in his search for a single, unifying truth. This certainly seems to have been true in the heady days of the mid-1480s. But much of this enthusiasm was dampened by Innocent VIII's condemnation of his theses, his provocative riposte, his flight to France, and imprisonment in the castle of Vincennes.[42] It was a chastened Giovanni who in 1488 found refuge in Florence, where he spent the last six years of his life, characterized by an increasing interest in biblical studies and a growing closeness to Savonarola. The disputations against astrology on which he embarked were, it was well known, only part of an intended sevenfold attack on Christianity's principal enemies.[43]

Can we on this basis assign an essentially religious motivation to the *Disputationes*?[44] It would be preferable to seek guidance from intellectual influences and developments in Pico before attempting to answer this. Two of the papers given at the recent Mirandola conference, which will go down as another milestone in Pico studies, are of considerable help at this point in my argument. The first, by Charles Trinkhaus, convincingly argues that the *Heptaplus* (1488–9) is a pivotal work that reveals Pico's vision of man and the universe within the coordinates of his Christian faith.[45] Of particular interest to us in this work is a chapter that warns against the vanities of astrology and contains a firm admonition against the use of talismans that was evidently directed against Ficino's recently written *De vita coelitus comparanda*.[46] At the same time, the work has certain points in common with earlier ones, which suggests that we are witnessing an evolution in Pico's epistemological position.[47] The crucial change in emphasis, however, is towards a theological standpoint that sees Christ as the only way to redemption, and religion as the only guide to ultimate happiness. The philosophical truth that Pico always sought is seen to be directed towards theological truth, a view, Trinkhaus concludes, that is wholly concordant with his devotion to Savonarola.

The second helpful paper, by Louis Valcke, shows how Pico's attitude changed after the fiasco of the Roman dispute, how the psychological blow he suffered brought him back to critical lucidity from the illusion that Plotinus' blend of reason and mysticism could establish harmony between Mosaic concepts and Greek philosophy.[48] For Valcke, the *De ente et uno* (1491) signals a radical dichotomy of philosophy and theology in Pico's thought. After it, the gap widens and we enter the devout, mystical period of Pico's life. This too points to the progressive strengthening of a religious thrust in his intellectual activity, culminating in the *Disputationes*.[49]

These and other such considerations[50] lend support to the view that Pico's final work is religious in motivation and apologetic in aim. Moreover, this view would seem to find corroboration in a parallel development, which I have already mentioned, in Pico's mode of life.[51] A turning point in his detachment from the world came in April 1491 when he gave Gianfrancesco his possessions in Mirandola and asked Girolamo Benivieni to distribute his excess wealth to the poor.[52] What is more, Pico frequented and corresponded with men of holy or reforming character, in particular Savonarola, the Carmelite Battista Spagnuoli, and Matteo Bossi, the abbot of the Badia in Fiesole, where Giovanni retired with increasing frequency.[53] It seems natural that someone like Pico should have translated his new-found spirituality into an apologetic plan of action, without in any way abandoning the path of rational investigation.[54] By the end of his life, Pico had attained 'una religiosità filosoficamente consapevole', to borrow Zanier's phrase.[55] His apologetic thrust embraced the ethical, the metaphysical, and the methodological. There is no reason for us to jettison the concepts of philosophical rigour and innovation in Pico, precisely because he himself felt no obligation to reject philosophical inquiry, which for him was the natural path to theological truth and Christian salvation. Thus the concept of the *vinculum* or *copula mundi*, which has come to be perceived as his intellectual hallmark and been wholeheartedly adopted in the humanist interpretation of Pico because it appears to make man master of his own destiny,[56] also, in a different perspective, places man in a unique position in the order of divine creation, and, far from distancing man from God, isolates and centralizes the dialogue between man and God. No surprise then that the *Disputationes* should give relatively little direct evidence of religious motivation. Pico was in the serious and exhaustive business of disputation, not of baring his soul. Where religion has a place on his agenda, he deals with it methodically and unambiguously.[57] When the scope of his argument allows it, as in the twelfth book that deals so perceptively with astrology's insidious infiltration across the ages into men's lives, he reveals the driving force and totality of his undertaking. For Pico, magic is now merely an amalgam of idolatry, astrology, and superstitious medicine to be confuted alongside the other enemies of Christianity, and astrology itself is a poison that destroys men's trust in religion, which is their *summum bonum*, 'as if miracles were nothing, as if divine prophecy did not exist, but everything came from the force of the stars'.[58]

There remains the question of Savonarola's precise involvement in the *Disputationes*. When the work finally appeared in print in July 1496, it was met with all manner of sweeping and unsubstantiated statements from both camps. Professional astrologers were of course outraged, and Lucio Bellanti from Siena in his reply of 1498 maintained that Pico's composition could only be explained by the cunning influence of Savonarola, who into the bargain astutely wrote a trivial little book in the vernacular to seduce the masses.[59] We also have the testimony of one of the friar's most devoted followers, Giovanni Nesi, the Florentine Neoplatonist, who, in his palingetic extravaganza *Oraculum de novo saeculo* (written September 1496), claimed that the Ferrarese Socrates, Savonarola, often helped the count with his judgement and advice in writing the disputations.[60] Modern scholars have with good reason tended to disregard such evidence, and it is accepted opinion that the contents of Pico's attack were unknown before it appeared in print to be read by, among others, Savonarola, who, in the summer of 1497, humbly simplified and popularized its message in the *Trattato contro gli astrologi*.[61]

I do not believe that this presents an accurate picture. First of all, the content of Giovanni's attack was in part known before July 1496. There are at least two defences of astrology written as early as the beginning of 1494 which reveal an awareness of its style and main directives: that by Gianbattista Abioso, which mentions an unspecified count (*comes*) identified later by Gianfrancesco as his uncle,[62] and that by Gabriele Pirovano of Milan.[63] Even more specific is the citing of one of Pico's chapters by Savonarola in his sermons on the Ark written at the beginning of the summer of 1494, when the *Disputationes* had not yet been completed and the count was still alive and busy working on it.[64] This is also true of Ficino's mention of it in his letter to Poliziano of August 1494, though here it is referred to in vaguer terms. Despite the climate of expectancy prevalent immediately before the work's appearance and expressed in Gianfrancesco's correspondence,[65] it would seem that the import of the *Disputationes* was known before their completion, and that the person with the most precise knowledge was Savonarola.[66]

Is it really true that Girolamo had not read his friend's book before it became available to the general public, as he claims in the *proemio* to his *Trattato*?[67] And was this *Trattato* truly his first and only attempt at popularizing the work? Before trying to answer these questions, let us quickly look at some instances of the friar's own involvement in the anti-astrological campaign, which he ardently supported, not only because this pseudo-science was superstitious and irreligious, but because astrology negated his Christian hierarchy, obstructed his moral reform, and constituted the greatest single threat to his own position as a prophet.[68]

An examination of Fra Girolamo's sermons and writings reveals that his own attacks on astrologers began with and ran parallel to both the period of his increasing public prominence and that of Pico's composition of the *Disputationes*.[69] I have already drawn attention to the sermons on the Ark that showed Savonarola incensed, in the summer of 1494, that astrologers should think they know more than the angels. It is possible that even before this, in the sermons on the psalm *Quam bonus*, supposedly delivered in the Duomo in Advent 1493, he strongly denounced the astrological practices of Roman churchmen: 'La chiesa si governa per mano d'astrologi. E non è prelato, né gran maestro, che non abbia qualche familiarità con qualche astrolago.'[70] In 1494 he also began the sermons delivered in Advent on the book of Haggai. In the fifteenth sermon, he depicted his ideal Florence as an angelic hierarchy threatened by astrologers:

Vorrebbe essere la città come una ierarchia angelica, con pace, con amore e con concordia, e però, se io ti prèdico e ti esorto alla pace e al governo pacifico, doveresti farlo volentieri e non contradirlo. Non ti reggere cogli astrologi, ma con gli angeli; non colla sola prudenzia umana, che non basta, ma con el vivere da cristiano.[71]

Astrologers, it is evident, posed a real problem for the prophet, for they distracted the people's attention, not only from his own admonition and counsel, but from the salvation that the Christian way of life alone could offer.

From the moment of Pico's death, Savonarola's assaults became more frequent, more direct, and more vehement. The sermons on Job for Lent 1495 were peppered with outbursts against astrologers and adduced arguments that were central to the as yet unpublished *Disputationes* and indeed to Girolamo's own *Trattato* of 1497.[72] What is more, from now on Savonarola's attacks are to be found in his books as well as his sermons. In the preamble to the *Compendio di rivelazioni*, which appeared in August 1495, he made it quite clear that judicial astrology was foremost among the impious divinatory arts that constituted the enemies of divine prophecy.[73] In his highly popular *De simplicitate Christianae vitae*, the first draft of which was written in autumn 1495, he maintained that the Christian life is independent of celestial influence but purposely refrained from elaborating because the *Disputationes* were about to appear.[74] By the time he came to write the *Triumphus Crucis* in the summer of 1497, they had already appeared and made their initial impact. Girolamo's work contained an entire chapter against astrology, including a heated digression directed against modern practitioners.[75] In the sermons on the prophet Amos for Lent 1496, when Savonarola returned to the pulpit after a ban imposed by the Pope the previous October, Florence witnessed another bitter outcry as he defended the inalienable rights of prophecy and railed against the abuses of the day:

Non è nessuno oggi che cavalchi o vadi a caccia se non a punto d'astrologia. Voi astrolagi promettete cose excelse e cose grandi alli vostri padroni. Promettete pur assai, ché io vi dico che presto sarete giunti alla rete insieme con loro. Voi avete guasto tutto el mondo colla vostra astrologia.[76]

The first edition of the *Trattato* itself bears no date, but in the text Savonarola states the time of writing as 1497.[77] His declared intention is to summarize and adapt Pico's main points in a simple but reasoned way for ordinary people, which he in fact does rather well.[78] But, on more than one occasion, he loses his composure when his personal feelings surge to the surface and he advocates burning, stabbing, and decapitating astrologers.[79]

Given his fundamental and personal antagonism to astrology and the intimate relationship between the two men, as well as the fact that he was closely acquainted with the detailed arguments of the disputations, as his explicit reference of early summer 1494 indicates, it does seem strange that Fra Girolamo should not have attempted to communicate and popularize parts of the count's book before 1498 (if we are to believe Garin's dating of the first edition of the *Trattato*).[80] In fact there is reason to believe that he could well have done so. In a letter sent from Mantua in February 1495, Battista Spagnuoli shared in Gianfrancesco Pico's unbridled enthusiasm for the manuscript *Disputationes*, which the Carmelite soon hoped to come and see for himself in Florence. At a certain point, he writes in passing: 'That translation of Girolamo's much desired for so long, everywhere sought after and nowhere to be found, I would gratefully receive, but would not know what to give to you or such a person in return'.[81] The reference is admittedly vague, and the precise Girolamo in question is not specified, but it at once springs to mind when we come to read an unquestionably specific reference contained in Gianfrancesco's *De studio*, which first appeared in July 1497 but bears a dedication dated January 1496. Speaking of his uncle's work, he talks of 'the summary which the famous Girolamo Savonarola has composed in the vernacular as well, in order to assist the unlettered'.[82] This, then, appears to be an accurate description of the *Trattato*. There is yet another reference, by the Dominican himself this time, in that chapter in the *Triumphus Crucis* that I have already mentioned, where he states that he too has published a book in the vernacular against astrology.[83] Savonarola is here writing in the summer of 1497, so that it is not possible to agree with Garin's dating of the *editio princeps* as 'posteriore al '97'.[84] Yet another serious challenge to Garin's dating is the one by Paola Zambelli, who has drawn attention to the mention of no less than two manuscript copies of a work by Savonarola 'contra li strologhi' in a Modenese catalogue that appears to have been compiled in 1495.[85]

My own belief is that the edition in which Savonarola states the time of writing as 1497 did appear in that year, but rather towards the beginning, given the reference in the *Trionfo*. I would submit, however, in the light of Zambelli's evidence and of the references in the sermon on the Ark, Spagnuoli's letter, and Gianfrancesco's *De studio*, that there also existed an earlier version, either in manuscript or in print or both, which had a restricted circulation before the *Disputationes* became available to the general public in July 1496, and that this earlier version, though probably bearing a different title (Gianfrancesco calls it his *Epitoma* or summary), was to form the basis of the *Trattato* which superseded it, having detailed knowledge of Pico's definitive published work.

I find little difficulty in believing contemporary claims that Fra Girolamo helped and advised Pico in his task, though not that he would not otherwise have written his attack. Garin, I feel, is more than a little naïve in accepting at face value all that Girolamo tells us in the *proemio*, and in supposing that Bellanti would necessarily be conversant with an earlier version. On the other hand, it is perhaps wrong to dismiss Bellanti's view that Savonarola's tract was part of a plan to win over popular support.[86] Ridolfi observed many years ago that the Dominican exploited the new instrument of printing with great astuteness and success.[87] Girolamo is also remembered as a deft politician and shrewd negotiator, as a man who could, when required, work cleverly and patiently behind the scenes.[88] Nor was he above using the spiritual and moral influence that he knew he possessed, to further his ends. It is not unreasonable to imagine that he would have wanted to marshal the young count's talents in the service of an anti-astrological stratagem in which the division of labour was clear.[89] Giovanni Pico, the brilliant polymath and renowned disputant, was admirably equipped to take care of the philosophical and technical aspects. Savonarola, with his rhetorical skills and propagational drive, could see to winning over the unsophisticated populace. This is not to suggest that Pico, like so many others, had succumbed to the friar's spell.[90] Fra Girolamo's shock announcement in the Duomo, less than a week after Pico's death, in which he publicly placed his young friend in the torments of Purgatory and was evidently incensed at his refusal to join the Dominican order, points to the fact that the prophet's ascendancy over Giovanni was far from total.[91] But it is equally a further example of how Savonarola could place Pico's reputation to good account in his mission of reform.

The friar's fiery revelations in the Duomo are a far cry from the esoteric world of Ficino and his talismans. Yet I hope that my survey of these three very different men's involvement in a controversy that reveals the untenability of syncretic, conciliatory dreams and reflects the longing for a return to purity that is itself utopian, has shown that the power of the stars was an issue around which the unrest and spiritual disorientation of an age could become polarized. Then there are the poor astrologers themselves, of course, for whom this confrontation represents a culturally less sophisticated crisis, and who, in direct response to the *Disputationes'* assault, adopted rearguard action that amounted to a veritable movement for renewal and astrological reform. But that is another story. Allow me to end with a simple plea, to William Craven and his followers, to accept at least Eugenio Garin's firm contention that the debate on astrology is of primary importance in pursuing our utopian desire to understand the Italian Renaissance.

Notes to Chapter 2

1. For the attacks in the third quarter of the 14th c. by Oresme and Heinrich von Langenstein (aka Henry of Hesse), who had both studied at the University of Paris, see L. Thorndike, *A History of Magic and Experimental Science*, iii (New York: Macmillan, 1934), 398–423 and 472–510. For Cardinal Pierre d'Ailly's defence and Jean Gerson's theological standpoint early in the 15th c., see Thorndike, iv. 101–13 and 114–31. See too S. Caroti, 'La critica contro l'astrologia di N. Oresme e la sua influenza nel Medioevo e nel Rinascimento', *Atti della Accademia Nazionale dei Lincei*, serie VIII, vol. 23, fasc. 6 (1979), 545–685.

2. See e.g. C. Vasoli, 'Le Débat sur l'astrologie à Florence dans la seconde moitié du XVème siècle: Ficin, Pic de la Mirandole, Savonarole', in *Divinations et controverses religieuses en France au XVIème siècle* (Paris, 1987), 19–33.

3. In attempting to establish beliefs, developments, and influences, reliance on the literally interpreted, unquestioned text is seductive. However, such reliance is patently not sufficient in a field where chronology is not always certain, where all the evidence does not lie in the relevant texts which do not all in any case survive (and if they do, not necessarily in the form intended by their author), and especially where the main protagonists often stage-managed campaigns, assumed oracular stances, feigned beliefs, or indulged in posturing and self-publicity for a variety of reasons, including fear of ecclesiastical censure.

4. D. P. Walker, *Spiritual and Demonic Magic from Ficino to Campanella* (London: Warburg Institute, 1958), 55. See too B. Copenhaver, 'Astrology and Magic', in *The Cambridge History of Renaissance Philosophy*, ed. C. B. Schmitt (Cambridge: Cambridge University Press, 1988), 264–300.

5. *Opera Omnia*, i (Basel, 1576), fo. 530.

6. Ibid., fos. 572–4.

7. Ibid., fos. 574–5, 904–5, 910–12.

8. He saw to it that Lorenzo de' Medici was able to read the work under attack in a fine manuscript prepared at the expense of Filippo Valori.

9. *Opera*, i, fo. 912.

10. Ibid., fo. 958.

11. *Opera* (Lyons, 1528), i, fo. 323.

12. *Disputationes adversus astrologiam divinatricem*, ed. E. Garin, i (Florence: Vallecchi, 1946), 60. In a letter written to Pico on 6 July 1488, Marsilio recalls that they had read Oresme's treatise against astrology together: *Opera*, i, fo. 890.

13. Attention has been drawn to the divergence between both Plotinus' natural magic and the natural magic claimed in the *Apologia* on the one hand, and what is actually contained in the third book of the *De vita* on the other; see e.g. P. Castelli (ed.), *Il Lume del Sole: M. Ficino medico dell'anima* (Florence: Opus Libri, 1984), 13–14 and 36–7.

14. F. Yates, *Giordano Bruno and the Hermetic Tradition* (London: Routledge & Kegan Paul, 1964), 60–1.

15. See P. Zambelli, *L'ambigua natura della magia: filosofi, streghe, riti nel Rinascimento* (Milan: Il Saggiatore, 1991), 270–1. In any case, as far as Christian orthodoxy is concerned, Copenhaver is clearly correct in saying that 'talismans, if cleared of demonic influence, are the limiting case of natural magic that falls on the safer side of the line' ('Astrology and Magic', 282). See too B. Copenhaver, 'Scholastic Philosophy and Renaissance Magic in the *De Vita* of M. Ficino', *Renaissance Quarterly*, 36 (1984), 523–54; id., 'Natural Magic, Hermetism and Occultism in Early Modern Science', in D. C. Lindberg and R. S. Westman (eds.), *Reappraisals of the Scientific Revolution* (Cambridge: Cambridge University Press, 1990), 261–301 at 270–5; E. Garin, 'Le "Elezioni" e il problema dell'astrologia', in *Umanesimo e esoterismo. Atti del V Convegno Internazionale di Studi Umanistici*, ed. E. Castelli (Padua: CEDAM, 1960), 17–31. The debate in recent years between Copenhaver and Zambelli on Ficino's Neoplatonic, Hermetic, and Arabic sources and their relative importance has served to draw further attention to the inconsistencies and ambiguities within the chapters on talismans and to the anxiety pervading his avowal of orthodoxy.

16. For useful short summaries of this critical attention see M. J. B. Allen, *The Platonism of M. Ficino: A Study of his 'Phaedrus' Commentary, its Sources and Genesis* (Berkeley and Los Angeles: University of California Press, 1984), 183 n. 27 and M. M. Bullard, 'The Inward Zodiac: A Development in Ficino's Thought on Astrology', *Renaissance Quarterly*, 43 (1990), 687–708 at 687–8.

17. He boasted that his predictions of the bishoprics of Francesco Salviati and Giovanni Niccolini had proved his powers as a *vates* (*Opera*, i, fos. 649, 668). Paolo Giovio tells us that Marsilio predicted the papacy of Leo X when the latter was still a mere child (*Supplementum Ficinianum*, ed. P. O. Kristeller, ii (Florence: Olschki, 1937), 250). It was his habit to record the exact moment of birth of his friends, and little that seemed to be of astrological significance escaped him (see e.g. *Opera*, i, fos. 820, 831; ii, fo. 1537). In 1489, the year of his *De vita*, he is also engaged in sending his horoscope, despite the disapproval of Plotinus, to Martino Uranio at his request, and in advising Filippo Strozzi on the best time to lay the foundation stone of his palace (see *Opera*, i, fo. 901 and *Supplementum Ficinianum*, ii. 307), and in a letter to Orsini of 26 June 1490 he talks of having been snatched from the jaws of voracious wolves, while at the same time requesting the Pope's date of birth and the star which was threatening his health in order to establish a beneficial remedy (*Opera*, i, fo. 911). See too Thorndike, *A History of Magic*, iv. 567–70.

18. This is especially evident in the correspondence with Cavalcanti (*Opera*, i, fos.

730–3). See E. Cassirer, *The Individual and the Cosmos in Renaissance Philosophy* (Oxford: Blackwell, 1963), 100 ; P. O. Kristeller, *The Philosophy of Marsilio Ficino* (New York: Columbia University Press, 1943), 212–13; A. Biondi in M. Ficino, *De vita*, ed. A. Biondi and G. Pisani (Pordenone, 1991), pp. xv–xvii.

19. He devotes the ninth chapter to showing that Christianity is independent of the stars and censuring popular astrologers (*Opera*, i, fos. 12–13).

20. I find it difficult to accept D. P. Walker's suggestion that the *Disputatio* (*Supplementum ficinianum*, ii. 11–74) was hastily put together much later, in 1493 or 1494 ('Ficino and Astrology', in G. C. Garfagnini (ed.), *Marsilio Ficino e il ritorno di Platone: studi e documenti*, i (Florence: Olschki, 1986), 341–9). There was no reason for Ficino to lie in announcing the completion of the work to Gazolti. Nor is it more likely that those passages in the *Theologia Platonica* (1482), the *De stella Magorum* (1482), and his commentary on Plotinus which are identical to parts of the *Disputatio* are sources of the latter, rather than the contrary (see Garin in Pico, *Disputationes*, i. 11–12). The work is also clearly listed by Ficino as the *Disputationes contra astrologorum iudicia* in an undated letter to Poliziano answering a request for titles of the books he had written (*Opera*, i, fo. 619).

21. *Opera*, i, fos. 849–53. In this letter he does, however, admit that the stars might possibly narrate God's glory in their function as mere signs.

22. Ibid., ii, fos. 1609–42.

23. These works were possibly spurred on by a tougher ecclesiastical line on providence and free will as a result of the important theological dispute on future contingents which ended in 1473 and involved important churchmen such as cardinals Bessarion and Francesco Della Rovere, the future Sixtus IV. See Vasoli, 'Le Débat sur l'astrologie à Florence', 22–3 and 'Marsilio Ficino e l'astrologia', in *L'astrologia e la sua influenza nella filosofia, nella letteratura e nell'arte dall'età classica al Rinascimento* (Milan: Nuovi orizzonti, 1992), 159–86 at 164–5.

24. In M. Ficino, *Lettere I. Epistolarum familiarum liber I*, ed. S. Gentile (Florence: Olschki, 1990), pp. xii–lxv.

25. See *Opera*, i, fos. 871–2.

26. His belief in the compatibility of Christianity and astrology is enshrined in his use of the *stella Magorum* theme, of doxographic Hermetic figures, and of imagery which equated ancient culture with Christianity (see S. M. Buhler, 'Marsilio Ficino's "De stella magorum" and Renaissance Views of the Magi', *Renaissance Quarterly*, 43 (1990), 348–71 and Vasoli, 'Marsilio Ficino e l'astrologia', 185–6). That this should escape ecclesiastical censure is hardly surprising, given the high level of tolerance towards the use of ancient pagan elements as rhetorical devices. Serious censure was reserved for the all-important step into the operative, experimental sphere, the step too far that Ficino took in the *De vita*.

27. *Opera*, i, fos. 875–9.

28. Ibid., fo. 944.

29. *Supplementum ficinianum*, ii. 76–9. See R. Marcel, *Marsile Ficin* (Paris: Société d'édition Les belles lettres, 1958), 558 ff.; C. V. Kaske, 'Ficino's Shifting Attitude towards Astrology in the *De Vita Coelitus Comparanda*, the Letter to Poliziano, and the *Apologia* to the Cardinals', in *Marsilio Ficino e il ritorno di Platone*, i. 371–81.

30. For a consideration of his earlier position see G. Zanier, 'Il problema astrologico nelle prime opere di G. P. della Mirandola', *La cultura*, 8 (1970), 524–51; p. 524 n. 1 summarizes the varying opinions of Thorndike, Di Napoli, Walker, Yates, and Garin.

31. The heavens are made of a different substance from the sub-lunar world and can act on earthly bodies only in the manner suited to their own nature, which is incorruptible and has exquisite sensitivity (light) and perfect actions (circular motion and heat). Celestial motion generates earthly motion, but not each single, finite motion. It is the universal cause of the special or secondary causes to which physical happenings on earth must be attributed. Similar arguments are given for light and heat. As for the moral order, in the world of souls—which for Pico is entirely distinct from the corporeal world—God either governs directly or by means of revelation and angelic spirits. In this way, the stellar intermediary is completely excluded.

32. See e.g. E. Garin, *Pico della Mirandola: vita e dottrina* (Florence: Le Monnier, 1937), 193; *Lo zodiaco della vita: la polemica sull'astrologia dal Trecento al Cinquecento* (Bari: Laterza, 1976), 100–1; G. Zanier, 'Struttura e significato delle "Disputationes" pichiane', *Giornale critico della filosofia italiana*, 5, 42 (1981), 54–86 at 81–2.

33. See P. Rossi, 'Considerazioni sul declino dell'astrologia agli inizi dell'età moderna', in *L'opera e il pensiero di G. P. della Mirandola nella storia dell'umanesimo. Convegno internazionale*, ii (Florence: Istituto Nazionale di Studi sul Rinascimento, 1965), 315–31; G. Desantis, 'Pico, Pontano e la polemica astrologica', *Annali della Facoltà di Lettere e Filosofia della Università di Bari*, 29 (1986), 155–91 at 157–9. In his opening book, Pico says he will show that astrology 'corrupts philosophy, adulterates medicine, weakens religion, creates and strengthens superstitions, fosters idolatory, does away with prudence, defiles morals, defames the heavens, makes men miserable, troubled, uneasy, and servile instead of free' (*Disputationes*, i. 44; my translation).

34. See typically *Lo zodiaco della vita*, 98–106 at 105.

35. See W. G. Craven, *G. P. della Mirandola Symbol of his Age: Modern Interpretations of a Renaissance Philosopher* (Geneva: Droz, 1981), 161. Other interpretations (notably Cassirer's, but also Saitta's and Kristeller's) which, like Garin's, see human freedom as the driving force in Pico's polemic are also attacked by Craven.

36. See L. Valcke, 'Pic de la Mirandole et son mythe, tels que vus par W. G. Craven', *Renaissance et Reformation*, 7/2 (1983), 79–88.

37. See Zanier, 'Struttura e significato delle "Disputationes" pichiane', 58–9. Even B. Soldati's first comprehensive modern treatment of Pico's work (in *La poesia astrologica nel Quattrocento: ricerche e studi* (Florence: Sansoni, 1906)), while missing the significance of the fundamental physical arguments in Book III and arriving at a generally negative evaluation, clearly identifies this layered structure. The occasional lack of structural rigour in the disputations can of course in large measure be imputed to their unfinished state at the time of his death.

38. The emphasis on man's weakness and insignificance which Craven (p. 153) claims to perceive in the *Disputationes*, in glaring contrast to the optimistic picture of man painted in the *Oratio*, should in fact be seen as the relatively

unemphatic adoption of a theme typical of the anti-astrological tradition, which had been used with much greater force in France in the fairly recent past by Oresme and Gerson (cf. S. Caroti, 'La critica contro l'astrologia', 662).

39. See Zanier, 'Struttura e significato delle "Disputationes" pichiane', 57 n. 11.

40. See V. Busacchi, 'L'opposizione ai procedimenti astrologici da G. Pico a G. Montanari e il loro influsso sul pensiero medico', in *L'opera e il pensiero di Giovanni Pico della Mirandola nella storia dell'umanesimo*, ii. 413–24 at 417–20; Zambelli, *L'ambigua natura della magia*, 76–118.

41. See A. Grafton, *Commerce with the Classics: Ancient Books and Renaissance Readers* (Ann Arbor: University of Michigan Press, 1997), 93–134, which appeared after this chapter was written. Grafton views the *Disputationes* as 'triumph of philology as well as philosophy', which 'retains its power to stimulate anyone interested in the origins of ancient science' (p. 122); in his opinion the work is Pico's 'most effective intervention in the public domain of knowledge and debate' (p. 134) and 'one of the most original pieces of humanist scholarship carried out in the Renaissance' (p. 126).

42. There had also been the humiliation in Arezzo, when in May 1486 he botched an attempt to abduct Mariotto de' Medici's beautiful wife: cf. E. Garin, *G. Pico della Mirandola* (Mirandola/Parma: P. Toschi, 1963), 35–8; H. de Lubac, *Pic de la Mirandole: études et discussions* (Paris: Aubier Montaigne, 1974), 364.

43. Gianfrancesco Pico in particular was at pains to publicize his lamented uncle's sevenfold plan and the fact that the most dangerous of Christianity's enemies was astrology. See G. Di Napoli, *G. P. della Mirandola e la problematica dottrinale del suo tempo* (Rome: Desclée, 1965), 235–6; H. de Lubac, *Pic de la Mirandole*, 326 and nn. 1–3; G. Desantis, 'Pico, Pontano e la polemica astrologica', 157; Zambelli, *L'ambigua natura della magia*, 215.

44. Many scholars have been reluctant to do so through understandable mistrust of Gianfrancesco's tendentious apologetics and the excessive zeal of his fellow Savonarolans.

45. C. Trinkhaus, 'L'*Heptaplus* di Pico come sommario tematico e concordanza del suo pensiero', in *G. P. della Mirandola. Convegno internazionale di studi nel cinquecentesimo anniversario della morte (1494–1994). Mirandola. 4–8 ottobre 1994*, ed. G. C. Garfagnini (Florence: Olschki, 1997), i. 105–25.

46. See too Zanier, 'Il problema astrologico nelle prime opere di G. Pico', 546–7; Garin, *Lo zodiaco della vita*, 88–9; Copenhaver, 'Astrology and Magic', 269.

47. The *Heptaplus*, for example, gives a non-astrological concept of the *spiritus* that is nonetheless strikingly similar to Ficino's. It also has certain similarities to the *Oratio*, such as the ever-present notion of man as *vinculum mundi*, and uses a method of interpretation analogous to the Cabala which, as a secret key to knowledge communicated by God to Moses, had aroused Pico's excitement in the *Conclusiones* and *Apologia*.

48. Valcke, 'G. P. della Mirandola e il ritorno ad Aristotele', *G. P. della Mirandola, Convegno*, cit., i. 327–49.

49. Valcke, on the other hand, is obviously disappointed to find Pico's final work devoid of theological argumentation. This is because he too undervalues the tactical nature of the disputations' technical approach, just as his reliance on Pico's praise of *mathematici* and scholastics fails to recognize that in his first book

the count is often courting public opinion and is not above giving a biased presentation of the 'authorities' he cites.

50. An important fact mentioned by Valcke that merits further investigation is that Pico's scholastic training was completed in the period of almost a year (1484–5) that he spent in Paris, where the schoolmen were deeply diffident of philosophical thought in general and of Neoplatonism in particular. Many years ago Hans Baron suggested that a Parisian and north European influence may have been present in the *Disputationes* ('Willensfreiheit und Astrologie bei M. Ficino und Pico della Mirandola', in *Kultur- und Universalgeschichte: W. Goetz zu seinem 60. Geburtstag dargebracht von Fachgenossen, Freunden und Schülern* (Leipzig and Berlin, 1927), 145–70). The suggestion is worth reconsidering. We know that the repercussions of Pico's mighty attack spread outward to Paris and beyond after 1496. But it is surely equally true that the severe line taken by Paris against astrology before then played a strong part in the build-up in hostility that culminated in that attack. One need only think of the testimony of practising astrologers across Europe, such as the Dutchmen Albert Pigghe or the Spaniard Pedro Ciruelo who, many years later, back in Salamanca, complained that, when he had been teaching in Paris in the 1490s, he had been forced to abandon prediction because of an attack by theologians. The reference is to the dramatic condemnation in 1494 of Simon de Phares, which mirrored the Florentine assault. Pico himself was impressed enough by the University of Paris's hostility towards astrology to mention it in his closing book.

51. For a succinct account of this development see Garin, *G. P. della Mirandola*, 48–53. Zanier's peremptory invalidation of biographical facts ('Struttura e significato delle "Disputationes" pichiane', 74 n. 50) is unacceptable in attempting to establish the motives and aims of someone whose interest and concern extend well beyond the field of abstract philosophy.

52. See H. de Lubac, *Pic de la Mirandole*, 377.

53. He continued his commentary on the Psalms, drafted short spiritual tracts, and on 15 May and 2 July 1492 wrote the two long edifying letters from Ferrara to his nephew Gianfrancesco that were to be part of the *aureae epistolae* that Europe later so much admired: see G. Di Napoli, *G. P. della Mirandola*, 196–200 and 230–5; H. de Lubac, *Pic de la Mirandole*, 366–7 and 377–8.

54. In his desire to see in Pico an early paradigm of modern man, Garin has, we have seen, tended to over-secularize his motivation, which he interprets as a humanist celebration of free initiative. He has, however, never denied or lost sight of the religious factor, and has increasingly favoured a duality of approach that stops short of contradiction while resisting convergence. Even Craven, when robustly rejecting the possibility of a humanist motive, admits that there is good evidence for a religious one (*G. P. della Mirandola*, 147–8, 153–4). Zambelli is refreshingly unambiguous in seeing a clear apologetic, even zealous, impulse behind Pico's attack on astrology, while at the same time recognizing its considerable importance in the history of ideas (*L'ambigua natura della magia*, 15–16, 183, 197, 240).

55. 'Struttura e significato delle "Disputationes" pichiane', 74; see too 86.

56. See e.g. Garin, *Lo zodiaco della vita*, 110.

57. A chapter deals with astrology's general harmfulness to religion (II, 5). Another shows that neither good nor bad religions are dependent on the heavens (IV, 10).

When it comes to considering miracles (IV, 14–16), there is no equivocation: miracles are miracles, they are not natural happenings; the *stella Magorum* was a temporary, fictitious star, not a permanent, natural one. Very occasionally Pico's hackles rise: he admits that he has violated the logical order of his attack because he cannot wait to destroy the doctrine of major conjunctions, a veritable plague that dares to subject religion to the stars (VI, 1).

58. *Disputationes*, i. 40–4; my translation. Pico was particularly anxious to uphold the power of divine prophecy: see IV, 4 (ibid. 442–56), where he appears to have Savonarola in mind (p. 446). See too E. Garin, 'Le "Elezioni" e il problema dell'astrologia', 36–7; Zambelli, *L'ambigua natura della magia*, 109 and n. 114.

59. *Liber de astrologica veritate et in disputationes Ioannis Pici adversus astrologos responsiones* (Florence, 1498), fo. 96ᵛ. For a similar claim by G. Pontano, whose angry manuscript reaction was suppressed by his editor Summonte, see G. Desantis ('Pico, Pontano e la polemica astrologica'). Bellanti adds a further dig in reminding the reader that, several years before, Paul of Middelburg had astrologically foretold the advent of a false prophet, and, further on in his defence, draws attention to his own prediction of Savonarola's violent death (*Liber de astrologica veritate*, fo. 111ʳ).

60. *Oraculum de novo saeculo* (Florence, 1497), pp. 16 a–b. See D. P. Walker, *The Ancient Theology: Studies in Christian Platonism from the Fifteenth to the Eighteenth Century* (London: Duckworth, 1972), 51–8.

61. See R. Ridolfi, 'Le predicazioni savonaroliane sull'Arca e le edizioni del 1536', *Bibliofilia*, 52 (1950), 17–37, and *Vita di G. Savonarola* (Rome: Belardetti, 1952), ii. 134. For the critical edition of the *Trattato*, see G. Savonarola, *Scritti filosofici*, ed. G. Garafagnini and E. Garin, i (Rome, 1982), 273–370 (notes: pp. 401–8), where Garin by and large follows Ridolfi (pp. 401–5).

62. *Dialogus in astrologiae defensionem cum vaticinio a diluvio usque ad Christi annos 1702.* The colophon claims that the work was written in 1492, sent to King Alfonso of Naples on 4 June 1494, and printed in Venice on 20 Oct. 1494 (sig. e.vᵛ). There is internal textual evidence that points to the date of writing as certainly after 1492 and probably at the end of 1493 or the beginning of 1494 at the latest (cf. sig. d.vʳ and d.iiiᵛ). The reference to Pico is at sig. a.iiiiʳ. In a letter to Mainardi written shortly after the publication of the *Disputationes*, Gianfrancesco identifies what appears to be Abioso's dialogue as an angry riposte to his uncle (cf. *Opera omnia* (Basel, 1573), fos. 1278–9). Abioso himself, in his *Vaticinium eventuum anni 1523* (Naples, 1523), presents his *Dialogus* of thirty years earlier as a demonstration of the ignorance and vanity of Pico's disputations (sig. b.iiʳ). See Zambelli, *L'ambigua natura della magia*, 103–5 and id., 'Fine del mondo o inizio della propaganda? Astrologia, filosofia della storia e propaganda politico-religiosa nel dibattito sulla congiunzione del 1524', in *Scienze, credenze occulte, livelli di cultura. Convegno Internazionale di Studi (INSR)* (Florence: Olschki, 1983), 291–368 at 361–4.

63. Pirovano's *Defensio astronomiae* (Milan, 1506) was reprinted at Basel as *De astronomiae veritate* in 1554, together with Bellanti's defence. Thorndike, confusing Galeazzo Maria Sforza with his son Gian Galeazzo, claims that the work was composed after the latter's death on 21 Oct. 1494 (*A History of Magic*, iv. 542), whereas the corrected historical reference suggests that it was composed before this date. In the text, Pirovano states the time of writing as the beginning of 1494

(*De astronomiae veritate*, 1554, p. 291), a date which other internal references tend to corroborate (cf. ibid. 266). Zanier rightly presents Gabriele as a follower of Raymond Lull and opponent of the Neoplatonists and of Ficino's attack on astrologers in his commentary on Plotinus (G. Zanier, *La medicina astrologica e la sua teoria: Marsilio Ficino e i suoi critici contemporanei* (Rome: Edizioni dell'Ateneo, 1977), 61–79). But Pirovano appears to have Pico foremost in his mind in his impassioned introduction denouncing the new opponents of the stellar science ('aggredior respondere hiis, qui totam vim Astrorum sua auctoritate ac disputationibus, vel potius imputationibus conantur evertere [. . .]', Pirovano, *De astronomiae veritate*, 222). Moreover, he makes it clear further on that he is also answering the arguments made by Pico 'longiori sermone vel dulciori rhetoricae lira' (ibid. 252), which, rather than referring to the limited attack in the *Heptaplus*, is more likely to be an indication that Pirovano was conversant with the nature of the count's exhaustive and eloquent confutation.

64. In his plans for the sermons for Advent 1494, written at the beginning of that summer, Savonarola refers explicitly to Pico's attack, summarizing an argument from *Disputationes* III, 3. See Ridolfi, *Vita di G. Savonarola*, i. 150 and ii. 134 n. 15, and id., 'Le predicazioni savonaroliane sull'Arca e le edizioni del 1536'; Garin, *Lo zodiaco della vita*, 96.

65. This expectancy is communicated particularly strongly in Gianfrancesco's excited correspondance with Battista Spagnuoli, the celebrated Carmelite from Mantua, which began immediately after his uncle's death. See G. F. Pico, *Opera omnia*, fos. 1296–8, 1340–2, 1353.

66. H. de Lubac (*Pic de la Mirandole*, 308) is of the opinion that the *Disputationes* were circulated, in part, during Pico's lifetime.

67. See Savonarola, *Scritti filosofici*, i. 275.

68. Savonarola's biographers are unanimous about the overriding importance of his prophetic role: Schnitzer emphasizes that the Dominican will always be an enigma to the historian who does not recognize the fact that he was above all a prophet (cf. J. Schnitzer, *Savonarola* (Milan: Treves, 1931)); Ridolfi waxes lyrical on those prophecies that came true (*Vita di G. Savonarola*); Weinstein traces the stages whereby the preacher of repentance evolved into the prophet of liberty (D. Weinstein, *Savonarola and Florence: Prophecy and Patriotism in the Renaissance* (Princeton: Princeton University Press, 1970)). Savonarola gathered together a compendium of his own past prophecies, which he published in Italian and Latin in 1495 in order to avoid misrepresentation. After the excommunication of May 1497, when his prophetic mission was constantly under attack, he took up the argument again in a more systematic manner in the *De veritate prophetica*, a dialogue on the validity and nature of prophecy which he finished at the end of 1497 (see *Compendio di rivelazioni e De veritate prophetica,* ed. Angela Crucitti (Rome: Belardetti, 1974)).

69. Savonarola began his *Trattato* of 1497 by reminding the reader that he had for some years been publicly denouncing astrology as a diabolic pseudo-science in his sermons: see *Scritti filosofici*, i. 275 and 402.

70. *Prediche sopra il Salmo Quam Bonus* (Venice, 1539), fo. 255^r. The Venice, 1528 first edition (which I have not seen) is the enlarged translation of a Latin autograph manuscript which is more of a treatise or meditation than a transcription of sermons, but may well be based on summaries of sermons actually delivered,

though, as Ridolfi points out, there is no real evidence of when or where, despite the claim that they were delivered in Santa Maria del Fiore during Advent 1493. See R. Ridolfi, *The Life of Girolamo Savonarola*, trans. C. Grayson (London: Routledge and Kegan Paul, 1959), 69–71.

71. *Prediche sopra Aggeo*, ed. L. Firpo (Rome: Belardetti, 1965), 258.
72. *Prediche sopra Giobbe*, ed. R. Ridolfi (Rome: Belardetti, 1957). See p. 298, where he uses the argument involving universal and particular causes; also pp. 47–8, 220, 321, 356, 381, etc.
73. *Compendio di rivelazioni*, 6.
74. See *De simplicitate Christianae vitae*, ed. P. G. Ricci (Rome: Belardetti, 1959), 30. The reference to the *Disputationes* was added in the first half of 1496, when Savonarola revised the original draft for publication (Aug. 1496). Girolamo Benivieni's translation appeared in Oct. 1496.
75. *Triumphus Crucis. Testo latino e volgare*, ed. M. Ferrara (Rome: Belardetti, 1961), 220–31 (IV, 3: Traditiones astrologorum penitus inutiles ac superstitiosas esse); the digression is at pp. 225–6. The Latin text was published towards the end of 1497, whereas the Italian translation, which Savonarola undertook himself, was edited and published after his death by Domenico Benivieni.
76. *Prediche sopra Amos e Zaccaria*, ed. P. Ghiglieri, ii (Rome: Belardetti, 1972), 26 (Pred. XVIII: 5 Mar. 1496). See too i. 83–4 (Pred. III: 19 Feb. 1496).
77. See *Scritti filosofici*, i. 351.
78. See ibid. 276–7.
79. See ibid. 291, 295–6, 368–9.
80. See ibid. 402.
81. G. F. Pico, *Opera omnia*, fo. 1352; my translation.
82. Ibid., fo. 23; my translation. For this reference and a convincing argument against Garin's dating, see Zambelli, *L'ambigua natura della magia*, 110–11.
83. See *Triumphus Crucis*, ed. Ferrara, 231.
84. Savonarola, *Scritti filosofici*, i. 402 n. 15.
85. See Zambelli, *L'ambigua natura della magia*, 111 n. 120; also Garin in Savonarola, *Scritti filosofici*, i. 402 n. 15. I am grateful to Prof. N. Harris, University of Udine, for further information on this evidence.
86. See Garin, in Savonarola, *Scritti filosofici*, 403.
87. See R. Ridolfi, *La stampa in Firenze nel secolo XV* (Florence: Olschki, 1958), 24.
88. See E. Garin, *L'età nuova: ricerche di storia della cultura dal XII al XVI secolo* (Naples: Morano, 1969), 99.
89. On Savonarola's admiration of Pico's eloquence, as recounted by Pietro Crinito in the *De honesta disciplina*, see Walker, *The Ancient Theology*, 48–51.
90. It is unlikely, as H. de Lubac remarks (*Pic de la Mirandole*, 388), that Pico would have been seduced by Savonarola's exalted prophetism.
91. There are two versions of Savonarola's announcement: one added as a postscript to the sixth sermon on Haggai, and a longer version elaborated by Gianfrancesco in his life of his uncle. See Ridolfi, *Vita di G. Savonarola*, ii. 134 n. 18.

CHAPTER 3

Luigi Pulci and the Generation of '94

Mark Davie

Luigi Pulci belonged to an earlier generation than that of '94. Born in 1432, he was nine years older than Boiardo and twenty-two years older than Poliziano; and he died in 1484, so that by the 1490s his presence was already a fading memory. While the influence of the *Morgante* on the development of chivalric narrative poetry is undisputed, what is perhaps less apparent is his standing with the generation immediately following his own. This chapter considers Pulci's relationship, first with Poliziano, a leading representative of the new culture which supplanted Pulci's in Florence in the course of the 1470s;[1] and second with Boiardo, whose *Orlando innamorato* provides the earliest evidence of the presence of the *Morgante* in the narrative poetry of the Valpadana.

A myth which goes back to Teofilo Folengo and Ortensio Lando, and which was reproduced by Poliziano's eighteenth-century biographer Mencke, claims that the *Morgante* was the product of a literary collaboration between Pulci and Poliziano, or even that it was written by Poliziano who then allowed Pulci to pass it off as his own. Folengo writes in the *Orlandino* (1526):

> Polizian fu quello ch'altamente
> cantò del gran gigante dal bataio,
> ed a Luiggi Pulzi suo cliente
> l'onor die' senza scritto di notaio;
> pur dopo si pentì; ma chi si pente
> po 'l fatto, pesta l'acqua nel mortaio;
> sia pur o non sia pur cotesto vero,
> so ben, chi crede troppo ha del liggero.[2]

It is true that neither Folengo nor the other authors who repeat this claim seem inclined to take it very seriously; but it must have had at least a degree of plausibility for their contemporaries, and it is reasonable to ask how it arose. The initial hint comes clearly enough from Pulci himself. In canto XXV of the *Morgante*, having finally embarked, after many distractions and digressions, on his promised theme of the betrayal and defeat of Charlemagne's army at Roncevaux, he breaks off as if a new thought had just occurred to him:

> Io avevo pensato abbreviàre
> la storia, e non sapevo che Rinaldo
> in Roncisvalle potrebbe arrivare;
> un angel poi da Ciel m'ha mostro Arnaldo,
> che certo un aüttor degno mi pare,
> e dice: — Aspetta, Luigi, sta saldo,
> ché fia forse Rinaldo a tempo giunto — ;
> sì ch'io dirò come egli scrive appunto. (*Morg.*, XXV, 115)[3]

Pulci does not spell out the identity of the 'angel da Ciel' at this point, although the phrase contains a thinly veiled allusion to his name; but any remaining doubt is removed when his help is acknowledged again in stanza 169:

> E ringrazio il mio car, non Angiolino,
> sanza il qual molto laboravo invano,
> più tosto un cherubino o serafino,
> onore e gloria di Montepulciano,
> che mi détte d'Arnaldo e d'Alcuïno
> notizia, e lume del mio Carlo Mano:
> ch'io ero entrato in un oscuro bosco;
> or la strada o 'l sentier del ver cognosco. (ibid. 169)

The 'Angiolino' who is 'onore e gloria di Montepulciano' is clearly Angelo Poliziano.

What then was the help for which Pulci thanked Poliziano so profusely? The admission in stanza 115 that 'Io avevo pensato abbreviàre / la storia' confirms the impression given by the first hundred stanzas of canto XXV, that after the numerous distractions in the earlier part of the poem, Pulci now meant to follow the canonical story of Roncevaux through to its conclusion without further delay. Poliziano's intervention seems to have made him have second thoughts about this decision, suggesting that he reintroduce the extraneous story of Rinaldo which he had abruptly cut short in the conclusion to canto XXIII for the first published version of the poem (printed in 1478).[4] This is

surprising, for as Pulci acknowledges in the very next stanza, there were
plenty of unsympathetic critics who would be ready to pounce on him
if his new poem (the five cantos of *La rotta di Roncisvalle*, printed as
cantos XXIV to XXVIII in the enlarged *Morgante* of 1483)[5] failed to
deliver the promised version of the Roncevaux story:

> E so che andar diritto mi bisogna,
> ch'io non ci mescolassi una bugia,
> ché questa non è istoria da menzogna;
> ché, come io esco un passo della via,
> chi gracchia, chi riprende, e chi rampogna;
> ognun poi mi rïesce la pazzia; (ibid. 116, 1–6)

In these circumstances, Poliziano's advice seems to have been that,
since his enemies would never be satisfied anyway, Pulci might as well
go his own way and let the critics do their worst:

> La mia accademia un tempo o mia ginnasia
> è stata volentier ne' miei boschetti,
> [. . .]
> e cosí fuggo mille urban dispetti;
> sí ch'io non torno a' vostri arïopaghi,
> gente pur sempre di mal dicer vaghi. (ibid. 117, 1–2, 6–8)

Pulci's appeal to his personal 'accademia' is a transparent reference to
Ficino's Accademia Platonica which had left him marginalized in
the cultural life of Florence after 1478; and Poliziano evidently encouraged Pulci to trust his own inspiration as no less valid than that of
his more fashionable rival.[6]

Pulci loses no time in making clear what this will mean. In the fifty
stanzas which follow, far from continuing the single-minded pursuit
of the Roncevaux story, he introduces the devil Astarotte to bring
Rinaldo and his companions back from the east to help the Christian
army in the battle. There ensues a long dialogue between Astarotte
and the sorcerer Malagigi, in which Pulci indulges his weakness,
apparent on several earlier occasions in the poem, for occult lore and
theological speculation[7]—a risky theme since it had been this which
had got him into trouble with Ficino and others in the early 1470s.

By stanza 169 his confidence was sufficiently restored for him to
break off once more in order to acknowledge his debt to Poliziano, in
the lines quoted above. His friend's advice had not only strengthened
his resolve to continue the narrative in his own way; it had also

encouraged him to maintain the element of variety which he could now see as one of the poem's strengths:

> la nostra istoria è sí fiorita e varia,
> ch'i' non posso in un luogo star mai saldo;
> e non sia altra oppinïon contraria,
> ché troppe belle cose dice Arnaldo; (ibid. 168, 3–6)

He is even bold enough to claim to have improved on the Roncevaux story itself, on the grounds that, without the intervention of Rinaldo, the rout of the Christian army would have been even more comprehensive, Charlemagne himself might have been captured and Gano might have escaped the punishment which he deserved (ibid. 170).

In stanza 169 Pulci thanks Poliziano for drawing his attention to both 'Arnaldo' and 'Alcuïno'. 'Arnaldo' appears to be a pure invention on Pulci's part, a cypher for the element of fantasy and humour which he had tried half-heartedly to eliminate in canto XXIII, but which Poliziano evidently encouraged him to retain. Alcuin, on the other hand, is a historical figure, to whom the Middle Ages ascribed Einhard's *Life* of Charlemagne, the most authoritative contemporary biography; and the rest of the *Morgante* is indeed a highly individual mixture of these two elements—the 'historical' story ending at Roncevaux, as it was enshrined in the long-standing epic tradition; and the largely comic material, associated especially but not exclusively with Rinaldo, which had predominated in the earlier poem.

The mixture remains in the distinctive last canto of the *Morgante*, which offers two summary versions of the life of Charlemagne. Concluding the poem with the emperor's death, Pulci recounts two orations which are given at his funeral: the first by a minstrel whom he calls 'Lattanzio' (XXVIII, 53, 2), who narrates the legendary exploits, supposedly belonging to Charles's youth, which were the subject of the romance tradition; and the second delivered by 'Alcuïno' (ibid. 67, 5), which gives a relatively sober account of his historical career. The first is derived largely from Andrea da Barberino's *Reali di Francia*, while the latter is based on the *Vita Caroli Magni* of Donato Acciaiuoli, a work largely based on Einhard but produced in the same circumstances as the *Morgante* in 1461.[8] It is fair to assume that it was Poliziano who reminded Pulci of the existence of Acciaiuoli's text, and that it is this which Pulci had in mind when he thanked his friend for directing him towards 'Alcuïno / [. . .] e lume del mio Carlo Mano'.

Acciaiuoli's work, while utterly different from Pulci's in scale and genre, shows the same uncertainty about how its subject matter was to be treated. Acciaiuoli had aspirations to be a serious historian, and the *Vita Caroli Magni* is cast in the form of a classical biography;[9] but he could not entirely discard the romantic accretions which accounted for so much of the Carolingian material—especially since, as a Florentine writer seeking to reaffirm the city's traditional alliance with France, he evidently felt obliged to include the legend of the city's refounding by the emperor after its destruction by the Huns. The figure of Charlemagne was clearly inherently problematic; he was required to fulfil too many roles in too many different contexts for any one text to embrace them all. Acciaiuoli's solution was to present the conflicting elements of the story, prefacing those about which he was dubious with a suitable warning, but in the end leaving the reader to decide what weight to give them.[10] And this is effectively what Pulci also does in canto XXVIII.

The *Morgante* remains to the end an unrepentantly ambivalent poem, epitomized in a stanza almost at the end of canto XXVIII in which Pulci first pays homage to his patroness, Lucrezia Tornabuoni, expressing his regret that she had died (in 1482) before the poem was finished, but also his confidence that she would have recognized his good intentions:

> E s'io ho satisfatto al suo desio,
> basta a me tanto e son di ciò contento:
> altro premio, altro onor non domando io,
> altro piacer che di godermi drento. (XXVIII, 136, 1–4)

But then in mid-stanza he breaks off and recalls Morgante, imagining him bending down from heaven to use his *battaglio* against any critics who might still be inclined to complain:

> E so ch'egli è lassù Morgante mio:
> però, s'alcun malivolo qui sento,
> adatterà il battaglio ancor dal Cielo
> in qualche modo, a scardassargli il pelo. (ibid. 5–8)

The two halves of this stanza reflect in microcosm the unresolved tension in the *Morgante* as a whole, between historical celebration and comic fantasy; and it is a tension which should be attributed, at least in part, to the influence of Poliziano.

Yet this is not quite the last page of the *Morgante*. The last seven stanzas of the poem (XXVIII, 146–52) are an extended tribute to

Poliziano, so that its concluding note, far from being hesitant or defensive, is an expression of confidence based on the help which Pulci expects to receive from the younger poet and the inspiration which he will draw from his example. The critics of the *Morgante*, he says, will be silenced

> [. . .] perché questo Agnol vi porrà la mano,
> nato per gloria di Montepulciano. (ibid. 145, 7–8)

Poliziano is comparable to all the poets of classical mythology (146, 1–4), and Pulci expects to accompany him 'per le famose rive / d'Eürote e pe' gioghi là di Cinto' (148, 1–2); his poetic talent, embracing both Latin and Greek ('le muse aüsonie ed argive', 148, 3), promises to produce a new flowering of 'nostro idïoma' (149, 5). What Pulci emphasizes is precisely the variety of Poliziano's writing—not only his mastery of three different languages, but his ability to mix styles and genres to create a new *docta varietas* which would validate Pulci's own more modest mixture of styles. For all the difference in the literary aspirations of the two poets, Pulci evidently saw a continuity between his own work and Poliziano's which encouraged him to conclude his poem with two stanzas (151–2) looking forward to a new golden age of vernacular poetry, under the patronage of Lorenzo's sons, in which Poliziano would be the leading light but in which Pulci himself would have a definite, if secondary, role to play.

If there is indeed such a continuity between the two poets, it is not difficult to see where we should expect to find it. As is well known, both Lorenzo and Giuliano de' Medici were launched on their public careers with a spectacular joust, Lorenzo in 1469 and Giuliano in 1475, and both occasions were commemorated with a specially commissioned poem—by Pulci in 1469 and by Poliziano in 1475. Pulci was apparently still trying to finish his *Giostra di Lorenzo de' Medici* in February 1474, at the height of his quarrels with Ficino and Matteo Franco; and by the time it was completed, preparations were already in hand for Giuliano's joust, and Poliziano had already been chosen as the poet who would celebrate it. So Pulci's *Giostra* ends with a stanza addressed to Poliziano, using the nickname 'compare' by which he was known in Lorenzo's circle.[11]

> Or sia qui fin, poi che convien posarsi,
> perché il compar, mentre ch'io scrivo, aspetta
> e ha già in punto la sua vïoletta.

Hor fa', compar, che tu la scarabilli, [. . .]

(*Giostra*, 159, 6–160, 1)

The tone is relaxed and companionable, with no suggestion of rivalry towards the younger poet. Already in 1474 Pulci has the confidence in his relationship with Poliziano to see him as a partner in a common enterprise, as he still would in the conclusion to the *Morgante* eight or nine years later. He could hardly have imagined, at the end of his *Giostra*, how different Poliziano's *Stanze* would be; yet the gulf between the two works evidently did nothing to undermine the friendship between the two poets, or Pulci's readiness to see Poliziano as his natural successor.

Pulci's *Giostra* is the first attempt in Florentine vernacular poetry to commemorate a public occasion in *ottave* with at least a minimum of literary aspirations.[12] It describes the pseudo-chivalric spectacle of the Medici joust using the forms and conventions of chivalric poetry. Clearly Poliziano's aspirations in the *Stanze* go a good deal further than that; but could he have written the *Stanze* without the precedent of Pulci's *Giostra*?

Pulci's poem begins with a description of the triumph of love in Florence, and of Lorenzo as a faithful devotee of Cupid:

> Par che 'l gaudio celeste qui si senta,
> con pace, con amore e con concordia,
> ché nol turbò la dea della discordia. (*Giostra*, 6, 6–8)[13]

When the plans for the joust are held up by the war against Venice in 1468, Lorenzo appeals to Venus to enable Cupid to tame the warlike heart of Borso d'Este:

> con quello stral che più tua virtù mostra
> e che più infiamma i generosi cori,
> chi m'ha negata la promessa giostra
> saetta al cor, sì ch'ancor lui innamori,
> e fia tua gloria magna, anzi fia nostra, (15, 1–5)

When Pulci embarks on the description of the event, he renews his appeal to the Muses and stresses the dignity of the theme:

> Non val qui il zufoletto melibeo
> a raccontar sì magna e bella giostra,
> anzi ogni gloria della città nostra. (22, 6–8)

There are clear parallels here with the opening of Poliziano's *Stanze,*

which also begin with a declaration that they will celebrate the glory
of Florence:

> Le gloriose pompe e' fieri ludi
> della città che 'l freno allenta e stringe
> a' magnanimi Toschi [. . .]. (*Stanze*, I, 1, 1–3)[14]

Poliziano, too, stresses the peace and prosperity which the city enjoys
thanks to Lorenzo—'E tu, ben nato Laur, sotto il cui velo / Fiorenza
lieta in pace si riposa' (4, 1–2)—and the benevolent influence of
'quella dea che 'l terzo ciel dipinge' (1, 4).

It must be admitted that the rest of Pulci's poem does not live up
to the promise of these opening stanzas. It consists largely of the
names of the participants in the joust, with descriptions of their
costumes, their coats of arms, their horses and the like. This part of
the text is based on an anonymous prose chronicle of the event; and
a comparison of Pulci's text with its source shows how he was not
content simply to reproduce the information given by the chronicler,
but was concerned to spell out the message which Medici propaganda
sought to convey through the event.[15] Pulci's poem leaves the reader
in no doubt that the essential purpose of the whole spectacle was to
celebrate Lorenzo's coming of age as the beginning of a new golden
age in Florence. And in this respect too, he offered Poliziano a precedent for what was surely his purpose in the *Stanze*—to spell out the
plans which Medici policy envisaged for Giuliano at the beginning of
his public career.

It is not surprising to find in the *Stanze,* with their fusion of classical
and vernacular traditions, echoes which could be of specific lines in
Pulci's *Giostra*, but which are more likely to be part of the common
stock of topoi of chivalric poetry. For instance, when Giuliano first
sees the vision of Simonetta, Poliziano draws on the commonplaces of
the traditional *innamoramento*, even down to such hackneyed rhymes
as *riso* : *paradiso* : *diviso*:

> Volta la ninfa al suon delle parole,
> lampeggiò d'un sì dolce e vago riso,
> che i monti avre' fatto ir, restare il sole:
> ché ben parve s'aprissi un paradiso.
> Poi formò voce fra perle e viole,
> tal ch'un marmo per mezo avre' diviso;
> soave, saggia e di dolcezza piena,
> da innamorar non ch'altri una Sirena: (*Stanze*, I, 50)

One could cite a stanza from Pulci's *Giostra* which is based on the same rhymes:

> E missegliela in testa con un riso,
> con parole modeste e sì soave,
> che si potea vedere il paradiso
> e sentir Gabrïel quando disse 'Ave' (*Giostra*, 9, 1–4)

But there is an even closer parallel with a stanza in *Morgante*, XVI, in the description of the captivating figure of Antea:

> E volsesi a Orlando con un riso,
> con un atto benigno e con parole
> che si vedeva aperto il paradiso,
> che si fermò a udir la luna e 'l sole.
> Ma Chiarïella diventò nel viso
> del color delle mammole vïole; (*Morgante*, XVI, 12, 1–6)

This has not only the rhymes *riso* : *paradiso*, but also the alternating series *parole* : *sole* : *viole*; it has a similar opening in the first line, 'Volta la ninfa [. . .]' / 'E volsesi a Orlando [. . .]'; and it describes both the heavens opening (l. 3) and the sun standing still (l. 4). The one feature for which the *Morgante* fails to provide a precedent is the abstraction of the physical description in line 5, where Simonetta's teeth and lips become 'perle e viole'.

It would be rash to press the claim that Poliziano drew directly on Pulci's stanza as his source, even though the coincidence of several points of resemblance seems to point in that direction. Rather, the stanza shows how Poliziano was able to use these tried and tested formulae from the poetic tradition, as Pulci had done, as part of a deliberate dialogue with the tradition: largely for humorous effect, exploiting the blatant hyperbole, in Pulci's case; as a point of departure for the more refined and elusive conception of love to which Giuliano must aspire, in Poliziano's.

The evidence of the *Morgante*, of Pulci's *Giostra*, and of Poliziano's *Stanze* combines to suggest that the relationship between the two poets is a reciprocal one, based on personal friendship and a shared attachment to the vernacular poetic tradition; and that this relationship survived the widening cultural gap between Pulci at the end of his life and the increasingly sophisticated Poliziano.

Geography and chronology both rule out any such mutual influence between Pulci and Boiardo. The presence of the *Morgante* in the

Innamorato is not in doubt, and recent research has confirmed the suspicion, voiced ten years ago by Pier Vincenzo Mengaldo, that the publication of the first *Morgante* in 1478 was decisive in prompting Boiardo to undertake his poem, as 'l'immediata risposta di Ferrara al tentativo di Firenze di affermare (o riaffermare) la propria egemonia anche nel genere per eccellenza padano della poesia cavalleresca'.[16] This seems to be confirmed by Stefano Carrai's impression that the presence of the *Morgante* is most conspicuous in Book I and diminishes in the course of Boiardo's poem.[17] However, Raffaele Donnarumma, in the most exhaustive survey yet undertaken of Pulci echoes in the *Innamorato*, concludes that on the contrary it is precisely because 'il primo *Innamorato* può essere letto come una risposta punto per punto a Pulci' that 'il riuso del *Morgante* nel I libro dell'*Innamorato* è [. . .] spesso camuffato e opacizzato'.[18] In Book II, in contrast, 'la presenza testuale del *Morgante* [. . .] è maggiore che nel I; ma soprattutto è più scoperta'; 'Pulci, insomma, inizia a diventare un modello da seguire, non più un modello cui opporsi' (p. 173). Finally, for Donnarumma, it is in Book III that Boiardo fully absorbs Pulci's example: 'Fra terzo *Innamorato* e primo *Morgante* c'è una convergenza che dimentica le diffidenze sottese al libro iniziale e supera le distanze ideologiche'; 'il pulcismo è, infatti, ciò che identifica il registro del III libro distinguendolo dai primi due' (p. 182).

When such detailed research leads to such divergent conclusions, it would be rash to attempt to synthesize or to adjudicate between them in a short essay such as this. Instead, two brief examples, one of the commonplace theme already discussed (that of feminine beauty and the male *innamoramento*), the other distinctively Pulcian (Pulci's anti-hero Margutte and his counterpart in Boiardo, Brunello), may serve to illustrate both the nature and the limits of Boiardo's absorption of Pulci's example.

Boiardo's poem opens with a scene analogous to those already considered in the two Tuscan poets; the appearance of Angelica at Charlemagne's court clearly belongs to the same genre as the appearance of Antea in the *Morgante* and that of Simonetta in the *Stanze*. Boiardo's version is striking for its economy; because he can count on his readers' ability to recognize the stereotype to which he is alluding, he needs only four lines to sketch in the essentials:

> Essa sembrava matutina stella
> e giglio d'orto e rosa de verzieri:

in somma, a dir di lei la veritate,
non fu veduta mai tanta beltate. *(Innamorato,* I, i, 21, 5–8)[19]

Bruscagli's notes to this stanza point out the parallels between the first two lines and Boccaccio's *Teseida* ('Ella sembiava matutina stella / e fresca rosa del mese di maggio', *Tes.,* I, 125, 3–4; 'più bella che rosa di verziere', ibid. 128, 3). There are comparable parallels closer to Boiardo's own time in the *Orlando laurenziano,* Pulci's source for the Antea episode:

> [. . .] questa bella Antea
> era più fresca che giglio o che rosa;
> e per le spalle una treccia scendea,
> ch'è d'or battuto, tanto par gioiosa,
> e tutta inanellata overo ricciuta;
> più bella treccia mai non fu veduta. *(Orlando,* XXX, 40, 3–8)[20]

There is no evidence for any diffusion of the *Orlando laurenziano* outside Tuscany, and in any case the phrases which it has in common with the *Innamorato* are, by this time, off-the-shelf clichés. But it is instructive to compare Boiardo's reaction to such phrases with Pulci's. Whereas for Boiardo they are an effective stylistic shorthand, alluding to an entire literary tradition with a few deft strokes of the pen, Pulci cannot resist indulging in an extended parody, taking the most hackneyed elements of the scene and doing them to death. This, for instance, is part of his version of the description of Antea:

> Avea certi atti dolci e certi risi,
> certi soavi e leggiadri costumi
> da fare spalancar sei paradisi
> e correr sù pe' monti all'erta i fiumi;
> da fare innamorar cento Narcisi, *(Morgante,* XV, 102, 1–5)

The parody centres on the stock rhymes *riso : viso : paradiso,* starting with the unexpected plural ('certi atti dolci e certi risi'), continuing with the disconcertingly concrete verb in 'da fare *spalancar* sei paradisi', and culminating in the hyperbole of 'da fare innamorar *cento* Narcisi'. Once it has been thus undermined, it is difficult for the series to be taken seriously when it recurs in XVI, 12 (quoted above) and again in XVI, 21:

> E cominciorno insieme a riguardarsi
> ognun più che l'usato intento e fiso;
> Rinaldo non potea di lei saziarsi,

> né crede ch'altro ben sia in paradiso;
> e la fanciulla cominciò a pensarsi
> che così bel già mai fussi Narciso.

Yet at the same time, Antea is not just a pretty face; she is, apart from anything else, an effective orator, and her gesture in XVI, 12 ('E volsesi a Orlando con un riso [. . .]') is the preliminary to addressing him with a speech which captivates him even more than her beauty. The same is true of Simonetta in the *Stanze* ('Volta la ninfa al suon delle parole [. . .]', I, 50), and also of Angelica in the *Innamorato*, although in Boiardo's stanza 23 all eyes are already fixed on her:

> Ogni barone e principe cristiano
> in quella parte ha rivoltato il viso,
> né rimase a giacere alcun pagano;
> ma ciascun d'essi, de stupor conquiso,
> si fece a la donzella prossimano;
> la qual, con vista allegra e con un riso
> da far inamorare un cor di sasso,
> incominciò così, parlando basso: (*Innam.*, I, i, 23)

Angelica has a 'riso / da far inamorare un cor di sasso', just as Pulci's Antea has 'certi risi / da far innamorar cento Narcisi' and Poliziano's Simonetta speaks with a 'voce [. . .] / da innamorar non ch'altri una Sirena'. There is an unbroken continuity between the three texts; all three poets take for granted the reader's familiarity with the conventions which are being alluded to; but Boiardo is either unaware of or is able to ignore the ironic overtones which seem inseparable from such a scene after Pulci's treatment of it.

Boiardo shows the same economy of effort in what is probably his most evident borrowing from Pulci, the figure of Brunello as a variation of Pulci's Margutte. In four stanzas at the end of II, xv and the beginning of II, xvi, Boiardo concentrates on two rudimentary points in Brunello's character: his love of food and drink, and his insolence in avoiding paying for them. Both are prominent aspects of the Margutte episode; Morgante and Margutte vie with each other in boasting about innkeepers they have cheated, in a joke which runs throughout their exploits together. Boiardo, however, draws on another part of Pulci's story:

> E benché i teverneri e' lor sergenti
> dietro li sian con orci e con pignate,
> lui se ne andava stropezando e denti,
> e faceva a ciascun mille ghignate. (*Innam.*, II, xv, 69, 1–4)

Brunello's defiant gesture in lines 3–4 is the same as Morgante's when
he devoured a whole elephant which he and Margutte had killed and
cooked:

> Margutte torna, e Morgante trovava
> che s'avea trangugiato insino all'osse
> il lïofante, e' denti stuzzicava
> con lo schidon del pin dove e' si cosse: (*Morgante*, XIX, 83, 1–4)

In a comic reversal of roles, Margutte is outraged at having been
cheated of his share, and is provoked to new heights of indignation by
Morgante's insouciant attitude:

> Dicea Margutte: — Io ho sempre mai inteso
> che gnun non si vorrebbe mai beffare:
> io mi vedea schernito e vilipeso,
> e costui stava il dente a stuzzicare,
> come se proprio e' non m'avessi offeso.
> Questo non posso mai dimenticare:
> e' si poteva pur far altrimenti
> che sogghignare e stuzzicarsi i denti. (ibid. 89)

The scene is doubly comic, both because Margutte becomes the
deceiver deceived, and because of his aggrieved repetition of the trivial
detail—of Morgante grinning complacently as he picked his teeth with
a tree-trunk—which added insult to injury. It takes just a couple of
phrases—'stropezando e denti', 'mille ghignate'—for Boiardo to recall
Margutte's complaint, and with him the comic potential of the earlier
scene.

In the same way, at the beginning of the next canto, Boiardo relies
on a single word to recall a colourful theme in Margutte's confession:

> E nel canto passato io dicea quando
> intrava quel giottone a ogni cucina,
> non aspettando a' figatelli inviti,
> pigliando e grossi sempre e rivestiti. (*Innam.*, II, xvi, 2, 5–8)

Fegatello was one of Margutte's favourite topics, first in his glutton's
creed:

> e credo nella torta e nel tortello,
> l'uno è la madre e l'altro è il suo figliuolo;
> e 'l vero paternostro è il fegatello,
> e posson esser tre, due ed un solo [. . .] (*Morg.*, XVIII, 116, 1–4)

and then in his exposition of culinary art, where he devoted two
whole stanzas to explaining how *fegatello* should be cooked:

> Del fegatello non ti dico niente:
> vuol cinque parte (fa ch'a la man tenga):
> vuole esser tondo, nota sanamente, [. . .]
>
> Piccolo sia, questo è proverbio antico,
> e fa che non sia povero di panni, [. . .] (ibid. 125, 1–3; 126, 1–2)

Boiardo's choice of this particular delicacy as the object of Brunello's greed would appear arbitrary if it did not serve to recall the whole of Margutte's 'arte'. But the detail also highlights two aspects of Pulci's Florentine humour which Boiardo does not take up, either because they are lost on him or because he chooses to suppress them. The first is the element of religious parody, where *fegatello* forms part of an extended 'gourmet's creed', with its versions of the Incarnation (116, 1–2) and the Trinity (ibid. 3–5).[21] But a further, equally subversive layer of meaning has become apparent with the recognition, thanks especially to Jean Toscan's monumental *Le Carnaval du langage*, of a highly developed code of sexual double meanings in fifteenth-century Florentine verse, the full extent of which in Pulci's work has still to be explored.[22] *Fegatello* is one of a series of allusions in the confession, some of them relatively transparent, which indicate the range and nature of Margutte's sexual tastes; and this in turn explains some details of the confession which otherwise seem mere gratuitous word-play.[23] In both these respects, Boiardo's use of the Margutte episode suggests that Pulci's poem, at least in its comic passages, was already partly foreign to an Emilian reader, but that Boiardo was nonetheless able to draw on it for an area of usage which had been outside his repertoire up to that point.

It is clear that Poliziano and Boiardo had both, in their different ways, moved on from the example established by Pulci. What they both retain, however, is Pulci's example of engaging in a creative dialogue with the preceding tradition—a tradition in which, for them both, Pulci himself had come to occupy a prominent place.

Notes to Chapter 3

1. See P. Orvieto, *Pulci medievale: studio sulla poesia volgare fiorentina del Quattrocento* (Rome: Salerno, 1978), esp. 'Crisi e decadenza del Pulci', 213–43; A. Rochon, *La Jeunesse de Laurent de Médicis (1449–1478)* (Paris: Les Belles Lettres, 1963), 251–6; I. Del Lungo, *Florentia: uomini e cose del Quattrocento* (Florence: Barbèra, 1897), 206–39 and 422–45.
2. *Orlandino*, I, 20, in T. Folengo, *Opere*, ed. C. Cordié (Milan and Naples:

Ricciardi, 1977), 633–4. See also [O. Lando], *La sferza de scrittori antichi et moderni di M. Anonimo di Utopia* (Venice: [A. Arrivabene], 1550): 'non vi voglio favellare di Luigi Pulci auttore del Morgante Maggiore anzi per più vero dire, di Agnolo da monte pulciano che ne gli fece cortese dono' (fo. 21ᵛ); F. O. Mencke, *Historia vitae et in literas meritorum Angeli Politiani, ortu Ambrogini* (Leipzig: in officina Gleditschiana, 1736), 627–8.

3. All references to the *Morgante* are to the edition by F. Ageno (Milan and Naples: Ricciardi, 1955).

4. The evidence for this edition, of which no copy survives, is provided by a letter from Duke Ercole of Ferrara, dated 11 Nov. 1478, to his envoy in Florence, asking him to obtain a copy of 'un libro chiamato Morgante' from 'uno che si chiama Alovise Pulçi, el quale se ne trova haver' (quoted in A. Luzio and R. Renier, 'Niccolò da Correggio', *Giornale storico della letteratura italiana* [hereafter *GSLI*], 21 (1893), 205–64 at 212 n. 2). See E. H. Wilkins, 'On the Earliest Editions of the "Morgante" of Luigi Pulci', *Papers of the Bibliographical Society of America*, 45 (1951), 1–22.

5. The first extant edition of the *Morgante* in twenty-eight cantos (Florence: Francesco di Dino, dated 7 Feb. 1482 [Florentine dating, i.e. 1483]) survives in two copies, one in the British Library and one, incomplete, in the John Rylands University Library, Manchester.

6. On Pulci's rivalry with Ficino see Orvieto, *Pulci medievale*, especially 'Per un'interpretazione dei cantari XXIV–XXVIII', pp. 244–83, and P. Orvieto, 'A proposito del sonetto "Costor che fan sí gran disputatione" e dei sonetti responsivi', *Interpres*, 4 (1981–2), 400–13. On the background to the quarrel see A. Della Torre, *Storia dell'Accademia Platonica di Firenze* (Florence: Carnesecchi, 1902), 820–30.

7. Pulci regularly dwells on the magic arts of Malagigi in the *Morgante*, including details which show his familiarity with occult lore; see *Morgante*, XXI, 70–5; XXII, 102–3; XXIV, 90 ff. He is at pains to disown his interest in the occult in XXIV, 104–13, probably to fend off accusations of heterodoxy. XXIV, 112 refers to a visit which he made to the reputed cave of the Sybil at Norcia, also mentioned in a letter to Lorenzo (4 Dec. 1470; no. XVI in L. Pulci, *Morgante e lettere*, ed. D. De Robertis (Florence: Sansoni, 1962; 2nd edn., 1984), 960–3). He alludes semi-seriously to his fascination in letter VI (p. 949): 'Io so che un gran mio amico [i.e. Lorenzo himself] è piú vago de' versi ch'io non sono degli spiriti.'

8. On the relations between Pulci's and Acciaiuoli's texts see M. Davie, 'Biography and Romance: The *Vita Caroli Magni* of Donato Acciaiuoli and Luigi Pulci's Morgante', in *The Spirit of the Court: Selected Proceedings of the Fourth Congress of the International Courtly Literature Society* (Toronto, 1983), ed. G. S. Burgess and R. Taylor (Woodbridge: Boydell & Brewer, 1985), 137–52; and id., *Half-Serious Rhymes: The Narrative Poetry of Luigi Pulci* (Dublin: Irish Academic Press, 1998), ch. 5.

9. The alternative Latin and Greek models of classical biography are themselves a source of tension in the work; Acciaiuoli's main source, Einhard, is closely modelled on Suetonius, while Acciaiuoli himself shows a clear preference for Plutarch. On Einhard and Suetonius, see Eginhard, *Vie de Charlemagne*, ed. L. Halphen (Paris: Champion, 1938), p. xi; on Acciaiuoli and Plutarch,

V. Giustiniani, 'Sulle traduzioni latine delle Vite di Plutarco nel Quattrocento', *Rinascimento*, 2nd ser., 1 (1961), 3–62.

10. Thus Acciaiuoli follows his account of Charlemagne's refounding of Florence with this disclaimer, before going on to reproduce the emperor's legendary campaign in the Holy Land and his meeting with Constantine: 'His rebus tam egregie a Carolo gestis addunt scriptores nonnulli rem maxime memoratu dignam, quam ego ut certam affirmare (quia nulla apud alios auctores eius rei mentio est) nec ut incertam relinquere ausim. Tradunt enim, cum Hierosolimo gravi barbarorum dominatu oppressa teneretur, Carolum Constantini Imperatoris precibus evocatum [. . .] ad liberandum sanctissimum locum [. . .] cum ingenti exercitu accessisse' (in J. B. Mencke, *Scriptores rerum Germanicarum*, 3 vols. (Leipzig: Martini, 1728–30), i, cols 813–32 at col. 827 D: 'To these distinguished feats of Charles's several writers add another which thoroughly deserves to be remembered, but which I hesitate either to affirm as a fact—since no mention of it is made by other authors—or to omit as unreliable. They relate that, when Jerusalem was harshly dominated [. . .] by the barbarians, Charles, responding to the entreaties of the emperor Constantine, went to liberate the holy site with a great army').

11. See P. Orvieto, 'Angelo Poliziano "compare" della brigata laurenziana', *Lettere italiane*, 25 (1973), 301–18.

12. On the very few, and modest, earlier examples (such as the descriptions of the joust which marked the visit to Florence of Galeazzo Maria Sforza and Pope Pius II in 1459), see R. Truffi, *Giostre e cantori di giostre: studi e ricerche di storia e letteratura* (Rocca San Casciano: Cappelli, 1911), 138–42; and P. Orvieto, in his edition of Pulci, *Opere minori* (Milan: Mursia, 1986), 59.

13. *La Giostra di Lorenzo de' Medici* is quoted from Pulci, *Opere minori*, ed. Orvieto, 61–120.

14. Quoted from A. Poliziano, *Stanze cominciate per la giostra di Giuliano de' Medici*, ed. V. Pernicone (Turin: Loescher–Chiantore, 1954).

15. See M. Davie, 'Luigi Pulci's *Stanze per la giostra*: Verse and Prose Accounts of a Florentine Joust of 1469', *Italian Studies*, 44 (1989), 41–58; and id., *Half-Serious Rhymes: The Narrative Poetry of Luigi Pulci* (Dublin: Irish Academic Press, 1998), ch. 3.

16. P. V. Mengaldo, preface to M. Praloran and M. Tizi, *Narrare in ottave: metrica e stile nell' Innamorato* (Pisa: Nistri-Lischi, 1988), 8.

17. 'La distribuzione nell'*Innamorato* dei riscontri discussi qui sopra evidenzia una tendenza al recupero di stilemi e di episodi pulciani maggiore nel primo libro, e tanto più cospicua man mano che ci si avvicina, a ritroso, verso l'inizio del poema' (S. Carrai, 'Primi appunti sulle presenze pulciane nell'*Innamorato*', in *Tipografi e romanzi in Val Padana fra Quattro e Cinquecento. Atti delle giornate di studio* (Ferrara, 11–13 febbraio 1988), ed. R. Bruscagli and A. Quondam (Modena: Panini, 1992), 107–16 at 113).

18. R. Donnarumma, 'Boiardo e Pulci: per una storia dell'"Innamorato"', *GSLI* 172 (1995), 161–212 at 166, 169.

19. Quoted from M. M. Boiardo, *Orlando innamorato*, ed. R. Bruscagli (Turin: Einaudi, 1995).

20. Quoted from *'Orlando', die Vorlage zu Pulcis 'Morgante'*, ed. J. Hübscher (Marburg: Elwert, 1886).

21. See the comment by L. Serra: 'Quanta diversità anche e proprio nel concetto di fegatello! Per Margutte entra, allegramente sacrilego, in un giuoco fra grossolano e raffinato, consapevolmente deridente del simbolo della Trinità; per Brunello è semplicemente il boccone più ghiotto e deliziosamente astutamente involabile' ('La sublimazione del grottesco: Brunello', in *Il Boiardo e la critica contemporanea*, ed. G. Anceschi (Florence: Olschki, 1970), 489–97 at 490).

22. See J. Toscan, *Le Carnaval du langage: le lexique érotique des poètes de l'équivoque de Burchiello à Marino (XVe–XVIIe siècles)*, 4 vols. (Lille: Presses Universitaires de Lille, 1981). For a thorough documentation of the homosexual culture in Florence to which many of these double meanings refer, see M. Rocke, *Forbidden Friendships: Homosexuality and Male Culture in Renaissance Florence* (New York and Oxford: Oxford University Press, 1996).

23. The most overt reference is in the phrase 'arare coll'asino e col bue' (*Morgante*, XVIII, 129, 3–4, with the facetious addition of 'col commello'), the meaning of which ('usare secondo e contro natura') was evident to Volpi in 1900, and cited by Ageno in her edition of 1955. With this clue—as well as Margutte's own cheerful summary, 'la gola e 'l culo e 'l dado', in 132, 2—one can see the relevance of a text by Burchiello in which *fegatello* refers to the active partner in homosexual intercourse, cited by Toscan (*Le Carnaval du langage*, 1599–1600).

CHAPTER 4

Boiardo's *Timone*

Peter Brand

Boiardo's *Timone*, which he labels *Comedia*, was intended, as we learn from the Prologue, for the entertainment of Ercole d'Este and his court in Ferrara. There is no evidence, however, that it was actually performed or that it was printed during the author's lifetime: the *editio princeps* is the Scandiano 1500 volume which was followed by some seven further editions during the next twenty years.[1] Nor do we have any firm evidence about its date of composition, generally assumed to be about 1490 but on highly conjectural grounds: indeed Boiardo could well have written it earlier than 1486, the date of the first performance of Plautus' *I Menechmi*, which is often credited with initiating vernacular comedy in the city. However, whatever the truth about its date of composition and possible performance, it is certainly one of the earliest vernacular comedies to survive and an illuminating example of the way the new *commedia erudita* was developing in the late Quattrocento.

Boiardo also informs us in his Prologue that his comedy is 'traducta de uno dialogo de Luciano', that is the dialogue 'Timon or the Misanthrope', although, as we might expect of a Greek dialogue turned into an Italian comedy, the translation is very free and there are substantial additions to Lucian's original text. Indeed given Boiardo's ignorance of Greek his vernacular 'translation' poses some intricate problems for the philologist, and a great deal of scholarly effort has been expended on establishing the genesis of the text via the possible intermediaries, Latin and the vernacular.[2] I do not wish here to add to this debate but to focus rather on the significance of *Timone* in the history of vernacular comedy in Italy and, to a lesser extent, on its place in the humanist tradition of Lucianic studies and the evolution of the Timon legend, later to attract Shakespeare and Molière.

Lucian's dialogues are very diverse and notably distinct as a genre from the other main dialogue traditions inherited by the Renaissance: the Platonic and the Ciceronian. Lucian in fact prided himself on the innovatory nature of his pieces—see his 'Double Indictment' where Dialogue charges Lucian with taking away from him his 'respectable tragic mask' and giving him another that was 'comic, satyr-like and almost ridiculous'; Lucian has dug up the old cynic Menippus, 'a really dreadful dog who bites unexpectedly: he grins when he bites', a mode akin to that of satirical comedy—and some of Lucian's dialogues are indeed reminiscent of Greek comedy, not only in their deliberate attempt to provoke laughter, but also in their structure and situations.[3] Some, such as the 'Dialogue of the Courtesans', are like a pastiche of Greek New Comedy, with their lovers and bawds, quarrels and misunderstandings. Others, including the *Timon*, are more reminiscent of Old Comedy with their sharp satirical edge and their fantastic characters (gods and personifications of abstract qualities). Some passages in *Timon* recall similar scenes in Aristophanes, and it has been suggested that this dialogue may in fact derive from a lost Middle Comedy by Antiphanes. It is not therefore surprising that Lucian's Dialogues have interested later playwrights and that Boiardo should have turned to Lucian for the subject of his entertainment for Ercole d'Este.[4]

Lucian's *Timon* opens with a monologue by the misanthrope who has been reduced to poverty, having squandered his inherited wealth in making generous gifts to his friends—who have now abandoned him. So he has turned his back on the world and retired to the country, and we find him labouring in the fields and cursing his fellow men. Zeus hears his complaints and sends down Riches to live with him but Riches complains that she does not want to return to Timon who has so maltreated her in the past; let him stay with Poverty. And a long discussion follows concerning the appropriate treatment of wealth and the need for reason. Eventually Riches is forced to go down to Timon, who is digging away with Poverty and Toil and other Virtues that accompany Poverty—Endurance, Wisdom, Manliness etc., who are now driven off on the approach of Riches. Timon at first threatens Riches, stressing the benefits he has enjoyed from his good friend Poverty, but Riches points out the advantages she can bring him if he treats her properly. Timon yields, not, however, in order to re-enter society and restore his honour, but so as to take revenge on his former toadies, who now return but are driven off with blows and clods of earth in a sequence of violent encounters. So the Dialogue ends on a quasi-farcical note and with an absence of any explicit moral conclusion. Timon is confirmed in his misanthropy, unable it seems to live sociably either with Riches or with Poverty as they have tried to persuade him to do.

This Timon is Lucian's reconstruction of a real fifth-century figure, probably quite distinct from Lucian's version. The comic poets of Lucian's day speak only of Timon's misanthropy without giving any explanation of the reasons for it, although the disloyalty of his friends seems to have been common knowledge: Mark Anthony, when his friends deserted him, is said by Plutarch and Strabo to have compared himself with Timon. Timon's discovery of the treasure and revenge on his fellows seems to have been Lucian's invention (unless he found it in Antiphanes). The Loeb editor comments that this would make a fitting conclusion for a comedy and that 'it is rather hard to imagine what other conclusion the comedy of Antiphanes could have had'. But if the coupling of misanthropy induced by disloyalty with a debate on the relative merits of wealth and poverty provided a suitable basis for Lucian's dialogue, it did not satisfy the comic dramatists who followed him, and the later adaptation of the misanthrope story to the conventions of Roman comedy produced some interesting solutions.

The differentiation of the characters and the sequence of oral exchanges in different settings and with attendant action seem to indicate a dramatic origin for Lucian's dialogue, and though we cannot document this in Antiphanes' lost comedy, we can compare it with a play by another dramatist who certainly influenced Lucian— that is Menander. The latter's *Dyskolos* centres on a misanthropic old miser (not a pauper) who has cut himself off from his fellows and is labouring away in the fields, violently assaulting anyone who intrudes on his property. He is shaken out of his misanthropy when he falls down a well and is saved by his stepson, who thus brings about something of a conversion, inducing the old man to dower and marry off his daughter. But the conversion is only half-hearted, and we subsequently see him calling for his strap to beat an errant cook. This is New Comedy, however, and in the final scene he is dragged groaning and protesting into the wedding celebrations to join in the dancing. By the addition of this sub-plot (which in fact includes two pairs of lovers) Menander is able to provide a conventional New Comedy framework for a perceptive portrait of a misanthrope and some serious discussion of the appropriate use of wealth. The young lover upbraids his father for his meanness: he should distribute his money generously, 'help everyone and enrich as many people as possible. Such generosity never dies, and if ever you have a fall, it will ensure the same generosity for you in turn'.[5] It is of course precisely the naivety of this view that Lucian exposes in his *Timon*.

The ingredients of the subsequent Quattrocento dramatization of Timon by Boiardo and others are thus in place: the confrontation of a misanthrope by young lovers who will eventually triumph over him but not perhaps change him, accompanied by debates on the right use of wealth. The earliest of these Renaissance adaptations of Lucian would seem to be Tito Livio de' Frulovisi's Latin version entitled *Claudi Duo*, dating from the early 1430s—by which time complete texts of Lucian's works were available in Italy.[6] The humanists characteristically moralize Lucian, and Frulovisi is no exception. His adaptation of the Timon dialogue was for Venetian schoolboys and was intended to provide them with linguistic and moral instruction. He stresses in his Prologue that he is not presenting bawds and prostitutes but figures who will demonstrate the need to use wealth with moderation and good sense. He introduces us therefore to a Timon figure, the young Plusipenus, whose extravagance has brought him from wealth to poverty, no longer able to indulge his sensual appetites and complaining to Jove of the god's ingratitude to one who has always paid him his due homage. The opening scenes thus parallel quite closely Lucian's 'Timon', and the attempts of Plutos (wealth) and Penia (poverty) to persuade Mercury to let them prevail continue in a wrangle on the merits of the two human conditions which basically follows Lucianic precedent. But Plusipenus is no misanthrope and the debates on friendship and loyalty do not concern Frulovisi. There is no room here for Lucian's witty cynicism—the personified virtues firmly ally themselves with Poverty until Jove orders them to change sides and accompany Plutos so that a reformed Plusipenus can enjoy the wealth that all men desire and honour. Lucian's irony all but disappears under Frulovisi's earnest moralizing.

Nevertheless Frulovisi's version of Lucian is a far from negligible work and anticipates some of the more significant developments of later Italian comedy. Already we have a local Italian setting (Ravenna) and some conscious adjustment to local politics. Lucian's characteristic disrespect for the gods is toned down by Frulovisi, who uses the incident of Riches' reluctance to obey Jove in order to put in a plug for obedience to one's lawful ruler (as Boiardo will do later). And the influence of the Roman theatre is clear. Frulovisi is one of the first to exploit the discovery in 1429 by Nicholas of Cusa of twelve hitherto unknown comedies of Plautus, which set off a long process of editing, translating, adapting, and performing in the Italian universities and courts, and which was to have a profound impact on the development of comedy all over Europe. Thus to Lucian's story of Timon Frulovisi adds a Roman-style sub-plot contrasting Plusipenus and his ultimately successful combination of wealth and virtue with the vicious Philaphrodita who squanders his inherited riches, and the cast includes not only the young lovers of Roman comedy but also a characteristic Renaissance figure: the much reviled Pedagogue. And against moralizing critics Frulovisi justifies his inclusion of a god on the stage by citing Plautus (*Amphitruo*) and indulges in several of those metatheatrical allusions so common in Plautus. It seems unlikely that Boiardo could have known Frulovisi's play, but the latter clearly anticipates the *Timone* in its adaptation of Lucian's dialogue to the conventions of Roman comedy.[7]

There is no record of any other Quattrocento dramatization of Lucian before Boiardo's *Timone* as far as I am aware, but there was of course a ferment of interest in the Dialogues, which were frequently translated into Latin throughout the century—by Guarino da Verona, Johannes Aurispa, Poggio Bracciolini, Lapo da Castiglionchio, and others, and a vernacular version of a substantial collection, including the 'Timon', enjoyed frequent editions in the early Cinquecento. It is worth remembering also, in connection with Lucian and the theatre, that the foremost Lucianist of the century, Leon Battista Alberti, also experimented with the dramatic form in his Latin *Philodoxus*, which adopts the personified virtues and vices of the Lucianic tradition. A mixed cast of gods and abstractions is found in the *Intercoenales* in the 'Virtus dea', and the typically Lucianic parallel between the affairs of the gods and those of humans which we find in Alberti's *Momus* will also recur in Boiardo's comedy.

Boiardo therefore inherited a lively Lucianic culture both in respect of the Latin and vernacular translations of Lucian's works and also in the interest shown in the Lucianic dialogue form by original writers such as Alberti and Pontano.[8] Closer to home, in Ferrara, was Pandolfo Collenuccio, another Lucianist who wrote both dialogues in the mould of Alberti and dramatic works—he translated Plautus' *Amphitruo* for example and composed a *sacra rappresentazione*, the *Commedia di Jacob e di Josef*, performed in Ferrara in 1504. Collenuccio's eclecticism is characteristic of course of writers of this period, when the vernacular was re-emerging after the long preoccupation with Latin and writers were experimenting with a variety of literary traditions and genres and seeking a stable form for their compositions. Nowhere was this more evident than in the theatre, where Roman comedy was vying for primacy with the sacred drama as well as absorbing inputs from other genres—the *novella*, the pastoral, and the dialogue.

Boiardo, we know, had already shown his skill in a variety of genres—romance, lyric, and pastoral—very much in response to the tastes and demands of the Ferrarese court; and Ercole d'Este's enthusiastic patronage of the theatre no doubt encouraged him to compose his comedy. What led him to choose the 'Timon' specifically of Lucian's works it is hard to say, but the subject of the correct use of wealth was a currently fashionable one, appropriate to the court and pertinent to the chivalrous ideals of the *Orlando innamorato*. Prasildo is a typical example of the generous knight

> [. . .] di cortesia pieno e di valore
> Molta ricchezza, di che egli abondava,
> Dispendea tutta quanta in farsi onore. (I, xii, 6)[9]

Thus to spend money liberally is a gentleman's duty, although how he is to acquire it is another matter. Orlando, offered the chance to achieve great wealth, declines disdainfully:

> [. . .] di periglio e di fatica
> L'onor de cavalier sol se nutrica.
> Ma l'acquisto de l'oro e de l'argento
> Non m'avria fatto mai il brando cavare. (I, xxv, 13–14)

and he scorns Rinaldo for wanting to carry off a gold chair as booty:

> Il conte li dicea che era viltate
> A girne carco a guisa de somiero. (II, ix, 33)

This aristocratic hauteur is transferred to the Timon story, the protagonist's father being stained with the money-making obsession (not mentioned by Lucian):

> ma gentileza ponto non apprese,
> perchè, lasciata ogni opera virile,
> solo a far roba pose la sua cura. (Argumento, ll. 3–5)

The play is thus immediately set in the local contemporary world, as is stressed in the Prologue:

> di greco oggi mi fece italiano [. . .]
> di novo son comedo divenuto
> per farvi cosa grata, e non mi pento
> che el dar piacere a molti è ben dovuto. (ll. 12, 19–21)

Boiardo knew little if any Greek and it seems clear that for his comedy he used a Latin version of Lucian (thought to be that by Bertoldo) as well as the vernacular prose translation of Lucian's dialogues published later by Zoppino in Venice in 1525; this appeared anonymously and was only attributed to Nicolò Leoniceno in the second, 1529, edition. This attribution is questionable and it has been suggested that this prose version of Lucian may in fact have been made by Boiardo (with the aid of Bertoldo's Latin translation).[10] He may therefore have gone back to his own earlier version in order to meet a request for an entertainment for the court. But whatever the means he employed to produce his comedy it remains clearly a dramatic transposition of Lucian's dialogue. Boiardo maintains the characters and the sequence of oral exchanges of the original and Lucian's witty debate on wealth and poverty survives largely intact. The comedy reverts virtually to dialogue here and the action is almost forgotten as one of the characters points out:

> [. . .] oh me tapino
> che abiam scordata cosa de importanza
> onde a venire abiam preso el camino. (II, 394–6)

If the colour and elegance of Lucian's prose is hardly matched by Boiardo's often clumsy *terza rima*, the Italian version nevertheless adopts a lively, colloquial diction with frequent recourse to popular proverbial idiom, reminiscent of the Quattrocento romance, even Pulcesque at times:

> tragualciando el bocon come uno ocello,
> che intrego giù passava per el collo,
> e tenea li occhi fitti nel piatello. (IV, 350–2)

A good deal of Lucian's comic spirit is in fact preserved in Boiardo's play, which is deliberately comic, seeking laughs from the confrontations between the human, divine, and abstract figures with their alternately earthy and pompous diction.[11] One has only to compare Boiardo's language with that of Galeotto del Carretto, who made a version of Lucian's dialogue a few years later, to appreciate Boiardo's achievement in this respect.[12]

Where Boiardo departs from Lucian's text it is most often in order to adapt the Greek dialogue to contemporary stage presentation. For comedy he is committed to a five-act structure, and he is really short of material for a play of that length. So apart from the new ending, which occupies all of the fifth act, he adds a Prologue and Argumento, and two scenes at the beginning of the fourth act where a new character is introduced, La Fama, who explains how she has spread the news of Timon's discovery of the treasure. New also is a soliloquy by Timon reflecting on his situation and preparing the way for the extra material to be added in the final act. But Boiardo also adapts the dialogue for stage presentation with some skill, accounting for the characters' movements, allowing time for their actions off-stage and giving directions for a split stage—one below for the earth-bound figures, and one above for the gods (which of course his audience would be familiar with from the *sacra rappresentazione*). He also establishes a rapport between the spectators and the figures on the stage with occasional direct address to the audience by Mercury, Fame, etc.

Most important, however, he creates a totally new ending appropriate to the comic stage by the addition of a subsidiary action involving a new set of characters of his own invention. Lucian's dialogue ends with Timon, having acquired his new wealth, denouncing the arch-parasite Thrasicles and climbing on a rock in order to repel the other toadies with stones. Boiardo repeats this scene at the end of his Act IV, and then opens his fifth act with the entry of a new character Auxilio (probably suggested by a similar figure in Plautus's *Cistellaria*) who announces to the spectators

> [. . .] per più farvi intendere
> quel ch'è in occulto voglio palesare:
> così potreti assai meglio comprendere
> lo effecto e il fin di questa comedia. (V, 23–6)

So he explains for our benefit that Timon has buried his gold in a nearby tomb (shades of Plautus' *Aulularia*), not knowing that a certain Timocrates has already hidden half of his own wealth there and has left in his will instructions for his son to open a letter, ten years after his father's death, informing him where this half of the inheritance was to be found. The miserly Timocrates had devised this means of preventing his free-spending son from running through his whole inheritance. Now, Auxilio tells us, the ten years are up, the son is in prison for debt,

and his servants have come to the tomb, in conformity with the terms
of the will. The remaining scenes of Boiardo's comedy work this story
through—the servants open the letter, recover the gold, and free their
master, who will now know how to conduct himself wisely and use his
wealth prudently.

Timon witnesses this happy ending but draws his own conclusions
from his experiences: since regaining his wealth he has been tortured
by anxiety about it and has lost his freedom, which is only to be found
in self-control:

> Libero è quel che a se solo obedisse,
> che strengie il freno a la cupiditate
> nè la avarizia el pongie [. . .]
> nè per Fortuna cangia qualitate. (V, 274–9)

He will return to his former way of life, 'inculta e solitaria':

> In qualche monte o in qualche selva strana
> mi pascerò de' fructi che vi nascano.
> e cacerò la sete a la fontana.
> E quando al verno e' rami se diffrascano
> nel tronco concavato de un gran rovero
> me faran letto le fronde che cascano. (V, 307–12)

So Boiardo reverts to his pastoral vein and Timon to his misanthropy,
chasing away Timocrates' servants and finally offering the audience the
loan of his belt to hang themselves on (his tree in the classical tradition).

Thus Boiardo quite cleverly preserves the character and conduct of
Lucian's misanthrope as well as his debate about the use of wealth
while equipping his play with a conventional Roman comic ending
and an acceptable moral lesson. His solution is in fact similar both to
Menander's and to Frulovisi's in that he provides a contrasting figure
to the misanthropic Timon, one who *does* succeed in dispensing his
wealth wisely and effectively, and who contributes to a sane and
harmonious society such as comic audiences could go home feeling
happy about (Timocrates' son shows his gratitude by freeing his slaves,
for example). And in the Roman comic tradition he ends his play
with an address by Auxilio to the audience warning us not to expect
the actors back on stage and explaining the outcome—reminiscent
of Plautus' *Cistellaria*, for example, or Terence's *Andria*—and later *La
mandragola*.

The question of closure was of course crucial to the theatre, and if
a dialogue could let things end much as they began, and even, in the

Lucianic vein, with a wry aftertaste, comedy had other conventions. Boiardo's mixed ending, combining a happy and an unhappy outcome, anticipates some of the more interesting developments of sixteenth-century theatre—from say Ariosto's *La Lena* (where the young lovers celebrate and the loveless Lena–Fazio–Pacifico triangle soldier on) to later Giraldian tragi-comedy where the virtuous are rewarded and the guilty suffer. Shakespeare's solution is similar, combining a tragic Timon with a triumphant Alcibiades.[13] Shakespeare breaks with the latter sixteenth-century view of Timon as a beast-like character, inhuman in his rejection of the natural bonds between a man and his fellows. His Timon is a tragic figure whose very nobility of spirit and idealism engender his misanthropy—his initial generosity and selfless love of his fellow men are presented as noble qualities, albeit misguidedly applied. The bitterness with which he reacts to his friends' ingratitude is a measure of his sensitivity, his greatness of soul:

> Poor honest lord, brought low by his own heart,
> Undone by goodness: strange, unnatural blood
> When man's worse sin is he does too much good. (IV, ii, 37–9)

He is, in Coleridge's words, 'a Lear of domestic or ordinary life'. In giving us a tragic Timon Shakespeare delves into the reasons for Timon's misanthropy and goes back to the time of his protagonist's prosperity—he adds a beginning to Timon's story, an *antefatto*, whereas Boiardo's main contribution is a *postfatto*, an aftermath. Both saw the need to supplement the bare bones of the Timon legend with some complementary material which would point up its moral significance—and in each case a bitter and misanthropic Timon is contrasted with another figure who is able to rise above his misfortune. In Boiardo's comedy Timocrates' son emerges from a debtor's prison to learn the proper use of his wealth; in Shakespeare's tragedy Alcibiades rises superior to the ingratitude of the Athenian rulers and learns to 'use the olive with (his) sword' (V, iv, 82).[14] The value of this counterpoint structure, which becomes so sophisticated in Shakespeare's theatre and is one of his major advances on the practice of his predecessors, was by no means obvious to the early Renaissance playwrights and we should give Boiardo due credit for his ingenuity in devising a suitable ending to Lucian's dialogue.

It does not seem exaggerated therefore to suggest that the enterprise and versatility of these late Quattrocento writers who were building a new vernacular literature on the basis of much recently discovered classical material provided the foundations for some of the more significant developments of the Cinquecento in the theatre as well as in other genres. The *Timone* can be seen as exemplifying the continuity of the culture of the 1490s in the passage between Quattrocento drama and the vernacular comedy that followed. If we may speak of crisis in the theatre in this period it was in the *sacra rappresentazione*, confronted with the rising tide of Roman comedy, now in inexorable advance. The so-called radicality of the 'rebirth' of regular comedy, often associated with Ariosto's *La cassaria* of 1508, has to be seen against the gradual acclimatization of Plautus and Terence in the Quattrocento, of which the *Timone* is an interesting example. Indeed the progress of comedy between the *Timone* and *La cassaria* does not seem dissimilar to that of the narrative poem between the *Innamorato* and the *Furioso*: in both genres Boiardo foreshadows the work of his more celebrated successor.

Notes to Chapter 4

1. The *editio princeps* of the *Timone* is that produced by Pellegrino de Pasquali and Gasparo Crivelli (Scandiano, 1500, repr. Bologna: Forni, 1977). There are modern editions by Luciano Serra (Reggio Emilia: Diabasis, 1994) and Antonia Tissoni Benvenuti and Maria Pia Mussini Sacchi in *Teatro del Quattrocento — Le corti padane* (Turin: UTET, 1983) (cited in this chapter).

2. See E. Rossi, 'Nota bibliografica circa il B. traduttore', *La bibliofilia*, 39 (1937), 360–9; G. Ponte, 'Matteo Maria Boiardo scrittore di teatro', *La rassegna della letteratura italiana*, 68 (1964), 286–302; E. Fumagalli, 'Da Nicolò Leoniceno a Matteo Maria Boiardo', *Aevum*, 59 (1985), 163–77.

3. Translations from Lucian's Dialogues are from the Loeb edition by A. M. Harmon, 8 vols. (London: Heinemann and Cambridge, MA: Harvard University Press, 1913–67). For the 'Double Indictment' see iii. 147. 'Timon' is in vol. ii.

4. See Christopher Robinson, *Lucian and his Influence in Europe* (London: Duckworth, 1979), 11–12; Graham Anderson, *Studies in Lucian's Comic Fiction* (London: Duckworth, 1976), 68. For Lucian's use of New Comedy see Philip Le Grand, 'Les Dialogues des courtisanes comparés avec la comédie', *Revue des études grecques*, 20 (1951), 176–231.

5. The translation is from the Penguin edition of Menander by Norma Miller (London, 1987) (Act V, ll. 805–10).

6. See the edition of C. W. Prévité-Orton, *Opera hactenus inedita T. Livii de Frulovisiis de Ferrara* (Cambridge: Typis Academiae, 1932). Frulovisi's other plays are redeemed from their inept love plots and poor dialogue by a keen satirical vein at the expense of local customs and even individuals—which probably owes something to Lucian. The use of allegorical characters returns, together with the poverty/wealth conflict, in Frulovisi's last play, *Eugenius*, where the protagonist

divorces his first wife Macrothyma (Patience), daughter of Eunus (Goodness) and Penia (poverty), in order to marry Wealth, whom he subsequently abandons in favour of gentle Patience. The plots of most of the plays centre on amorous intrigue with deception and disguise, including in one play (*Corallaria*) a young woman who cross-dresses in pursuit of a man.

7. See Robinson, *Lucian and his Influence*; Natale Caccia, *Luciano nel Quattrocento in Italia* (Florence, 1907); E. Mattioli, *Luciano e l'umanesimo* (Naples: Istituto Italiano per gli Studi Storici, 1980). For Lucian and the Cinquecento dialogue in Italy see V. Cox, *The Renaissance Dialogue* (Cambridge: Cambridge University Press, 1992).

8. See F. Tateo, *Tradizione e realtà nell'umanesimo italiano* (Bari: Dedalo, 1967), 228, 307; D. Marsh, *The Quattrocento Dialogue: Classical Tradition and Humanist Innovation* (Cambridge, Mass.: Harvard University Press, 1980), 100–10.

9. Quotations from the *Innamorato* are from the edition by Aldo Scaglione, 2 vols. (Turin: UTET, 1966).

10. See the article by Fumagalli cited in n. 2 above.

11. For a useful comparison of Boiardo's text with Lucian's see M. Aurigemma, 'Il *Timone* di Matteo Maria Boiardo', in *Il Boiardo e la critica contemporanea. Atti del convegno di studi su Matteo Maria Boiardo*—Scandiano–Reggio-Emilia, 1969, ed. G. Anceschi (Florence: Olschki, 1970); and on Boiardo's comic vein see the perceptive article by Antonio Franceschetti, 'Ispirazione comica e dimensione umana nel *Timone* del Boiardo', *Yearbook of Italian Studies* (1987), 75–89.

12. Galeotto del Carretto's version is reproduced in Antonia Tissoni Benvenuti's *Teatro del Quattrocento*. It is in five acts in *ottava rima* with a Prologue, Argumento, and Commiato, but has no staging or performance instructions. Galeotto follows closely the Latin translation printed in Venice, 1494. He modernizes the dialogue, removing Greek references, but does not otherwise modify the subject matter significantly.

13. For Shakespeare's *Timon of Athens* see H. J. Oliver's Introduction to the Arden edition (London, 1965), pp. xlviii–li. Shakespeare scholars consider it unlikely that Shakespeare knew Boiardo's comedy, although a case has been made out for this (see R. W. Bond, 'Lucian and Boiardo in *Timon of Athens*', *Modern Language Review*, 26 (1931), 52–68. G. Bullough gives a version of Boiardo's *Timon* as an analogue of Shakespeare's play in his *Narrative and Dramatic Sources of Shakespeare*, 6 vols. (London: Routledge, 1966), vi. 229.

14. For another treatment of the Timon legend contemporary with Shakespeare see the anonymous English *Tymon*, ed. J. C. Bulman and J. M. Nosworthy (Malone Society Reprint, Oxford: Oxford University Press, 1980), where the clumsy secondary plot seems to have little or no relevance to the main one.

CHAPTER 5

Rugiero and the Dynastic Theme from Boiardo to Ariosto

Marco Dorigatti

For the modern reader, accustomed to the Aristotelian unity of action that has prevailed in the modern novel, Boiardo's work, built on a multiplicity of stories, is one that defies any attempt at being summarized, let alone classified. It has, however, two main narrative poles. One is the *innamoramento* of Orlando, which is the name of a specific genre as well as a variant title of the work itself (*Inamoramento de Orlando*), while the other may be called *invenzione di Rugiero* since it is Boiardo's own expression. The background war opposing Christians and Saracens need not be counted as a 'third' thematic component, as it is an inseparable part of the Orlando story, one that Boiardo inherited from the Carolingian tradition together with its main character. Moreover, these two narrative poles are distinct entities. In fact, whereas Orlando's *innamoramento* follows an established pattern whereby a hitherto chaste character of the Carolingian tradition is turned into a lovelorn figure, the *invenzione*, or story of Rugiero, originates from a different genre, the classical epic. With plot and characters of its own, the *invenzione* runs along parallel lines with the *innamoramento*, forming what is in effect a poem-within-the-poem.

Both narrative poles are also clearly discernible in Ariosto, but their relative significance has long been a matter of dispute. At least since Ruscelli's 1556 'Annotationi'[1] it has been held that the true link between Boiardo and Ariosto was provided by the story of Orlando, whose fall into madness as a result of his unrequited love was said to constitute both a response to Boiardo and the true novelty of *Orlando Furioso*. In fact, Orlando's love-sick madness and his 'furore' were already present in embryonic form in Boiardo; hence Ariosto cannot be credited with the invention of this motif.[2] Nor can it be held as the ultimate cause that prompted Ariosto to continue Boiardo's *Orlando innamorato*, for in *Orlando furioso*, especially the 1516 version, the story of Orlando is by no means the central theme, but a more marginal one. What lies at the root of Ariosto's poem is, arguably, the *invenzione* of Rugiero, which is the topic to be explored here. Beginning with Boiardo we shall first examine how the theme of Rugiero came into being, and then trace its development in his continuators, including Ariosto.[3]

There are two things to note about Rugiero in Boiardo's work. The first is that of the two main themes that make up *Orlando innamorato*—the story of Orlando and the story of Rugiero—that of Orlando is a purely literary motif, whereas that of Rugiero has a historical as well as a literary significance. The second observation to be made is that his appearance comes quite late in the course of the poem.

Rugiero is first mentioned at the very end of Book I, when Boiardo suspends the story of Orlando, saying that it is now necessary to abandon 'il cantar della storia amorosa' in order to turn to 'cosa assai maggiore' (*Inn.*, I, xxix, 55, 8), a new subject intended for the next book:

> Cosa maggior, né di gloria cotanta
> fu giamai scritta, né di più diletto,
> ché del novo Rugier quivi si canta,
> qual fu d'ogni virtute il più perfetto
> di qualunque altro che al mondo si vanta. (*Inn.* I, xxix, 56, 1–5)[4]

In Book II we find that Boiardo was not content with introducing this character alone; he introduced at the same time a new cast of characters, and this in a romance that was already overcrowded. It is as if, having reached the end of Book I, Boiardo had lost interest in the Orlando story and discovered a worthier subject. Orlando does not disappear altogether, but from Book II he seems to take second place.

This has the effect of creating a dichotomy in the second part of *Orlando innamorato*, with one narrative pole centring on the titular protagonist and the other on Rugiero, the new-found deuteragonist; their stories run parallel and very rarely cross. Indeed, Rugiero and Orlando meet only twice in *Orlando innamorato*. Rugiero has a first glimpse of Orlando at the end of Book II ('Cognobbe Orlando a l'insegna del dosso', II, xxxi, 27, 1), when the two engage in a brief combat; yet it is not until the middle of Book III that they have the opportunity to exchange a few words. This happens when Rugiero breaks into the argument Orlando is having with the 'nano', his abstract remark signalling a sense of loss ('Disse Rugier: — Non è solo un parere, / e ciascun loda la sua opinione [. . .] —', III, vii, 39, 1–2). For Orlando, Rugiero is an outsider as well as a newcomer. They have, after all, very little in common, and in the proem to Book III Boiardo seems to refer to their stories as distinct and separate. He must have been aware of this duality, for in a rare transition from Rugiero's story to Orlando's he speaks of the need to gather these separate narrative strands together, 'accioché queste storie che son sparte, / siano raccolte insieme a una sustanza' (*Inn.*, II, xvii, 38, 5–6). The addition of Rugiero's story halfway through the poem alters its original conception to the point of endangering its structural unity, but it also highlights what must have been a bold decision on the part of the author.

The scale of such a literary venture can be judged by the fact that Book II of *Orlando innamorato* registers the introduction of no fewer than nine major characters, namely, in order of appearance: Rugiero (II, i, 4, 4), Agramante (II, i, 16, 2), Rodamonte (II, i, 16, 8), Atalante (II, i, 73, 8), Frontalate (II, ii, 68, 5), Mandricardo (II, iii, 8, 1), Brunello (II, iii, 39, 8), Bradamante (II, vi, 23, 5), and Alcina (II, xiii, 55, 1). Even a cursory glance at these names is enough to reveal that they are all instrumental, in one way or another, to the story of Rugiero. One suspects that Boiardo added them to play as second leads in support of Rugiero's main lead, to which we must now turn our attention.

Since Boiardo meant Rugiero, and possibly Bradamante,[5] to become the founders of the House of Este these are no ordinary characters. The link between fictional characters and historical figures is not as explicit as it will be in Ariosto. Duke Ercole I (1431–1505), the dedicatee of Book I, is not mentioned anywhere in it. In Book II he is twice alluded to (II, xxi, 59; xxv, 50), although in one case he appears almost indistinguishable from the mythological Hercules. As for Alfonso (1476–1534), Ercole's son, he was still in his infancy at this time, 'un Febo piccolino' (II, xxvii, 58).

Vague as the allusions to Este figures are, it is significant that they begin to occur only with Book II, thus coinciding with the introduction of the new dramatis personae. However, neither Ercole nor Alfonso is ever alluded to in connection with his legendary ancestor. The only explicit link between Rugiero and the House of Este can be found in the title of Book II, announcing 'la Inuentione de Rugiero terzo Paladino Progenitore de la Inclyta casa da Este'.[6] To learn about Rugiero's origins one has to wait until Book III. For it is here, only five cantos from the end, that Rugiero and Bradamante first meet (III, iv, 52), and during their only tête-à-tête conversation Rugiero tells her his line of descent culminating in the revelation 'Rugier son io; da Troia è la mia gesta' (v, 37, 8). Unfolding over some twenty stanzas (III, v, 18–37), Rugiero's genealogy is exceptional by any standard in Boiardo. Although it is far from easy to disentangle (Ariosto for one stumbled on a few details), it can be arranged in the shape of a genealogical tree (see Table 5.1).

Speaking to an attentive Bradamante, Rugiero begins with the 'primo sdegno' that ignited the war with the Greeks and caused the fall of Troy. Not satisfied, the Greeks want to extinguish any remaining 'sangue troiano' (III, v, 19, 4). With Hector dead, Polissena having been slain before the eyes of her mother (Hecuba), and Andromache (Hector's wife) having died in order to save her child, Astyanax is the last surviving vestige of Hector's blood.

At this point, departing from the main Trojan legend according to which Astyanax was hurled from the walls of Troy by the Greeks, Rugiero tells how the child was saved by a knight who took him to the 'Isola del Foco' (Sicily).[7] Here Astyanax grew up, eventually becoming Lord of Messina (23, 1–2) and marrying the Queen of 'Saragosa' (Syracuse).

What happens in Sicily is more or less a 're-run' of the Troy events. Like his father, Astyanax dies in the struggle against the Greeks, but leaves a pregnant widow whom the Greeks are now pursuing. Messina comes under siege, and she has no alternative but to flee. Having crossed the Strait of Messina ('sola sola / sopra ad una barchetta piccolina', 27, 1–2), she arrives at 'Regio' (Calabria), where she gives birth to Polidoro.

From Polidoro onwards the succession develops rapidly through Polidante, Floviano, and the twin brothers Clodovaco and Constante. At this point the line of descent splits into two main branches. From Constante descends the branch leading to Pepin and Charlemagne, and from Clodovaco the branch leading to Bovo of Antona (Hampton, modern Southampton). The latter branch is said to be 'lignaggio anco più fino' (29, 5), for it includes the first of Rugiero's close ancestors, namely Rugiero I, 'paladin novo' (29, 7). Yet with Bovo, one of his descendants, the genealogical line splits again, as

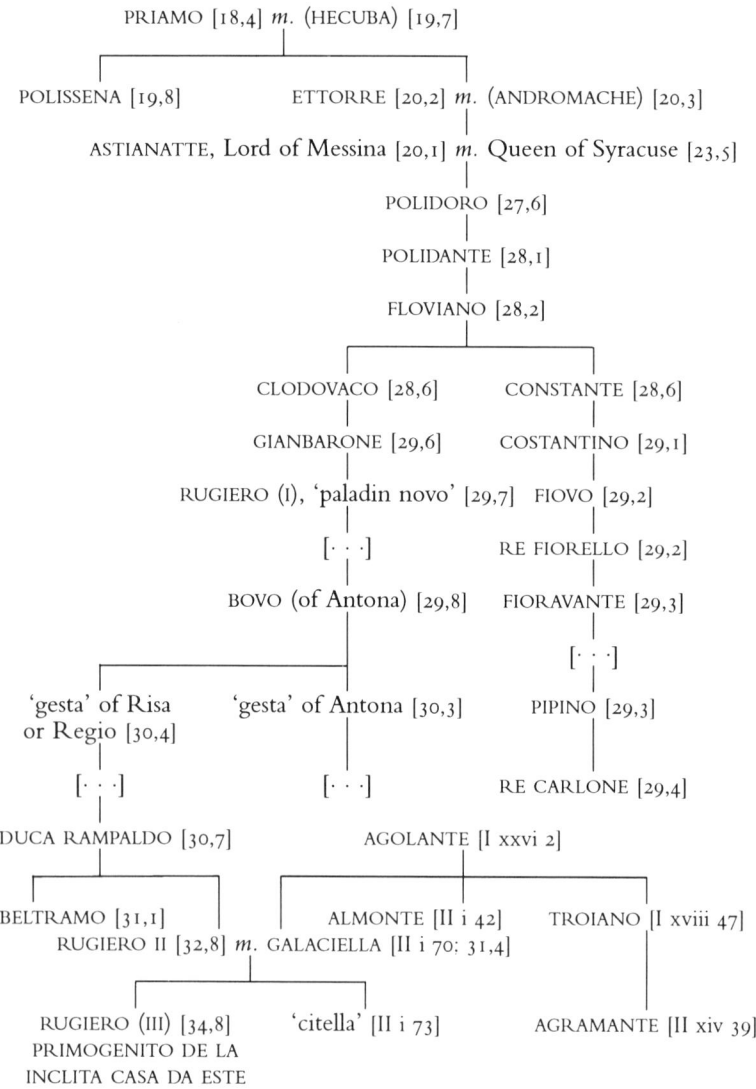

Table 5.1. Rugiero's genealogical tree according to *Orlando innamorato*. Brackets contain textual references; when the stanza only is given Book III, canto v, is intended. Names in parentheses are not explicitly mentioned in the text.

some of Bovo's descendants remained in Antona whilst others settled down in Risa (Reggio Calabria). Finally, it is within this latter 'gesta' that Rugiero III is able to point out to Bradamante (who has remained breathless all along) his close relations: his grandfather Rampaldo, Duke of Risa (30, 7); his uncle Beltramo (31, 1); his mother Galaciella (31, 4); and his father Rugiero II (32, 8).

Geographically at least, the provenance of Rugiero's close ancestry is not inconsistent with the Este policy of dynastic relations, as the Este family had strong links with southern Italy. Ercole I, the ruler of Ferrara at the time of Boiardo, had spent his youth in Naples; in 1473, after his return to Ferrara, he married Eleanor of Aragon, whose marriage further consolidated the traditional alliance between the Este dynasty in the north and the Aragonese in the south. That Rugiero should also come from this geographical area is therefore not surprising.

It is true, however, that all attempts to trace this legendary founder in any of the genealogical sources available to Boiardo have proved vain. Rugiero does not figure in Boiardo's own *Carmina de laudibus Estensium* (*c.*1463), or in the *Historiae Ferrariae* by Pellegrino Prisciani (1435–1518), which provided the official version of the Este descent, or in Ricobaldo's *Istoria imperiale*, which was translated into the vernacular and enlarged by Boiardo himself.[8] Rugiero does figure, however, in a Latin poem by Boiardo's uncle, Tito Vespasiano Strozzi. Entitled *Borsias*, this poem contains the so-called *Origo Estensium principum*.[9] But as demonstrated by the German scholar Walter Ludwig, who discovered the complete version, it is Strozzi's *Origo* that appears to be based on Boiardo, rather than the other way round.[10] And although the correct chronological order should have been revealed simply by the fact that Strozzi went so far as to give 'Rugerus' a mentor called 'Atlas', it still shows that Boiardo's genealogy received official recognition.

In reality, Rugiero, like Bradamante, was borrowed from literary sources. His original name was Riccieri, and the work featuring him and other members of his family is *Aspremont*, a popular narrative originating in the fourteenth century, of which different versions are known.[11] The events of the battle of Aspramonte were as familiar to Boiardo as they were to his audience. In it Orlando gained his horse (Brigliadoro), his sword (Durindana), and the equally famous horn (oliphant): 'sì come io credo che vi sia palese' (cf. *Inn.*, II, xi, 8). The version used by Boiardo is almost certainly a prose narrative,

Aspramonte, by Andrea da Barberino (*c*.1370–*c*.1431).[12] This work tells, among numerous other things, how Galiziella—Agolante's daughter, Almonte's sister, and herself a warrior—fell in love with, and eventually married, Riccieri of Risa. His brother, Beltramo, who was also in love with Galiziella, but unrequitedly, killed him and burnt Risa to the ground. At this point Andrea da Barberino states that the fate of Galiziella, whether she died or survived, is not known.

It needs to be observed that Andrea's work is more than just one version of *Aspramonte*, because in a way it combines them all. So encyclopedic is his knowledge of chivalric matters that whenever he finds disagreement amongst his sources he often lists all the variant versions of events, as indeed he does when considering Galiziella's fate:

> E ancora si dice che in quello fuoco fu gittata Galiziella; alcuno dice che Almonte vi fece gittare un'altra femina, e segretamente mandò Galiziella in Africa in su una nave e fella menare in prigione. *Alcuno altro è detto di lei che ella ebbe uno figliuolo maschio e una femmina.* (Andrea da Barberino, *Aspramonte*, Book I, ch. xliv)[13]

Feeble as the hint was, it prompted Boiardo to imagine that Galiziella survived and had two children, Rugiero and an unnamed 'citella', whose birth is recounted in almost identical terms in *Orlando innamorato*, II, i, 72–3. It may be noted, however, that the Riccieri mentioned by Andrea da Barberino, namely Galiziella's husband who was killed by his brother Beltramo, corresponds to Boiardo's Rugiero II. As for Rugiero III, in *Aspramonte* Boiardo could find only a hint of the possibility that he might have been born, and even this remained mere speculation. Boiardo would thus be justified in claiming paternity for his 'novo Rugier' (I, xxix, 56, 3).

Born against all the odds, Rugiero comes to symbolize the ideal prototype of the Este ruler. Boiardo calls him 'giovane reale' (*Inn.* II, xxi, 31, 6; xxxi, 31, 1), and the name that he gave him, Rugiero instead of Riccieri, is reminiscent of the Norman rulers of Reggio Calabria, namely Roger I (1088–1101) and Roger II (1105–54). In spite of his obscure origins in *Aspramonte* he is chosen to become the founder of a dynasty. His image is redrawn accordingly, so that behind the story of Rugiero it is possible to see a reflection of the history of the Este family, and it is this possibility that will now be explored.

What is remarkable about Rugiero's line of descent is not its mixture of classical and vernacular sources; it is the fact that almost all its members died an unnatural death, invariably through betrayal. The list begins with Hector 'e 'l tradimento del caval di legno, / come il condusse il perfido Sinone' (III, v, 18, 4–5),[14] and continues with his son, Astyanax, 'occiso a modo tristo / da un falso Greco, nomato Egisto' (v, 22, 7–8), the cause of death being 'tradimento' (v, 24, 4). Whilst it could be argued that this outcome was decreed by Virgil rather than Boiardo, it is still the case that those members not borrowed from Virgil are equally prone to die in the same manner, although for this group a tendency to die prematurely was already visible in their respective sources, notably *Aspramonte*. However, Boiardo may have chosen them for this very reason, because their untimely deaths fitted the general Virgilian pattern. In Boiardo, the risk affects particularly those who embody the legitimate line of descent; it threatens the dynasty rather than the individual.

Take for example Duke Rampaldo, the father of Rugiero II. He lives peacefully with his family at Risa, his ducal authority being characterized as 'bon governo e bona guisa' (III, v, 30, 6). And yet one learns next that 'il duca Rampaldo e' soi figlioli / a tradimento fôr morti con dôli' (III, v, 30, 8). Boiardo explains how it happened:

> La voglia di Beltramo traditore
> contra del patre se fece rubella;
> e questo fu per scelerato amore
> che egli avea posto alla Galacïella; (*Inn.* III, v, 31, 1–4)

Nor was Rugiero II, the heir to the dukedom, spared:

> Morto fu poscia con estremo oltraggio,
> né maggior tradimento vidde il mondo,
> perché Beltramo, il perfido inumano,
> traditte il patre e il suo franco germano. (*Inn.* III, v, 33, 5–8)

So Beltramo, the brother of Rugiero II, having lustfully desired his sister-in-law, Galaciella, was led to betray both father and brother; not satisfied, he handed over the city to the besieging Almonte: 'Risa la terra andò tutta a ruina, / arse le case, e fu morta la gente' (34, 1–2). As a family tragedy involving incestuous lust as well as struggle for power it looks rather like an anticipation of *Hamlet*. Like Claudius, Beltramo is both a usurper of his brother's rights and a seducer of his sometime sister-in-law: 'The story is extant, and writ in choice Italian' (*Hamlet*, III, ii, 250). Although these events had already been told by Andrea da Barberino, his Beltramo did not figure in the stemma of a ducal family; in Boiardo, it is the theme of 'tradimento' that is accented.

Nor are these the only instances of betrayal, for the most notable victim of all was to be Rugiero III himself, the primogenitor of the 'inclyta' House of Este. His end is the first thing Boiardo tells us:

> pur gli fece fortuna estremo torto,
> ché fu ad inganno il giovinetto morto. (*Inn.* II, i, 4, 7–8)

Betrayal by relatives appears to account for the most likely cause of death affecting the male descendants of an otherwise noble family. Summing up the story of his descent, Rugiero has to confess to Bradamante that it amounts to a 'lunga diceria de tanti mali' (*Inn.* III, v, 37, 6).

The question arising at this point is why Boiardo should repeatedly stress this sombre aspect, certainly not a flattering one. That *Orlando innamorato* may have any historical significance has sometimes been denied; Bacchelli, for example, believed that 'Quel che Boiardo non guardava, era la politica'.[15] Yet to find a link between fiction and reality one need look no further than the chronology of the poem's composition. Each of the three books of *Orlando innamorato* is connected to a specific war threatening Ferrara. In particular, the end of Book I (completed in 1478) coincides with the outbreak of the Florence–Ferrara war of 1478–80; the end of Book II (1482) with the outbreak of the Venice–Ferrara war of 1482–4; and finally the end of Book III (1494) with the well-known descent into Italy of Charles VIII of France in 1494. Just as the end of each book is marked by an outbreak of war, so is the beginning marked by a period of restored peace. Thus the poem's composition took place in a tidal alternation between war and peace, and the author invoked these changes in the political climate as sufficient reasons for interrupting or resuming his narration.

As a governor in the service of Duke Ercole I, Boiardo was aware of the forces threatening Ferrara, particularly the Venetian Republic and the Papacy. As a small principality set amongst more powerful neighbours, Ferrara's only element of political stability was provided by the Este dynasty itself, which had secured for the city three centuries of almost uninterrupted internal peace. The antiquity of the Este dynasty was therefore not just a matter of prestige. Boiardo, and later Ariosto, strove to strengthen this element by stretching the family's line of descent back to Trojan times.

This is because the Este family had no possessory title over Ferrara. Ferrara was a papal fief that they could only rule in their capacity as papal vicars *in temporalibus*, and the Papacy was careful to preserve its sovereignty intact. Nicolò II (r. 1361–88) had been the first ruler fortunate enough to be granted a vicariate for life, and it was not until nearly a century later that Borso obtained the title of Duke (1471) and the privilege to designate his own successor. In this connection it is worth observing that an early ancestor of Rugiero (Astyanax) is referred to as 'segnore' (*Inn.* III, v, 23, 2), in contrast to Rampaldo, who is the first ruler of Risa to be called 'duca' (ibid. 30, 7). Any change of ruler was subject to papal approval, which also had a price: in 1473 the investiture bull cost Ercole 5,000 'fiorini larghi'.[16] Although over the centuries successive Este rulers had *de facto* turned their vicariate into virtual sovereignty, Ercole I had yet to obtain the right of hereditary succession, a right so vital for the existence of every dynasty. Technically, he was a feudal vassal of the Church for Ferrara and the Romagna territory.

In an age when there was a common belief in the historical truth of Virgil's *Aeneid* and Homer's *Iliad*, the Trojan motif had a special significance, not least because it was connected to the foundation of Rome. The legacy of imperial Rome is one that many Italian city-states strove to revive; it was a way of manifesting their political aspirations through a rich symbolism. Frances Yates calls it the 'Imperial Theme'.[17] In Ferrara specific references to imperial Rome can be seen in the cycle of frescoes at Palazzo Schifanoia completed in 1470, six years before Boiardo began his poem.[18] So potent was the 'Imperial Theme' that many European monarchies, including France and England, sought Trojan ancestors through whom to link their origins and destinies with imperial Rome. With Aeneas and other descendants of Hector having already been 'adopted', Boiardo had to make do with Rugiero, though in a way his Rugiero is even nobler than the progenitor of Rome: unlike Aeneas, he descends from Hector in an unbroken line. His Trojan ancestry allows Boiardo to assign the origins of the House of Este to a time pre-dating the Papacy, thereby implying its autonomy and validating its claim to full sovereignty. Accordingly, the continuity of the dynastic line becomes the leitmotif of Rugiero's Trojan descent, and his account also highlights the crucial necessity of preserving an unbroken line. This is because like Rugiero's ancestors the Este descendants were torn by internal conflicts. This danger was rooted within the family, with consequences for the political stability of Ferrara. An episode that must have left a deep impression on Boiardo, who witnessed it, is the 'velaschi' conspiracy, which will provide an insight into the Este family.

It began on 21 August 1471 when Borso d'Este died and his twenty-year rule came to an end. Only a few months earlier (14 April) he had become the first member of the Este family to be made Duke of Ferrara; Count Boiardo was among the 'splenditissimo apparato'[19] escorting him to Rome for his investiture by Pope Paul II. The succession should have been smooth. Before his death Borso had officially designated Ercole—his half-brother and a legitimate son of Nicolò III—to succeed him. Ercole's accession to the ducal throne, which took place on the same day that Borso died, restored the legitimate line that had been interrupted for thirty years, and generated 'grandissimo trionfo et alegreza'.[20]

Unfortunately, Borso also had a nephew named Nicolò d'Este (1438–76), the son of Marquis Leonello (r. 1441–50), who was one of Nicolò III's numerous bastards (see Table 5.2). Therefore neither Leonello nor his descendants had any claim to the princedom; Boiardo even refuses to mention Leonello despite his having been a humanist patron. It is true that Borso, too, was a natural son of Nicolò III, but unlike Leonello he chose not marry and left behind no troublesome pretenders.

Refusing to recognize Ercole's rights to the ducal throne, Nicolò d'Este envisaged a different course of events that would give him power. The rivalry between the two contenders came into the open as soon as it became clear that Borso was going to die. On 24 July 1471, fearing for his life, Nicolò fled to Mantua and sought the protection of his uncle, Marquis Lodovico Gonzaga,[21] who warned him 'ch'essendo egli scioccamente uscito per le porte, gli sarebbe stato grandissima fatica à uolere entrare nella città per le finestre'.[22] Undaunted, Nicolò perpetrated a conspiracy to kill Ercole and usurp his place, and to this end he enlisted a number of conspirators, in both Ferrara and Mantua, who called themselves 'velaschi' after the 'vela' that featured in Nicolò's coat of arms. Ercole's featured a 'diamante', so Nicolò was now bent on studying how the Sail could cut through the Diamond.

Meanwhile, the family contention had turned into a political affair. Mantua and Milan took sides with Nicolò, Venice with Ercole, and all were ready to intervene. Ercole soon realized that as long as Nicolò was alive his dukedom was under threat, so he decided to get rid of Nicolò (unimaginatively perhaps) by poisoning him. The person charged with this task happened to be Count Nicolò Ariosto, the poet's father and a trusted member of the Gonzaga household, yet secretly acting on

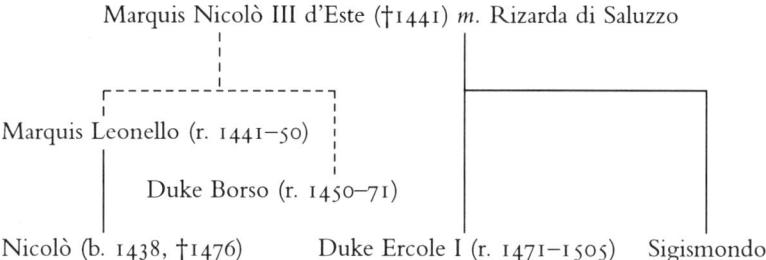

Marquis Nicolò III d'Este (†1441) *m.* Rizarda di Saluzzo

Marquis Leonello (r. 1441–50)

Duke Borso (r. 1450–71)

Nicolò (b. 1438, †1476)   Duke Ercole I (r. 1471–1505)   Sigismondo

Table 5.2. Genealogical diagram showing the Ferrara branch of the House of Este from Nicolò III to Ercole I. Broken line signifies illegitimate descent, b. born, *m.* married, † died, r. ruled.

Ercole's behalf. Count Ariosto sent Nicolò in Mantua a consignment of delicate foods, which concealed a poisoned knife and a spare quantity of venom. Nicolò's steward, a certain Cesare Pirondoli, who had been corrupted, was then supposed to execute the actual poisoning. This was planned for 8 December 1471. But at the crucial moment poor Cesare panicked, thinking he had accidentally poisoned himself. Troubled about his conscience, he sent for a confessor, got the whole machination off his chest—and his head onto a pole.

This incident could have had serious consequences for the traditional alliance between Mantua and Ferrara, so Lodovico Gonzaga pretended not to know that Ercole d'Este was behind the assassination plot; similarly Ercole pretended not to know that Gonzaga knew. As for Count Ariosto, he fell out of favour with the Gonzagas, and from then on the interests of the Ariosto family became inextricably tied to the fortunes of the Estes; his immediate reward was the post of governor of Reggio Emilia.

Ercole, however, was still under the same threat, although this did not materialize for nearly five years. Meanwhile, in 1473 Ercole married Eleonor of Aragon; in 1474 Count Ariosto had by Daria Malaguzzi Valeri, his wife, a child named Ludovico; and in that same year Boiardo became himself the victim of an attempted poisoning.[23] In January 1476 he left Scandiano and moved to Ferrara to take up a new post; his only duty, apparently, was to be the Duke's 'compagno'. Residing at the ducal palace he was thus ideally placed to witness the events that were to follow. Later that year, in July, Ercole and Eleonor had a child who was christened Alfonso. During this period Nicolò had been assembling an army, and was now ready to claim the throne that had been his father's.

The opportunity presented itself on 1 September 1476, when Duke Ercole was out of Ferrara. Shouting *Vela! Vela!* Nicolò and his conspirators suddenly invaded Ferrara in an attempt to turn the city against Ercole. But they were mistaken. The people of Ferrara, traditionally loyal to the ruling family in a way that baffled Machiavelli, responded to their *Vela! Vela!* with *Viva il Diamante!* Nor had Nicolò reckoned with the fact that Sigismondo, Ercole's brother, was in Ferrara, and in no time he organized a resistance force which soon defeated Nicolò's army.

The plot was thus foiled, and all the 'velaschi' rebels captured. The axe did the rest: Nicolò was first beheaded in Castel Vecchio, and then the severed head was carefully stitched back onto its neck. Finally, he was dressed in sumptuous clothes and given a lavish state funeral. Writing to Lodovico Gonzaga, Ercole reassured him that Nicolò was 'fatto seppellire *honorificentissimamente* e come si conveniva ad uno della nostra casa'.[24]

These events must have been fresh in Boiardo's mind when he was shaping the Este family tree. He almost certainly met Nicolò, for both were part of the retinue escorting Borso to Rome on the occasion of his ducal investiture, and he was in Ferrara in September 1476 when Nicolò invaded it. Consequently, even assuming Rugiero's line of descent was largely invented, his insistence upon betrayal by family members has a familiar ring. Like Beltramo in Rugiero's genealogy, who betrayed both father and brother, so did Nicolò. To be precise, his intended victim was his uncle, Ercole. The man who fits Beltramo's description more closely is perhaps Leonello, as he failed to comply with the last will of his father (Nicolò III) and usurped the rights of his half-brother (Ercole). But what matters is that betrayal was taking place within the ducal family.

Moreover, Boiardo had already referred to the 'velaschi' conspiracy in his Latin epigrams (*Epigrammata*). Written even as the noise of battle was still in the air—'Haec inter strepitus agitataque condimus arma / Territaque insueto est nostra Thalia sono' (I, 9–10)[25]—they celebrate the victory of the Diamante over the Vela. The very fact that Boiardo openly discussed such a politically sensitive issue shows to what degree he was involved in the political affairs of Ferrara. His loyalty to Ercole has never been in question, and it comes out most clearly in his *canzoniere*:

Doe cose fòr mia spene, e sono ancora:
Ercole l'una, il mio Signor zentile,
l'altra il bel volto ove anco il cor se posa. (*Amorum libri*, 174, 8–10)[26]

This is also attested by Taddea, Boiardo's widow. Writing to Duke Ercole on 29 March 1495 she tells him how Matteo used to say to her, 'Mogliere mia, non te pigliare desperatione de la morte mia; perché io lascio a te et a mio figliolo una nobile hereditate de nostri parenti che mai vi abandonarano.' And her letter continues: 'Ma sopra tuti lo Ill.mo Sig.re Nostro, la excellentia del quale son certissimo ve tenirà diffesi molto bene da ogni impeto et hostile impazzo per lo amore che sempre a me ha dimostrato per cagion de la mia vera servitude verso quella.'[27] Finally, according to Lovise Roseto, a court scribe, his work would have been precisely 'uno libro de Orlando, che compone el Conte Mathio Maria *Boiardo per la Excellentia del Signore Nostro*'.[28]

The significance of the Rugiero motif can only make sense if read against the peculiar background of Ferrarese politics and Boiardo's proximity to the ducal family. His intention to present Ercole as the legitimate descendant of Rugiero appears to have been endorsed by Ercole himself, who encouraged the poet and even gave him special leave to work on the poem. And since his effort to legitimize the Este family received the personal support of the Duke, it fitted the Este strategy of basing their claim to power on hereditary succession.

What Boiardo celebrates in Book II, therefore, is not only the advent of peace, but also the restoration of the legitimate line of descent: 'ora è il mal vento e quel verno compìto, / e torna il mondo di virtù fiorito' (*Inn.* II, i, 2, 7–8). This had been broken by Nicolò III's death in 1441 and revived with the ascent of Ercole I in 1471. It was then challenged by Nicolò d'Este, who was finally overcome by Ercole in 1476, and it is in the wake of this turbulent period that Boiardo's encomiastic idea was conceived. With this theme he imparted a new direction to his work, effectively putting it to the service of dynastic policy—something that he described as 'inventione de Rugiero'.

In *Orlando innamorato* Boiardo made a number of important predictions concerning Rugiero, almost all prophetically announced by Atalante at the council on the eve of the Moors' invasion of France

(*Inn.* II, xxi, 53–5). The key events in the progress of Rugiero's story should have been the following:

(a) Rugiero was to follow Agramante on his invasion of France;[29]
(b) Atalante was to follow Rugiero to France;[30]
(c) due to Rugiero Charlemagne was to be defeated;[31]
(d) Rugiero was to convert, be baptized, and become a Christian;[32]
(e) Rugiero was to be betrayed and die at the hand of Gano of Maganza;[33] this was to happen in war,[34] and Frontino, his horse, was to die with him;[35]
(f) Rugiero's descent was to be Christian, and as illustrious as any in the world.[36]

Of these future developments only the first, Agramante's attack on France, is started in Boiardo (*Inn.*, II, xxii ff.), while the others are just promised. One can also notice a possible contradiction in the fact that Rugiero was to defeat Charlemagne (c), yet convert to Christianity (d). This was just one of the challenges facing the continuators, and their solutions will help us to understand, if only by contrast, Ariosto's own treatment of the theme of Rugiero.

Before Ariosto's 1516 *Orlando furioso* there were three continuations of Boiardo: Nicolò degli Agostini's *Il quarto libro de linamoramento de Orlando* (Venice: Giorgio de' Rusconi, 1505); Raffaele Valcieco da Verona's *El Quinto e Fine de tutti li Libri de lo inamoramento de Orlando* (Venice: Giorgio de' Rusconi, 1514); and Nicolò degli Agostini's *Il Quinto Libro Dello inamoramento de Orlando* (Venice: Giorgio de' Rusconi, 1514).[37] The latter two appeared when Ariosto's composition was in an advanced stage.

In Agostini's Book IV, Rugiero reaches the river bank where Boiardo left Fiordespina, at the very end of his poem (III, ix, 25), ardently in love with Bradamante whom she thinks a (male) knight (IV, iv, 35). Predictably enough, Rugiero's arrival relieves Bradamante from her predicament, leaving Fiordespina 'sconsolata / quasi piangendo per la disperazione' (iv, 48, 1–2). Three cantos later Rugiero, finally alone with Bradamante in a 'vago loco', proposes to her and she accepts, on condition that he convert to the Christian faith. Mindful of his loyalty to Agramante, Rugiero hesitates at first, but is soon persuaded: 'Né fu mirabil cosa se sì presto / rimase vinto subiugato e preso, / ché 'l vago volto angelico e modesto / aria spezato i sassi e il mar acceso' (vii, 23, 1–4).

However, there is no question of marriage in Agostini; what we have

is something different. No sooner has Bradamante baptized Rugiero
than he wants to know her (carnally, that is); there is hardly time for a
brief prayer to the wood, so that 'testimon al sponsalizio sia' (vii, 26,
8). The graphic scene that follows—'I lieti basi, i suspirar cocenti, / el
manegiarsi insieme, el stringer spesso', etc. (vii, 36, 1–2)—'non è certo
tale da poter essere inclusa nelle antologie scolastiche, ma è tale che,
più di un lungo discorso critico, illumina per contrasto il processo
dell'invenzione ariostesca nella storia di quei due personaggi'.[38]

Although from this point onwards Rugiero and Bradamante are
frequently seen together, there are no new developments concerning
their story, except perhaps for the fact that the Trojan descent as told
by Boiardo has not gone unnoticed by Agostini. When Rugiero and
Bradamante meet Marfisa, the latter relates an account of her descent
which happens to be almost identical with Rugiero's: 'Marfisa
cominciò [. . .] / et li narrò de Greci el primo sdegno / ch'ebbero con
Troia e del crudel Sinone [. . .]' (x, 61, 1–4). Although this leads to
the revelation (useful to Ariosto) that Rugiero and Marfisa are brother
and sister, Agostini's rehearsal of Boiardo's Trojan descent remains an
extraneous appendage; the very fact that it is retold almost identically
suggests that Agostini could not quite make sense of it.

Valcieco's 1514 *Quinto libro* is an eighteen-canto sequel to Agostini's
Quarto libro. Valcieco was determined to bring to an end whatever
story still remained unfinished. But the price that he had to pay for
his resolve is a prevailing sense of haste and anticlimax. We may disregard the fact that his Book V features, amongst other things, the
death of Angelica, struck by lightning, and turn instead to Rugiero,
for whom nothing less remarkable lies in store. Valcieco is in fact the
first continuator to narrate his death. This happens when, during the
battle of Paris, Rugiero falls asleep in a meadow. Gano notices him,
and betrays his location to the pagans, who take him prisoner and
condemn him to death:

> Poi ch'ebbeno ligato el gioven stretto,
> el re Agramante con facia rubesta
> el brando in mano recosse el maledetto,
> e presi li capilli con tempesta
> del bon Rugiero, cavalier perfetto,
> poi con un colpo li tagliò la testa:
> così rimase morto sopra el piano,
> speme e conforto de ciascun cristiano. (Valcieco, V, xiv, 63)

A self-congratulatory note transpires soon after, when the author declares 'or *consumatum est la profecia*' (xiv, 65, 8). Yet, for Valcieco, Rugiero's decapitation (in the manner of St John) was not to be the end of his story, for he promised to come back with another sequel: 'el libro de Rugino' (xiii, 3). It never came, but the mention of Rugino (Rugiero's son) is interesting nevertheless. Boiardo never thought of Rugino, although his existence must have been implied if Rugiero's line was to continue. Even as Ariosto was publishing his 1516 *Furioso* (where Ruggiero's son is also alluded to), Pierfrancesco de' Conti da Camerino was writing a book entitled *El Sexto libro del innamoramento Dorlando nel qual si tratta le mirabil prodece che fece il giouene Rugino figliolo di Rugier da Risa e di Bradamãte sorella di Rinaldo da mõte albão.*[39]

Agostini's own Book V came out in October 1514, only seven months after Valcieco's. This continuation adds little to the Rugiero story because, unlike Valcieco, Agostini chose to delay his own version of Rugiero's death to yet another sequel. What is surprising is to find that the marriage of Rugiero and Bradamante, already consummated in Agostini's own Book IV, is at last formally celebrated in Paris. The wedding ceremony is even attended by Agramante and other pagans despite the fact that they regard Rugiero as a renegade. The news of his conversion, however, proves too much for Atalante, who hangs himself 'a un alto ramo' (V, i, 61, 8). Rugiero's indifference to the death of the person who played a fatherly role in his life causes Agramante to react angrily: 'Ma gran fatto non è, se non ti dole / de lui avendo ancor manco pensiero / di quel sommo Macon che regge il Sole, / il qual renegato hai sì de leggiero' (i, 79, 2–5). The wedding has no real consequence, for Rugiero resumes his former, 'premarital', role, while Bradamante gradually falls into the background—and vanishes. The reader is left wondering whatever happened to their marriage, consummated in the 1505 sequel, formalized nine years later, and then simply forgotten.

It is clear from this that the special significance attached by Boiardo to the story of Rugiero was lost in both Agostini and Valcieco, whose treatments result in little more than purely fictional incidents. Both show genuine admiration for Boiardo—for Agostini he is 'un novo Orfeo' (IV, i, 1, 4), for Valcieco 'el maestro et io el scolaro' (V, i, 5, 8). Yet, given the apparent nonchalance with which they often trivialize Boiardo, their eloquent protestations betray an acknowledged inadequacy in dealing with the very model they proclaim to revere. On the other hand, neither had any links with the Este family, and so it is understandable that they should fail to penetrate the full implications of the Rugiero theme. These become apparent only if viewed from the perspective of Ferrara, to which we must now return.

As a Ferrarese, Ariosto took the story of Rugiero far more seriously than any other continuator. He did not use it as an incidental episode, but gave it a structural function, so that in the 1516 *Furioso* it emerges as the poem's central motif—one that is sustained throughout and scrupulous in its adherence to Boiardo's indications. Ariosto's treatment of the Rugiero story can thus be seen as a faithful attempt to carry out Boiardo's legacy; indeed, it may have been the very reason that induced Ariosto to continue Boiardo's work.

In the title preceding Book II of *Orlando innamorato*, Boiardo referred to the story of Rugiero as 'la inventione de Rugiero'; and in 1512, writing to Gian Francesco Gonzaga, Marquis of Mantua, Ariosto indicates that he has begun a literary work 'continuando la inventione del conte Matheo Maria Boiardo'.[40] One is struck by the coincidence that on the only occasion that Ariosto explicitly mentions Boiardo's work he refers to it by the same word— 'inventione'—already used by Boiardo. If, with the expression 'inventione del conte Matheo Maria', Ariosto meant Boiardo's 'inventione de Rugiero', this would provide external evidence that what prompted him to write a continuation of Boiardo was not his *Innamorato* as a whole, but specifically the story of Rugiero—the 'inventione' rather than the 'inamoramento'.

The question rests on the meaning of 'inventione' in the two poets. In Boiardo there are at least three different possibilities. Firstly, it may be a Latinism (from *invenire*) referring to the 'finding' or 'discovery' of Rugiero jealously guarded by Atalante on Mount Carena. Secondly, it may have the rhetorical meaning of 'literary invention', hence 'fictional story'. And thirdly, it may signify 'invention' in the modern sense of the word, something that is specially devised. Of these possibilities, the first seems the least likely, but the other two are serious contenders. Boiardo uses this word only on one other occasion (*Inn.* I, ii, 31, 3, 'lodano tutti quella invenzïone'), where the intended meaning is clearly the third (an idea aptly devised by Charlemagne). This would suggest that Boiardo regarded the story of Rugiero as his own 'invention'.

Ariosto's case is more complex. The term 'inventione' occurs twice in *Orlando furioso*, but in two different senses. In the Ruggiero and Alcina episode (*Fur.* VII, 19, 7 ABC,[41] 'invenzïoni e poesie') it clearly stands for 'literary composition'; whereas in the Olimpia episode added to the 1532 edition (*Fur.* XI, 26, 1–2 C, 'Come trovasti, o scelerata e brutta / invenzïon, mai loco in uman core?') it denotes a technological invention, namely firearms. In Ariosto's case, therefore, evidence is not conclusive. It may be added, however, that when alluding to Boiardo's work as a 'literary composition', Ariosto tends to use less abstract words, such as 'istoria' or 'istorie', so it is possible that his usage of 'inventione del conte Matheo Maria' may convey a different meaning.

But perhaps the best indication comes from Ariosto's practice itself. He does not begin his continuation from the end of *Orlando inna-morato*, as all other continuators do, but rather from Book II, the novelty of which was precisely 'la inventione de Rugiero'. Ariosto's procedure makes sense, for in order to set the story of Ruggiero and Bradamante at the centre of his work, he has to rewrite large portions of that story, beginning with Agramante's expedition to France (*Inn.* II, xxii, 3 ff.)—an expedition, it may be recalled, that cannot proceed without Rugiero. All this points to the conclusion that it was Rugiero's story, rather than Orlando's, that provided the initial impetus to Ariosto's poem.

Rajna noticed that as the curtain is raised on *Orlando furioso* Rug-giero looks ten years older, having partly lost his former joviality.[42] Even so, his career progresses as forecast by Boiardo: he is baptized in due course (*Fur.* XXXVII, 59 AB; XLI, 59 C) and, finally, his union with Bradamante is crowned with 'nozze splendide e reali' (*Fur.* XL, 46, 1 AB; XLVI, 73, 1 C). In Ariosto these crucial events have been deferred to the conclusion, thus revealing that the Ruggiero story serves as the poem's main structural component.

According to Boiardo, however, Rugiero's story did not have a happy ending, and the suggestion of his impending death is one with which Ariosto wrestled for a long time. Bradamante learns about it as early as canto III (24, 7–8 ABC). But whereas she seems unmoved by this prospect, Atlante's grief is such as to cause him to precede Ruggiero to the grave. Even in his afterlife, Atlante does not cease to worry about his protégé. Speaking from his tomb, he informs Ruggiero of his premature departure, whilst also reminding him that his astrological signs are not favourable:

> Ruggier, se ti guardò, mentre che visse,
> il tuo maestro Atlante, tu lo sai.
> Di te senti' predir le stelle fisse,
> che tra' cristiani a tradigion morrai;
> e perché il male influsso non seguisse,
> tenertene lontan m'affaticai:
> né obstare al fin potendo alla tua voglia,
> infermo caddi, e mi mori' di doglia.   A
> (*Fur.* XXXIII, 68 A; 64 B; XXXVI, 64 C)

From the holy hermit who baptizes Ruggiero we learn about the cause and circumstances (invented by Ariosto) of Ruggiero's death:

> che per la morte che sua donna diede
> a Pinabel, ch'a-llui fia attribuita,
> serìa, e per quella ancor di Bertolagi,
> morto dai Maganzesi empi e malvagi.   A
> (*Fur.* XXXVII, 61, 5–8 AB; XLI, 61 C)

Through the hermit's mouth, Ariosto reveals important clues as to how Ruggiero's story should have evolved. His death was to remain shrouded in secrecy for a long time. Meanwhile, Bradamante was to give birth to a child, 'che pur Ruggier fia detto' (*Fur.* XXXVII, 64, 2 AB; XLI, 64, 2 C): he was destined to become Marquis of Este ('dominio giusto avrà del bel paese, / e titolo onorato di marchese', ibid. 64, 8). His father's death was not to remain unavenged, for one day, just before dawn, he would appear to Bradamante in the shape of a ghost (like Hamlet's father), revealing to her the names of the culprits and the place of his burial:

> Avea Dio ancora al servo suo predetta
> di Ruggier la futura aspra vendetta:
>
> ch'in visïone alla fedel consorte
> apparirà dinanzi al giorno un poco;
> e le dirà chi l'avrà messo a morte,
> e, dove giacerà, mostrerà il luoco:
> ond'ella poi con la cognata forte
> destruggerà Pontieri a ferro e a fuoco;
> né farà a Maganzesi minor danni
> il figlio suo Ruggier, com'abbia l'anni.   A
> (*Fur.* XXXVII, 65, 7–8, 66 AB; XLI, 65–6 C)

Ariosto had even set a time limit to Ruggiero's life. In the 1516 *Orlando furioso* he is said to die within four years from being baptized ('devea *quattro* anni, e non più, star in vita', XXXVII, 61, 4 A); in the 1532 version his life was prolonged by three more years ('da quel dì ch'ebbe la fede, / dovea *sette* anni, e non più, stare in vita', XLI, 61, 3–4 C). This shows how uneasy Ariosto must have felt about this detail, and also how seriously he took Boiardo's predictions concerning Ruggiero.

Even after the 1516 *Furioso*, Ruggiero's death continued to trouble Ariosto. Valcieco thought nothing of it, but Ariosto was understandably reluctant to execute the death of the Este founder. However, there must have been a time when he seriously considered doing so. As C. P. Brand points out, 'The *Cinque Canti* may well have been motivated by the sense that the *Furioso* was incomplete in respect of the Ruggiero story, which is there carried on beyond the wedding with a purer, nobler, worthier Ruggiero, moving, one assumes, to a tragic death worthy of the Estensi.'[43]

Ariosto's *Cinque canti* have long been a matter of debate, not least because of the uncertain date of their composition. Even so, whether this text pre-dates or post-dates the 1521 edition, what is beginning to emerge is that rather than constituting an addition to be inserted in the poem's final canto (*Fur.* XL, 45 AB), this long fragment may have been intended as a continuation to follow from the end of the *Furioso*.[44] Although Ariosto later abandoned this idea, it is significant in that it represents an attempt on the part of the poet to bring Ruggiero's story to its ultimate (Boiardan) conclusion, confirming that even after the 1516 *Furioso* it was still this story, rather than Orlando's, that was motivating Ariosto. In order to understand his uneasiness to give poetic representation to that part of Boiardo's legacy we ought to consider the Ruggiero story from the dynastic perspective.

Ariosto is unique among the continuators in inheriting from Boiardo not just the fictional material of the Rugiero story but its special significance as well. His procedure is different also because his work, structurally, does not continue any previous sequels to Boiardo. Although Ariosto certainly did not ignore these, especially Agostini's Book IV, his *Orlando* joins onto Boiardo's more directly; he effectively repudiates the lengthy accretions that had been appended to Boiardo, replacing them with a new, alternative, version. Nor does he begin his narration from the point where Boiardo left it.[45] Instead, he shifts the beginning of his *Furioso* much further backwards, the exact point at which his poem superimposes onto Boiardo's being *Innamorato* II, xxii, 2–3.[46] By so doing Ariosto commits himself to rewriting long segments already narrated by Boiardo, and for the first part his poem is an act of 'riscrittura' as well as 'scrittura'. But it also causes a retardation, which is due to the problem facing Ariosto at the beginning of *Orlando furioso*.

In inheriting Boiardo's subject matter Ariosto also inherited its incongruities. As already mentioned, there is a dichotomy in *Orlando innamorato*, a conflict between the original *innamoramento* of Orlando and the subsequent *invenzione* of Rugiero. This structural imbalance is one that not even Ariosto could entirely redress, and it is the principal factor accounting for the 'delay' in resuming Boiardo's proper narration. Of the two main stories left unfinished by Boiardo—Orlando's and Rugiero's—the latter was by far the less developed, and so Ariosto's most urgent concern, in the first eight cantos or so, was to bring that story to a similar level of development as the other.

This can be clearly seen in his proem to *Orlando furioso*. As is well known, Ariosto's proper narration follows a *proposizione* (the stating of the subject matter), a dedication, and an *antefatto* (a résumé of preceding facts), each of the three parts occupying two stanzas (I, 1–2, 3–4, 5–6), respectively. Yet we may observe that in fact the subject matter is stated twice, and that there is not one but two different *proposizioni*. The first, and more obvious, relates to Orlando:

> Dirò d'Orlando [. . .]
> [. . .]
> che per amor venne in furore e matto   A
> (*Fur.* I, 2, 1–3 ABC)

whilst the other concerns Ruggiero:

> Voi sentirete fra più degni eroi
> [. . .]
> ricordar quel Ruggier [. . .].
> [. . .]
> L'alto valore e' chiari gesti suoi
> vi farò udir [. . .]   A
> (*Fur.* I, 4, 1–6 ABC)

These two statements of subject matter appear as unrelated here as they were in Boiardo. However, unlike Boiardo, it was possible for Ariosto to introduce both subjects concurrently, while also establishing a more explicit connection between Ruggiero and the Este family, notably

Ippolito and the other 'Erculea prole'. This accounts for the fact that the theme of Ruggiero is not announced in the *proposizione* (where it would be expected), but rather in the dedication. By this means, the Este progenitor is introduced to his living descendants as 'quel Ruggier, che fu di voi, / de li avi e maggior vostri il ceppo vecchio' (*Fur.* I, 4, 3–4 A).

It is surprising, however, that the proem makes no mention of Bradamante, given that the creation of a new dynasty also requires a female founder. To understand the reason for this one needs to bear in mind her particular situation in *Orlando innamorato*. Whereas Rugiero had been acknowledged by Atalante as the progenitor of an illustrious descent (*Inn.*, II, xxi, 55, 2–4), Bradamante never was. Her relation with Rugiero had just started, and Ariosto recalls with utmost accuracy how she fell in love with Rugiero even though she only saw him once ('ben che concesso ancor Fortuna trista / non l'ha più nanzi d'una dolce vista', *Fur.* II, 32, 7–8 A). Hence Ariosto's immediate pre-occupation was to assign to Bradamante a dynastic role, and it is notable that in order to do so he had to invent a new character solely for this purpose: Melissa.

Melissa is a character whose only function is that of guiding and protecting the future Este progenitors, Bradamante in particular. On her first appearance in canto III Melissa acts as the author's inter-mediary who officially appoints Bradamante to her special mission: 'e qui son stata acciò ch'io ti riveli / quel c'han di te già statuito i cieli' (*Fur.* III, 9, 7–8 ABC). She patiently instructs Bradamante in the history of the Este family (*Fur.* III, 23–62 ABC), and through her agency Ariosto fills one of the most urgent gaps left open by Boiardo. Now that Bradamante's story has reached the same level of devel-opment as Ruggiero's, and both founders designated, the tale of their reunion and founding of the House of Este can effectively begin. In the proem Bradamante had yet to become an Este progenitor, and so Ariosto could not present her in that capacity.

The genealogical review put on display by Melissa for the benefit of Bradamante in canto III may not fire the imagination of modern readers; Rajna sums it all up when he confesses: 'Pur troppo qui si passa ad una parte, di cui il poema farebbe a meno con molto vantaggio'.[47] In reality, this genealogical sequence serves a clear pur-pose from Ariosto's viewpoint. Here and elsewhere he consolidates the link between the legendary ancestors and the Este family by filling in the intervening descendants, most of whom were missing in

Boiardo. The display begins with Bradamante's own son—not named here, but resembling his mother 'ne' sembianti e nel giocondo aspetto' (*Fur.* III, 24, 2 ABC)—and culminates with Duke Alfonso I, Cardinal Ippolito I, and two 'Sigismondi', being the brother and the son of the late, and much lamented, Duke Ercole I (*Fur.* III, 58 AB). In the 1532 edition Ariosto updated the Este family tree by adding the younger offspring, most notably Duke Alfonso's five children: Ercole II (b. 1508), Ippolito II (b. 1509), Francesco (b. 1516), Alfonso II (b. 1527), and Alfonsino (b. 1530).[48]

While retaining the basic line of descent as found in Boiardo—principally *Inn.* II, xxi, 56–9, but also II, xxvii, 52–8, which described the pavilion ornamented with pictorial representations of the 'dodeci Alfonsi'—Ariosto amplifies Ruggiero's modern descent considerably. Boiardo had devoted to the subject a mere eleven stanzas; Ariosto has 139, particularly the two segments devoted to the male and female lines of descent in canto III (23–61 AB; 23–62 C) and canto XI (57–71 AB; XIII 57–73 C), respectively. But this is not all, for he sets Boiardo's half-fictitious, half-historical genealogy into a more rigorous and coherent mould. As a result, his portrayal of the Este family sounds more historical, and is therefore more convincing.

Inevitably, Ariosto's account of Ruggiero's descent also covers the period plagued by the struggle for succession. Ariosto was only two years old when the Diamond was fighting the Sail, finally cutting it into pieces in 1476; but he must have heard much about this stormy period in later years, not least from his father, who was one of the participants. The impression left on Boiardo by this dramatic episode can be measured by the fact that in the *Innamorato*, with the single exception of Ercole, he passed over in silence all other rulers who were his contemporaries. Particularly notable is his silence concerning Leonello, Nicolò's father. This posed a delicate problem for Ariosto, as he could not avoid mentioning him without breaking the chronological sequence, or making his silence speak even louder. Ariosto therefore does name Leonello, albeit through Melissa's mouth, but his mention—'Vedi Lionello, e vedi [. . .]' (III, 45, 1 A)—is as swift and brief as could possibly be, and clearly uneasy. Like Boiardo, what Ariosto magnifies is the advent of Ercole's reign and the restoration of the legitimate line of descent: Ercole, Melissa prophesies, 'avrà per sua virtù la signoria, / più de trent'anni a lui debita pria' (*Fur.* III, 47, 7–8 A).

Just as the memories of past power struggles were beginning to fade, Ariosto happened to witness one of the darkest episodes in the history of the Este family, and one that brought back, uncalled, the spectre of Nicolò d'Este twenty-nine years after he had died. Melissa's genealogical review does not end on a celebratory note, for it has an epilogue as dramatic as unexpected. Having watched the parade of her future descendants, Bradamante notices that Melissa skipped silently over two Este figures who had drawn her attention,

> e dimandò: — Chi son dua, che sì tristi
> tra Ippolito et Alfonso avemo visti?
>
> Veniano suspirando, e gli occhi bassi
> parean tener d'ogni baldanza privi;
> e gir lontan da loro i' vedea i passi
> dei frati sì, che ne pareano schivi. —   A
> (*Fur.* III, 59, 7–8; 60, 1–4 AB; 60–1 C)

The two unnamed figures are Giulio and Ferrante d'Este, the brothers of Cardinal Ippolito, Duke Alfonso, and Sigismondo. They look miserable because in 1505 they conspired to seize power.[49] The pretext for the conspiracy, if not the real cause, is said to be the jealousy between Giulio and Ippolito. Both were paying court to Angela Borgia [*Fur.* XLVI, 4, 6], the cousin and lady-in-waiting of Lucrezia Borgia, when she came to Ferrara in November 1505 on the occasion of Lucrezia's marriage to Alfonso. During this visit Angela apparently remarked, facetiously, that Giulio's eyes were worth more than the Cardinal's whole person. This trivial incident took a tragic course when Giulio was set upon by a band of assassins and partly blinded in the presence of Ippolito. Despite Giulio's insistence, Alfonso was less than willing to punish Ippolito. This only added to Giulio's grudge, and he began to conspire with Ferrante. Their plan was to kill Alfonso and put Ferrante in his place, and it involved other people dissatisfied with Alfonso's policy, notably Albertino Boschetti, Gherardo de' Roberti, Francesco Boccaccio, and Gian Cantore, a priest in Alfonso's service. The plot, however, was foiled before it was put into action. In September 1506, the conspirators were publicly executed, while Giulio and Ferrante had their death sentences commuted to life imprisonment in the dungeons of Castel Vecchio. (Ferrante died in 1540; Giulio was released in 1559, and died in 1561.)

It is to Ariosto's credit that this episode has not been suppressed in *Orlando furioso* even though Cardinal Ippolito, the poem's dedicatee and Ariosto's master, does not emerge in a good light. This latest conspiracy extends the chronicle of family betrayal to the present, adding an uncanny resonance to Boiardo's theme of *tradimento*. Boiardo and Ariosto share the same concern for the dynastic line. But whilst in Boiardo betrayal by family relatives was relegated to that part of Rugiero's genealogical tree preceding the foundation of the House of Este, in Ariosto it can be found among Ruggiero's living descendants, which makes it more disquieting.

The 1505–6 conspiracy offers an unusual insight into Ariosto's attitude towards the Este family. This is made possible by the fact that Ariosto treated this subject in one other work besides *Orlando furioso*: a terza rima eclogue which must have been written before September 1506 since it makes no mention of the conspirators' execution, which took place in that month. The eclogue gives a more personal and open account than can be found in the poem, and it was not published in its entirety until 1812.[50]

Tirsi and Melibeo, the eclogue's interlocutors, relate the author's opinion on the recent events through a dialogue conducted under an Arcadian veil which slightly masks the participants' names: 'Alfenio' (Alfonso), 'Iola' (Giulio), 'Fereo' (Ferrante), 'Eraclide' (Ercole), etc. In spite of this pastoral setting, Ariosto's remarks are strikingly frank. Ferrante is accused in no equivocal terms of making an attempt on Alfonso's life with intent to seize power (adumbrated under 'mandre e ville'):

> Così, s'al pensier l'opra succedea,
> Fereo non a lui solo e mandre e ville,
> ma, quel ch'è più, la vita tòr volea. (*Egloghe*, I, 34–6)

Not only did Ferrante plot to kill Alfonso, but also 'gli altri dui suoi frati' (l. 101), Ippolito and Sigismondo. Nor is Giulio spared similar accusations, for Ariosto goes so far as to insinuate an unsubstantiated rumour that he was not a legitimate son of Ercole and Eleanor of Aragon, but the fruit of Ercole's relation with his mistress 'Ardeusa' (Isabella d'Arduino):

> Nol partorì ad Eraclide Ardeusa,
> nascostamente compressa da lui
> ne li secreti lustri di Padusa? (*Egloghe*, I, 64–6)

Giulio and Ferrante are presented as the chief instigators of this machination ('il capo e il petto', l. 89), and they could not put it into effect without a group of accomplices ('le braccia e' piedi', l. 90):

> Che altri aveano a questa impresa eletto
> io vedo, ché dui soli erano pochi
> a dare a tanta iniquitate effetto. (*Egloghe*, I, 91–3)

These are listed by name: 'Silvan' (Albertino Boschetti), his 'ribambito suocero' (Gherardo de' Roberti), 'Boccio' (Francesco Boccaccio), and 'Gano', also called 'Ingan' (Gian Cantore). The eclogue's vehemence can be judged from the fact that Ariosto does not hesitate to use the word 'tradimento' ('chi altri al tradimento è che prestasse / favor o col consiglio o con la mano', ll. 113–14). His inexorable account knows no mitigating circumstances or compassion for any of the participants, and all the blame is laid on Giulio and Ferrante.

This version of events could not contrast more sharply with that in *Orlando furioso*. When replying to Bradamante's question as to the identity of the two shadows that have caught her attention, Melissa suddenly appears uneasy, and the tone of her voice changes:

> Parve ch'a tal dimanda si cangiassi
> la maga in viso, e fe' degli occhi rivi,
> e disse: — Ah sfortunati, a quanta pena
> lungo instigar d'òmini rei vi mena!   AB
> (*Fur.* III 60, 5–8 AB; 61 C)

It is difficult to reconcile Melissa's portrayal of the two Este brothers with the image of 'Iola' and 'Fereo' in the eclogue. Here they are presented as 'sfortunati', the victims whose long suffering makes them deserving of compassion ('quanta pena'). No condemnation is attached to either of them: both were led astray—it would seem—by frequenting the wrong type of company. Responsibility for the dark affair is shifted onto the other conspirators, who had already been executed. Giulio and Ferrante were only unwilling participants; what caused the conspiracy was 'lungo instigar d'òmeni rei'.

Thus, through Melissa's mouth, Ariosto puts forward the 'official' version of events. Far from suggesting that either brother may have been illegitimate, here Ariosto invokes the legitimacy of their birth as the main argument in his plea for mercy:

> O bona prole, o degna d'Ercol bono,
> non vinca il lor fallir vostra bontate:
> di vostro sangue i miseri pur sono:
> qui ceda la iusticia alla pietate. —   A
> (*Fur.* III, 61, 5–8 AB; 62 C)

The discrepancy between the eclogue's intransigent stance and the *Furioso*'s reconciliatory view is highly indicative. That is not to say that there is contradiction in Ariosto. Whatever his personal opinions might have been (and the eclogue was eloquent in this respect), these seem to lose all relevance in the poem. Here, other considerations prevail, not least the poet's awareness of the 'public' nature of this work and the special position assigned in it to the ruling dynasty. Hence Ariosto's conduct in *Orlando furioso* is aimed at minimizing any damage to the Este family that might arise from this episode. Now that the worst consequences have been averted, Ariosto seems to argue, Giulio and Ferrante no longer pose any threat to the dynastic line, while their harsh punishment is a stigma on the whole family and an unnecessary reminder. Yet the fact that Ariosto's plea for mercy went unheard suggests that the rest of the family did not take their restored security for granted, and that concern for the dynastic line prevailed after all.

Ariosto returns to the 1505–6 conspiracy at the very end of *Orlando furioso*, where its link with the theme of Ruggiero becomes apparent. On the eve of the wedding of Ruggiero and Bradamante, Melissa adorns the bridal chamber with a pavilion that she has specially brought from Thrace (*Fur.* XL, 49 ff. AB; XLVI, 76 ff. C). Embroidered in the pavilion is a series of scenes, one of which is rather extraordinary. It represents a pensive Cardinal Ippolito in the act of counselling Alfonso, and revealing to him the treacherous plot that some of his dearest relatives have been hatching. The Cardinal is even credited with the merit of uncovering the plot, thus effectively saving Alfonso and the State.

> Si vede altrove, a gran pensier intento
> per salute d'Alfonso e di Ferrara,
> che va rimando per strano argumento,
> e truova, e fa veder per cosa chiara
> al giustissimo frate il tradimento
> che gli usa la famiglia sua più cara:
> e per questo si fa del nome erede,
> che Roma a Ciceron libera diede.   AB
> (*Fur.* XL, 68 AB; XLVI, 95 C)

This stanza is exceptional in *Orlando furioso*. It combines the 'Imperial Theme' with a rather direct allusion to the conspiracy, here called a 'tradimento'—a word which, in the poem, Ariosto uses nowhere else in relation to the Este family. Because of its explicitness this version of events is remarkably closer to the eclogue than to the previous reference in canto III. It is the last example in a long process that has seen the theme of 'tradimento' progressing from the lower roots of Ruggiero's genealogical tree to the upper branches, where it affects Alfonso and 'la famiglia sua più cara'.

However, there is another side to Ariosto's attitude towards the Este family, one that is private and sheds a different light on the theme of Ruggiero. Ariosto did not enjoy the same frank relationship with Cardinal Ippolito or Duke Alfonso as Boiardo did vis-à-vis Duke Ercole; their status was different. The son of a ducal official and a member of that small municipal nobility who depended on the princely court for their living, Ariosto spent his working life in the service of the Este family. Whereas Boiardo could relate to Ercole as an equal, Ariosto was a 'famiglio', an employee of the Cardinal since 1504. Boiardo's letters to the Duke exude cordiality and genuine friendship; Ariosto's are marked by deference due to his awareness of a social distinction. As Antonio Franceschetti points out:

Quello che cambia [. . .] sostanzialmente nel *Furioso* rispetto al poema precedente è il tono umile e deferente che caratterizza il rapporto fra il narratore da un lato, collocato su un piano servile, e dall'altro il destinatario, a livello nettamente superiore insieme a tutti gli altri Estensi nominati nel corso dell'opera; mentre il Boiardo si rivolge fin dal primo verso dell'*Innamorato* ai 'signori e cavallier' della corte situandosi alla loro stessa altezza [. . .] l'Ariosto assume questo aspetto dimesso e ossequioso che nell'ambito della tradizione encomiastica non ha precedenti altrettanto evidenti e marcati [. . .].[51]

With an annual salary of 240 lire Ariosto often complains of his struggle to support his large family.[52] In March 1513, when Giovanni de' Medici was elected Pope Leo X, Ariosto had great hopes that his long-standing friendship with him might bring better prospects, but he was disappointed. Writing from Rome on 7 April 1513, Ariosto thus describes his papal audience:

È vero che ho baciato il piè al papa, e m'ha mostrato de odir volentera: veduto non credo che m'abbia, ché, dopo che è papa, non porta più l'occhiale. Offerta alcuna, né da Sua S.ta né da li amici mei divenuti grandi novamente, me è stata fatta, li quali mi pare che tutti imitino il papa in veder poco.[53]

Yet it is not until more than a year after the publication of *Orlando furioso* (22 April 1516) that Ariosto's difficult relations with the Este family begin to emerge. In August 1517 he left Ippolito's service and entered Alfonso's, having refused to follow the Cardinal to his episcopal seat at Eger, in Hungary. His departure (25 October 1517) almost coincides with the first of Ariosto's *Satire*. Addressed to his youngest brother, Alessandro, and Ludovico da Bagno (both of whom had followed Ippolito to Hungary), the *Satira* marks the rupture of Ariosto's relation with his demanding master, and gives vent to a catalogue of grievances ranging from the meagre salary to the cool reception of his *Orlando furioso*:

> S'io l'ho con laude ne' miei versi messo,
> dice ch'io l'ho fatto a piacere e in ocio;
> più grato fòra essergli stato appresso. (*Satire*, I, 106–8)[54]

Significantly, the *Satira* also contains a direct invocation to Ruggiero:

> Ruggier, se alla progenie tua mi fai
> sì poco grato, e nulla mi prevaglio
> che li alti gesti e tuo valor cantai,
>   che debbo far io qui, poi ch'io non vaglio
> smembrar su la forcina in aria starne,
> né so a sparvier, né a can metter guinzaglio? (*Satire*, I, 139–44)

Ariosto may not simply be referring to the Cardinal's ingratitude for his encomium in *Orlando furioso*. More than the lack of reward for what was essentially an unpaid service, the poet seems to point to a more profound uneasiness, the lack of appreciation or understanding for his work. José Guidi describes the disillusionment pervading Ariosto's *Satira* as a 'secrète brûlure', a 'cuisant regret' resulting from 'le fait pour le poète de constater que ce qu'il croyait être sa fonction principale ne lui a en définitive rien rapporté'.[55]

There can be no doubt that Ariosto's *Satira* marks a significant change in his attitude towards the Este family. However, the grievances referring to the period spent by the poet in the Cardinal's service may have been coloured by the rupture of their relationship in 1517.

The *Satira*'s disenchanted view is in marked contrast with the hopeful, if deferential, tone of a letter written to the Cardinal in 1509, which—incidentally—contains the only other mention of Ruggiero outside the poem. While congratulating the Cardinal on the Este victory against the Venetians in the battle of Polesella (22 December 1509), Ariosto reveals to him his intention to include this heroic deed in the embroidered pavilion adorning Ruggiero's bridal chamber (*Fur.* XL, 70 AB; XLVI, 97 C). Since Ariosto's idea is clearly meant to please, presumably he would not mention it unless he were anticipating a cordial approval on the part of the Cardinal. 'Me ne sono alegrato'—writes Ariosto referring to the Este victory—'ché oltra l'util pu<blico la mia Musa ha>verà historia da dipingere nel padaglione del mio <Ruggiero a nova la>ude de V. S.; alla quale mi racomando.'[56]

It is difficult to reconcile this letter with the *Satira*. This view of Ruggiero is more passionate and fervent, and also consistent with the spirit informing the 1516 *Furioso*. Thereafter, the *Satira* signals a turning point in Ariosto's relations with the Este family and a disillusionment that was to leave its mark on the 1521 and 1532 versions of the poem. These reveal that whilst the encomiastic passages have been retained, they have hardly been modified or expanded. Even though Alfonso had by then replaced Ippolito as Ariosto's master, Alfonso is not acknowledged in this new role and his portrayal has been preserved almost entirely unaltered. Ippolito's case is no less remarkable: the Cardinal had died in Ferrara on 2 September 1520, yet Ariosto does not think his death even worth mentioning. Nor does Ippolito, Alfonso, or any other living member of their family, figure in the *Cinque canti*, begun after the 1516 *Furioso*. Given this, it is not surprising that in the 1532 version, which introduces extensive and substantial additions, the references to the Este family have remained virtually unchanged, as if Ariosto had lost interest in Ruggiero's living descendants. What we have is an anachronistic *tableau vivant* of the Este family as it stood before 1516. As Alberto Casadei observes: 'Le sezioni encomiastiche non vengono ridotte dalla prima alla terza stampa e sono soggette a correzioni assai limitate: si notano piccole aggiunte, ma non modifiche della loro struttura complessiva.'[57] Instead, in the 1532 edition Ariosto devotes increasing attention to historical developments affecting a larger, European, scale. Within this markedly changed historical frame, the destiny of Ferrara is viewed with anxiety. In a typical addition to this version, Ariosto envisages Ferrara as a self-sufficient stronghold, 'd'argini e di mura / [. . .] munita', so that she may 'contra tutto il mondo star sicura / [. . .], senza chiamar di fuori aita' (*Fur.* XLIII, 59, 3–6 C). The Este family continues to play an essential role in the security of Ferrara, for Ariosto can see no alternative to the Este rule, notwithstanding his personal opinions on individual members of the family.

This explains why, after the 1516 *Furioso*, Ariosto continued publicly to endorse Alfonso and Ippolito, even while—privately—he was
fighting both of them in a legal battle over the property of disputed
lands.[58] Legal proceedings started in 1519 and dragged on, leaving the
poet disheartened. He confessed to his friend Mario Equicola:

È vero ch'io faccio un poco di giunta al mio *Orlando furioso*, cioè l'ho com-
minciata; ma poi da l'un lato il Duca, da l'altro il cardi[le], havendomi l'un tolto
una possessione che già più di trent'anni era di casa nostra, l'altro un'altra
possessione di valore appresso di dece mila ducati, *de facto* e senza pur citarmi
a mostrare le ragion mie, m'hanno messo altra voglia che di pensare a
favole.[59]

This pessimistic vein, personal and political, runs through the late
Ariosto. His private resentment was compounded by the realization
that the future of Ferrara was no longer in the hands of the Este rulers,
having fallen into those of more powerful masters, notably Francis I
and Charles V. Significant in this respect is the addition of fifty-nine
stanzas (*Fur.* XXXIII, 1–59 C) featuring pictorial representations of
the most important developments since 1516.[60] Here, given the scale
of the forces at play, the tiny Este enclave does not even enter the
political equation, and what preoccupies Ariosto is the fate of the
Italian peninsula as a whole. A typical instance of this is when he
admonishes the French invader that he stands to gain 'vittoria e onore,
/ qualor d'Italia la difesa prenda'; but if he intends 'porle il giogo e
farsene signore, / comprenda [. . .] / ch'oltre a quei monti avrà il
sepulcro aperto' (*Fur.* XXXIII, 12, 3–8 C).

In the final version of *Orlando furioso* Ariosto responded to this climate
of crisis by giving his poem a different direction, the sense of which,
according to Lanfranco Caretti, becomes apparent if the 1532 text is
viewed 'non come il sereno approdo di una omogenea linea di sviluppo,
ma come la laboriosa e ardua ricomposizione, nella poesia, di un
universo terremotato: risarcimento letterario [. . .] delle illusioni perdute
e della grave crisi politica, al tempo della caduta libertà italiana e dei
grandi conflitti europei'.[61] This is particularly true of the story of
Ruggiero which, in the poem's final version, becomes an almost
exclusively literary theme, having lost the vibrancy and political
resonance that it had in the first edition. The abandonment of the *Cinque
canti* in the intervening years marks the moment when the poet
ultimately gave up the idea of pursuing this story beyond the confines
of the 1516 *Furioso*. By 1532, Boiardo's 'inventione de Rugiero' had

been superseded by a new historical climate, and seemed to have lost its power to inspire the poet.

Thus, the version of Ariosto's poem which most coherently establishes a direct link with his Boiardo—in terms of poetic affinity, narrative inventiveness, and sensitivity to the dynastic theme—is the 1516 *Orlando furioso*. In this version the story of Orlando's 'innamoramento' is only briefly developed, and what stands out is the epic story of Ruggiero and Bradamante, culminating in their marriage and the foundation of the House of Este. This theme represents both the climax of Ariosto's poem and the fulfilment of Boiardo's dynastic aim—something which makes the 1516 *Orlando furioso* the only legitimate continuation of *Orlando innamorato*.

Notes to Chapter 5

1. 'ANNOTATIONI, / ET AVVERTIMENTI DI / IERONIMO RVSCELLI, / SOPRA I LVOGHI DIFFICILI, ET / IMPORTANTI DEL FVRIOSO [. . .]', in *ORLANDO FVRIOSO / DI M. LODOVICO ARIOSTO* [. . .], Venetia, Valgrisi, 1556, sig. a2^v.

2. I have discussed the Boiardan origin of Orlando's madness in 'Concordanze, rimario e testo critico: il caso del Boiardo', *Studi e problemi di critica testuale*, 40 (1990), 51–67, and 'Reinventing Roland: Orlando in Italian Literature', in K. Pratt (ed.), *Roland and Charlemagne in Europe: Essays on the Reception and Transformation of a Legend* (King's College London Medieval Studies, 12, 1996), 105–26.

3. For the sake of consistency character names will be spelt as they appear in their respective texts; hence Boiardan names such as Rugiero, Atalante, and Rodamonte will become, when referring to Ariosto, Ruggiero, Atlante, and Rodomonte, respectively.

4. Matteo Maria Boiardo, *Orlando innamorato*, ed. G. Anceschi, 2 vols. (Milan: Garzanti, 1978) (reproduces the text of *Tutte le opere di Matteo Maria Boiardo*, ed. A. Zottoli, 2 vols. (Milan: Mondadori, 2nd edn., 1944).

5. This is because there is nothing in *Orlando innamorato* explicitly linking Bradamante to the House of Este, or suggesting that she is to become one of their founders. Nor is there any mention of her being destined to marry Rugiero, but only the beginning of a romance. Her part, particularly in Book II, is limited and fragmentary. Rugiero only discovers her feminine identity at III, v, 40, and the poem ends with Bradamante still not knowing what his face looks like (cf. III, v, 43). Initially, Boiardo appears to have been uncertain about her very name: see Dorigatti, 'Concordanze, rimario e testo critico', 56.

6. Cited from the 1487 edition (Venice: Piero de' Piasi, 1487), which differs somewhat from the Zottoli edition at this point. See M. M. Boiardo, *Orlando innamorato* (*Ristampa anastatica dell'ed. Piero di Piasi, 1487*), ed. N. Harris (n.p.: Arnaldo Forni Editore, 1987).

7. By saving Astyanax whilst letting Andromache die instead, Boiardo makes a

significant departure from Virgil, whose version of events tells the exact opposite. Boiardo was obviously anxious to establish a direct blood relation between Hector and Rugiero. See E. Paratore, 'L'*Orlando innamorato* e l'*Eneide*', in *Il Boiardo e la critica contemporanea. Atti del convegno di studi su Matteo Maria Boiardo (Scandiano–Reggio Emilia, 25–27 aprile 1969)*, ed. G. Anceschi (Florence: Olschki, 1970), 347–75 at 370–1.

8. On Boiardo's *volgarizzamento* of Ricobaldo's *Istoria imperiale* see A. Sorrentino, 'La leggenda troiana nell'epoca cavalleresca di Matteo Maria Boiardo', *Bulletin italien* [of Bordeaux University], 17/1 (1917), 22–35 at 34; and G. Ponte, 'Matteo Maria Boiardo volgarizzatore, rifacitore, manipolatore di opere altrui', *Il Boiardo: notiziario di informazione e bibliografia boiardesca*, 4 (1994), 2–3. See also A. Rizzi, 'M. M. Boiardo's version of Riccobaldo Ferrarese: the *Historia Imperiale* (1471–73)', unpublished Ph.D. thesis (University of Kent at Canterbury, 2000).

9. First published by G. Bertoni in 'Gli Estensi nel poema del Boiardo', in *Nuovi studi su Matteo Maria Boiardo* (Bologna: Zanichelli, 1904), 232–5.

10. W. Ludwig, *Die 'Borsias' des Tito Strozzi: Ein lateinisches Epos der Renaissance. Erstausgabe mit Einleitung und Kommentar* (Munich: Fink, 1977).

11. See A. Franceschetti, 'L'*Orlando Innamorato* e la tradizione dell'*Aspremont*', *GSLI* 157 (1970), 513–33.

12. P. Rajna, *Le fonti dell' 'Orlando furioso': ristampa della seconda edizione 1900 accresciuta d'inediti*, ed. F. Mazzoni (Florence: Sansoni, 1975), 511–17, indicates two other manuscript versions of *Aspramonte* which, however, seem less convincing.

13. Andrea da Barberino, *Aspramonte*, ed. M. Boni (Bologna: Palmaverde, 1951). My italics.

14. For Hector see also *Inn.* III, i, 27, 8 ('a tradimento poi lo occise Achille'), and III, ii, 6, 6–7 ('Ettòr, l'anima franca, / occiso fu nel campo a tradimento').

15. R. Bacchelli, *La congiura di Don Giulio d'Este* (1931; repr. Milan:, Mondadori, 1983), 63.

16. See O. Rombaldi, 'La politica e la guerra: 1454–1494', *Il Boiardo: notiziario di informazione e di bibliografia boiardesca*, 3 (1994), 9–10 at 9.

17. F. Yates, *Astrea: The Imperial Theme in the Sixteenth Century* (London: Routledge & Kegan Paul, 1975), 130 ff.

18. See L. Zorzi, 'Ferrara: il sipario ducale', in *Il teatro e la città: saggi sulla scena italiana* (Turin: Einaudi, 1977), 3–59.

19. COMMENTARIO / DELLE COSE DI / FERRARA, / Et de' Principi da Este, / Di M. Giovambattista Giraldi [. . .], IN VENETIA. / Appresso Giouanni de' Rossi. / [M. D. LVI], p. 15.

20. Letter by Nicolò Ariosto to Lodovico Gonzaga, 21 Aug. 1471, cited in M. Catalano, *Vita di Ludovico Ariosto ricostruita su nuovi documenti*, 2 vols. (Geneva: Olschki, 1931), i. 20.

21. Nicolò's mother was Margherita Gonzaga, Lodovico's sister and Leonello's first wife.

22. Giraldi, *Commentario delle cose di Ferrara*, 107.

23. The poisoner, a certain Simon Bojoni, had been instigated by Taddea Pio, Boiardo's aunt. Early in Book II of *Orlando innamorato* one notices the poisoning of a ruler, Alessandro, 'che un suo fidato l'ebbe a velenare' (II, i, 6, 6), and the result is fatal: 'Evi da poi sua morte dolorosa, / come Antipatro, il falso traditore, / l'ha avelenato con la coppa d'oro' (ibid. 29, 5–7).

24. Letter cited in Bacchelli, *La congiura di Don Giulio d'Este*, 89. On Nicolò d'Este see also A. Cappelli, 'Nicolò di Lionello d'Este', in *Atti e memorie delle RR. Deputazioni di storia patria per le provincie Modenesi e Parmensi*, 5 (1870); Catalano, *Vita di Ludovico Ariosto*, i. 17–23; and G. Bertoni, 'Gli *Epigrammata* di M. M. Boiardo', in *Nuovi studi su Matteo Maria Boiardo* (Bologna: Zanichelli, 1904), 79–82.

25. *Tutte le opere di Matteo Maria Boiardo*, ii. 702.

26. Matteo Maria Boiardo, *Canzoniere (Amorum Libri)*, ed. C. Micocci (Milan: Garzanti, 1990), 228.

27. Cited in G. Bertoni, 'M. M. Boiardo ed Ercole I d'Este', in *Nuovi studi su Matteo Maria Boiardo*, 4.

28. Letter to Duke Ercole, Feb. 1483, quoted in G. Bertoni, 'Usi e costumanze di corte nel poema del Boiardo', in *Nuovi studi su Matteo Maria Boiardo*, 240. My italics.

29. 'Tu vôi condurre il giovane soprano / di là dal mare ad ogni modo in Francia' (*Inn.* II, xxi, 54, 1–2).

30. '[. . .] tu [Atalante] potrai venir con seco ancore, / anci verrai' (ibid. 61, 6–7).

31. 'per lui serà sconfitto Carlo Mano' (ibid. 54, 3).

32. 'Il celo e la fortuna vôle / che la fé di Macone e Trivigante / perda costui, che è tra' baroni un sole' (II, xvi, 53, 4–8); 'ma il giovanetto fia poi cristïano' (II, xxi, 54, 5); '[. . .] che morirà dannato, / se Dio per sua pietate non lo aiuta, / o se persona non li mette in core / di batezarse e uscir di tanto errore' (III, viii, 58, 5–8).

33. 'al fin serà Rugier poi per te morto' (II, xxi, 54, 8); '[. . .] Gano di Maganza, / pien de ogni fellonia, pien de ogni fele, / lo uccise a torto, il perfido crudele' (III, i, 3, 6–8). Boiardo's decision to make Rugiero fall victim to the House of Maganza can be seen as an implicit response to the rumours that were being spread, especially in Venice, claiming that the House of Este descended from the treacherous Gano.

34. '[. . .] in guerra serai morto a tradimento' (II, xvi, 35, 8).

35. '[. . .] Rugier possa l'appellò Frontino, / sin che seco fu morto il bon ronzone' (II, xvi, 56, 5–6).

36. 'ma resterà sua genealogia / tra Cristïani, e fia de tanto onore, / quanto alcun'altra che oggi al mondo sia' (II, xxi, 55, 2–4).

37. Cf. N. Harris, *Bibliografia dell'*'Orlando innamorato' (Ferrara: ISR and Modena: Franco Cosimo Panini, 1988), i, nos. 6, 11b, and 12, respectively.

38. C. Dionisotti, 'Appunti sui *Cinque canti* e sugli studi ariosteschi', in *Studi e problemi di critica testuale* (Bologna: Commissione per i Testi di Lingua, 1961), 369–82 at 378.

39. Perugia, *c.*1516–17. No copy of this edition is known; the earliest surviving text was printed in Milan in 1518, which is the source of the title quoted above. See Harris, *Bibliografia dell'*'Orlando innamorato', i, nos. 14 and 15c.

40. Letter addressed to Marquis Gian Francesco II Gonzaga, dated Ferrara, 14 July 1512. See *Lettere*, ed. A. Stella, in Ludovico Ariosto, *Satire, Erbolato, Lettere* (Milan: Mondadori, 1984), no. 12, p. 151.

41. The letter A denotes the first edition of *Orlando furioso* (Ferrara: Giovanni Mazocco dal Bondeno, 1516); B the second (Ferrara: Giovanni Battista da la Pigna, 1521); and C the third (Ferrara: Francesco Rosso da Valenza, 1532). The

text of A is quoted from the copy in the Biblioteca Comunale Ariostea, Ferrara [S.16.1.21], and also, especially for B, from Ludovico Ariosto, *Orlando furioso secondo l'edizione del 1532 con le varianti delle edizioni del 1516 e del 1521*, ed. S. Debenedetti and C. Segre (Bologna: Commissione per i Testi di Lingua, 1960). The text of C is quoted from Ludovico Ariosto, *Orlando furioso*, ed. C. Segre (3rd edn., Milan: Mondadori, 1982).

42. 'Nell'Ariosto quella freschezza e quel profumo sono svaniti pur troppo; Ruggiero si direbbe invecchiato di dieci anni almeno': Rajna, *Le fonti dell' 'Orlando furioso'*, 55.

43. C. P. Brand, 'Ariosto's Continuation of the *Orlando Innamorato'*, in C. H. Clough (ed.), *Cultural Aspects of the Italian Renaissance: Essays in Honour of Paul Oskar Kristeller* (Manchester: Manchester University Press, and New York: Alfred F. Zambelli, 1976), 377–85 at 379–80.

44. This hypothesis has been put forward by A. Casadei, '*I Cinque canti* o l'ultima eredità di Boiardo', *Italianistica*, 21 (1992), 739–48.

45. See Brand, 'Ariosto's Continuation of the *Orlando Innamorato'*, 378.

46. The opening stanza of the 1516 *Orlando furioso* has been 'assembled' from the two stanzas referred to above, the first of which provided Ariosto with the hapax legomenon 'antichi amori' (*Fur.* I, 1 A: 'Di donne e cavallier li antiqui amori'), and the second with a succinct account of Agramante's expedition to France. I have discussed the relevance of this Boiardan source as the starting point of the *Furioso* in my D.Phil. thesis: 'The Significance of Boiardo in the Making of *Orlando Furioso*, with Special Reference to the 1516 Edition of Ariosto's Poem', Oxford University, 1994, 63–4.

47. Rajna, *Le fonti dell' 'Orlando furioso'*, 133.

48. Cf. *Fur.* III, 58–9 C.

49. See especially Bacchelli, *La congiura di Don Giulio d'Este*. Some reservations about Bacchelli's interpretation of the conspiracy have been expressed by C. Dionisotti, 'Documenti letterari d'una congiura estense', *Civiltà moderna*, 9 (1937), 327–40.

50. L. Lamberti and U. Lampredi, 'Poesia di M. Lodovico Ariosto', *Il poligrafo*, 2 (1812). A critical edition of the eclogue can be found in Ludovico Ariosto, *Opere minori*, ed. C. Segre (Milan and Naples: Ricciardi, 1954), 224–35, from which quotations are taken.

51. A. Franceschetti, 'Il Boiardo e l'avvio del Furioso', in B. M. Da Rif and C. Griggio (eds.), *Miscellanea di studi in onore di Marco Pecoraro* (Florence: Olschki, 1991), 111–30 at 121.

52. The figure for Ariosto's annual salary is derived from *Satire*, ed. Segre, in Ludovico Ariosto, *Satire, Erbolato, Lettere*, 580 n. On Ariosto's social position see also C. Dionisotti, 'Chierici e laici', in *Geografia e storia della letteratura italiana* (Turin: Einaudi, 1967), 73–5.

53. Letter to Benedetto Fantino, dated Rome, 7 Apr. 1513, in Ariosto, *Lettere*, ed. Stella, no. 14, p. 154.

54. *Satire*, ed. Segre.

55. I. Guidi, 'Imagination, maîtresse de vérité: l'épisode lunaire du *Roland Furieux'*, in *Espaces réels et espaces imaginaires dans le 'Roland Furieux'* (Paris: Université de la Sorbonne Nouvelle, 1991), 47–85 at 80–1.

56. Letter to Cardinal Ippolito, dated Rome, 25 Dec. 1509, in Ariosto, *Lettere*, ed. Stella, no. 5, p. 139.

57. A. Casadei, *La strategia delle varianti: le correzioni storiche del terzo 'Furioso'* (Lucca: Fazzi, 1988), 21.

58. See Catalano, *Vita di Ludovico Ariosto*, i. 507 ff.

59. Letter to Mario Equicola, dated Ferrara, 15 Oct. 1519, in Ariosto, *Lettere*, ed. Stella, no. 26, p. 172.

60. On this passage added to the final version see Casadei, *La strategia delle varianti*, 61–71.

61. L. Caretti, 'Codicillo', appendix to 'L'opera dell'Ariosto', in *Antichi e moderni: studi di letteratura italiana* (Turin: Einaudi, 1976), 103–8 at 108.

CHAPTER 6

❖

Poliziano's *Stanze per la giostra*: Postmodern Poetics in a Proto-Renaissance Poem

Martin McLaughlin

To use a word like 'postmodern' of an early Renaissance text might seem at first sight irresponsibly anachronistic or simply a modish inaccuracy. It certainly requires some definition and justification. As for a definition of the term, postmodernism embraces, according to recent surveys, at least two major areas of reference: firstly, it is used to refer to contemporary (late twentieth-century) culture in a very broad sense, being applied both to the arts (postmodern literature, architecture, theatre, etc.) and to the general cultural condition of our time; but secondly it refers more specifically to a set of textual practices that inform works of literature. As Edmund Smyth has said recently, 'post-modernism' is used to characterize: 'any creative endeavour which exhibits some element of self-consciousness and reflexivity. Fragment-ation, discontinuity, indeterminacy, plurality, metafictionality, hetero-geneity, intertextuality, decentring, dislocation, ludism: these are the common features such widely differing aesthetic practices are said to display.'[1]

I am not going to claim that all these characteristics are present in the unfinished narrative poem *Le stanze per la giostra* (1475–8), written by Angelo Poliziano (1454–94).[2] In any case, even if it could be shown that all these qualities inform the text, that would still not make Poliziano a postmodern writer in any but a superficial sense; all it would do is to suggest that *Le stanze* is a less well-known predecessor of other self-referential, fragmented, or intertextual works, such as Cervantes's *Don Quixote* or Sterne's *Tristram Shandy*, to which today's postmodernists are indebted. What I do want to suggest, however, is that since a surprisingly high number of these elements, perhaps even all of them, are present in this and other works by this most precocious of Italian humanists, then it is worth enquiring why this should be, and to try to establish the significance of any analogies that can be drawn between Poliziano's position vis-à-vis the classical tradition, and our own relationship to modernism and the Western literary canon. Poliziano will, I hope, be seen to possess a strikingly modern or even postmodern sensibility and a strong penchant for intertextuality—indeed he is probably the inventor of the latter term, at least in its Latin form. In what follows I want to proceed in three stages: first to reconsider the context and structure of the poem; second, to review the main critical approaches to the text; and finally to examine its textual practices and what they can tell us about Poliziano's poetics, postmodern or otherwise.

Context and Structure

The background to the poem is a tale of two jousts. The joust of 7 February 1469 was won by the 20-year-old Lorenzo de' Medici and his victory was celebrated in a vernacular poem which was written by Luigi Pulci (1432–84), but which took five years to write, and was almost out of date by the time it was finished in 1474.[3] Pulci's poem was eclipsed not just in terms of topicality but also in originality and poetic sophistication by a text written by someone twenty-two years his junior. Poliziano's poem celebrates the second joust, which was won by Lorenzo's brother Giuliano de' Medici on 29 January 1475. Work began on the text shortly after Giuliano's victory, but the poet interrupted the *Stanze* three years later in 1478, presumably because by that stage both the heroine and the hero of his poem were dead: in 1476 Simonetta Cattaneo Vespucci died, a tragedy that Poliziano worked briefly into what now is the end of Book II of his poem, when he says that the hero had a vision of Simonetta being swept up in a dark cloud and turned into a figure of Fortuna to guide him (II, 33–4). Even more famously, in April 1478 the hero of the poem, Giuliano, called by the Latinate name Iulio in the poem, was killed in the violent Pazzi conspiracy of that year. On this point Oscar Wilde might have remarked that to have one protagonist die may be an accident, but to lose two starts to look like carelessness; in any case this double misfortune effectively ended Poliziano's work on the poem:

the text is truncated almost violently by this second death, and ends early in the second book with the hero invoking the aid of supernatural deities for the forthcoming joust.

In terms of structure, Poliziano's *Stanze per la giostra* contains a total of 171 octaves, a curiously similar number of stanzas to those in Pulci's joust poem (160 octaves). But although Pulci's poem is also structurally imbalanced, in that nearly two-thirds of it is concerned with what the combatants wore, nevertheless he does eventually narrate the joust, and his poem does have a discernible beginning, middle, and conclusion. By contrast, Poliziano's *Stanze* has a beginning, a controversial central section, and no apparent conclusion. That central section, almost exactly a third of his poem (55 out of 171 octaves), is devoted to an ekphrasis or descriptive digression describing Venus' garden and the reliefs carved on her palace doors; then the poem breaks off before the narrative reaches the joust, and although one critic has argued that the work was complete by this stage, this interpretation has found few followers.[4]

Critical Approaches

Thematic

The general thrust of critical inquiry into the poem has concentrated on thematics and structure.[5] In terms of theme, critics have predictably highlighted the centrality of the theme of love, and the mythical atmosphere with which Poliziano endows the poem. Ida Maier identifies 'la toute-puissance de l'Amour' as the main theme, while Maria Luisa Doglio sees the paradoxical juxtaposition of *dolce* and *amaro* as pervading the poem, first applied to love, but in the end referring to the fate of the two protagonists.[6] Amongst critics writing in English, David Quint argues that 'the thematic enterprise of the *Stanze* [. . .] is the transformation of historical events into poetic myth. [. . .] From the outset love displaces the tournament as the center of interest.'[7] He also feels that there is an element of civic education in Iulio's movement from solitary hunter to lover and participant in a 'tournament quite literally in the civic arena' (p. xvii). Unlike Quint, who sees Neoplatonic elements only in Iulio's final prayer, the majority of recent critics have considered the whole poem as broadly Neoplatonic. Ferruolo, for instance, stresses in particular the aura of brightness that surrounds Simonetta, and the importance of light imagery for contemporary theorists influenced by Platonic notions of beauty.[8] Carrai also gives a Neoplatonic interpretation, quoting an important passage from Ficino's commentary on Plato's *Symposium* (1469), on the distinction between the earthly and celestial Venus (II, 7), and stressing the fact that the protagonist has to tame the impulses of 'Venere terrena' with the restraint of heavenly, contemplative love and the aid of Minerva and Glory.[9] Berman sees Neoplatonic influences more in the account of Iulio's dream, and regards the three divinities invoked at the end of Book II by Iulio as a Neoplatonic triad: Minerva as goddess of Contemplation, Amor as Desire, and Gloria as Will.[10] Terpening stresses the importance of the reliefs on the doors of Venus' palace: sight was a crucial sense in Neoplatonic theory, and what the eyes beheld in the two doors was a universal history of love, from its highest to its lowest form.[11] Love, whether with Neoplatonic overtones or not, is certainly the dominant theme of the *Stanze*, but this does not take us very far in characterizing the poem's distinctive qualities. Other elements, such as structure and style, are also of importance.

Structural

Structurally critics have been exercised mainly by the question of the long description of the realm of Venus, which was initially seen as an ornamental, but otiose mythical digression. However, McNair demonstrated that the ekphrasis was in a sense 'the central arch' of the poem, since all the action in *Le stanze* initiated from Venus' couch, on which she reclined having conquered Mars, the traditional patron of Florence. He pointed out that Venus, but not Mars, was present in Poliziano's main classical source for the poem, Claudian's *Epithalamium* for the Emperor Honorius and Maria, and concluded that the vision at the end of Book I, of Mars and Venus reclining together sated after the act of love, must therefore derive from another source, Lucretius' *De rerum natura*. The allusion in the opening stanza to the peaceful, harmonious city ruled by Lorenzo was then shown to be connected with the more arcane version of the myth of Venus and Mars, the one in which the fruit of their union is their daughter, Harmonia; the poem was thus both a celebration of Giuliano's victory in the joust and a homage to Lorenzo's harmonious, beneficent rule.[12] In a further refinement of the structural question Branca suggested that the echoes in the poem of Petrarch's *Trionfi,* which were more popular in the late Quattrocento than his *Canzoniere*, were so strong that this text too could be seen as a series of Triumphs: first the Triumph of Forza and Castità in Iulio's pursuit of hunting and rejection of Amore (I, 1–22); then a Triumph of Amore (I, 39–67); to be followed by a Triumph of Fortuna and Death (II, 35–7), which in turn is overcome by a Triumph of Fame over 'Morte e Tempo' (II, 15, 42–6).[13] As we shall see, this motif of the Triumph is an integral element in the poem, though not exactly in the sequence that Branca outlines.

Neoplatonic

However, it is Mario Martelli's interpretation, recently made more accessible in an important volume of essays, which is the most persuasive and authoritative, on both a thematic and structural level.[14] Adopting a Neoplatonic perspective, he sees the poem as embodying a platonic ascent up the ladder of being. The wood represents the lowest level of the ladder, that of matter (indeed the Greek word for 'matter', *hyle*, means 'wood' or 'forest'); the beautiful doe that distracts Iulio in the hunt is then seen as the second stage of this process, that of 'natura' and 'bellezza sensibile' or sensual beauty; Simonetta occupies the third level, representing the 'anima razionale' which experiences desire for divine beauty: but she is still only an intermediate stage, standing for the earthly, active life, or the four cardinal or civic virtues, which encourage the young Iulio to come of age politically, an action to be symbolized by his participation in the joust; finally, Venus' realm is seen as the fourth, supernatural level, and Venus herself is in Platonic terms the 'mente angelica', the lavish attention to the vegetation and animals in her realm being explained by the fact that the 'mente angelica' is synonymous, in Pico della Mirandola's almost contemporary interpretation, with 'paradiso', which derives from the Greek word 'paradeisos' meaning 'garden' or 'park'. This garden is as superior to the 'pratello' on which Simonetta sat (I, 37) as Venus is superior to Simonetta, hence it merits this longer description. As for the digression or ekphrasis, Martelli argues that the earlier symbolic transition from the life of the senses (the doe) to that of the rational soul (Simonetta) could take place without interruption as it does when the doe metamorphoses into Simonetta in the space of one line: 'ivi sotto un vel candido li apparve / lieta una ninfa, e via la fera sparve' (I, 37, 7–8); but the shift from the active life to the contemplative life is too great not to be emphasized by a pause, which signals the digression's importance also in structural terms. To this convincing Neoplatonic interpretation I would add only that almost every one of the many plants and animals mentioned in the first half of Book I finds an exact echo in all the flora and fauna which live in harmony in Venus' realm, where the animals are no longer victims of the hunt.[15] The realm of Venus then represents a Golden Age or a Platonically Ideal existence in which hunting is not necessary, a point to which I shall return.[16]

Allegorical

But alongside this vertical Neoplatonic ascent, one should add a horizontal, linear gloss. Branca suggested a sequence of four Petrarchan Triumphs, of Chastity, Love, Fortune, and Fame, but I would argue that there really are only three major turning points, not mentioned explicitly by critics, yet clearly signalled in the text: they concern Amore and those favourite Renaissance dualities, *Fortuna* and *Virtú*. These shifts can be observed first by considering Iulio's changing notions of virtue. He initially celebrates 'antica virtú' in song (I, 11), and regards *Fortuna* and *Amore* as the enemies of his own particular kind of celibate virtue, since it was the advent of these two forces which in his view ended the Golden Age (I, 21). Thus at the outset the opposing forces for Iulio are on the one side *Virtú*, on the other *Fortuna* and *Amore*. However, from this point onwards in the poem, every time virtue is mentioned it is associated with Love: Simonetta is described as surrounded by 'ogni virtú' (I, 46); the next virtuous example is the lovelorn Lorenzo (II, 6), whose 'virtú' is sharpened by the pangs of love (II, 14), while all the Tuscans become full of 'virtú' as a result of the assault of Cupids (II, 19). By the end of the poem Iulio is pleading for the protection of Amore and twice asks for the aid of Minerva's 'virtú' (II, 41), as his own strength ('virtú'), which he had exalted at the beginning of the poem, is now seen to be inadequate:

> [. . .] dolce Amor, [. . .]
> fa' sí del tuo furor mio pensier pregno
> che spirto di pietà nel cor li crei:
> mie virtú per se stessa ha l'ale corte
> perché troppo è 'l valor di costei forte. (II, 44)

Each of the three forces in turn thus triumphs over the other two. At the outset Virtue is all-powerful: Iulio's opening speech portrays himself as the exemplar of Virtú (i.e. both chastity and the manly strength—*vir-tus*—required in the hunt) against the twin evils, as he sees them, of *Fortuna* and *Amore*:

> Fortuna, invidiosa a lor quiete,
> ruppe ogni legge, e Pietà misse in fondo;
> Lussuria entrò ne' petti, e quel furore
> che la meschina gente chiama Amore.   (I, 21)

Once he sees the beautiful Simonetta, however, and falls in love with her, we reach the first turning point, as Love now holds sway over the other two forces: 'ch'a Virtute e Fortuna Amor pon legge' (I, 59).

The second shift comes in Book II, when at first the premonition of the death of Simonetta suggests that Fortuna is now all-powerful against Love and Virtue: 'Ma che puote a Fortuna esser disdetto, / ch'a nostre cose allenta e stringe il morso?' (II, 35). However, Fortune's triumph is short-lived, since the poet then immediately argues in the next stanza that since Fortuna rules so much of our lives, it is best to ignore her and to entrust oneself entirely to Virtue: 'Beato qual da lei [Fortuna] suo pensier solve, / e tutto drento alla virtú s'involve!' (II, 36). At the end of the following octave he explicitly reshuffles the position of the three powers once more and claims that the man who trusts entirely in his own Virtue will not only be immune to Fortune but will actually conquer her: 'Da sé sol pende, e 'n se stesso si fida, / né guidato è dal caso, anzi lui guida' (II, 37). By this stage the poem has come full circle, with Virtue once more preeminent. However, the love-inspired virtue (and we have observed that after the opening scene virtue is always associated with Love throughout the text) which is exalted at the end of the second book is totally different from the virtuous chastity ('virtú') vaunted by Iulio at the outset of Book I. In the final stanzas of the poem, after this series of triumphs of first Amore, then Fortuna, and finally Virtú, Iulio now asks for the aid of Amor, Minerva, and Gloria (II, 41–4). These last three deities are, as has been observed by critics, clearly meant to combat the negative forces mentioned at the end of the very first stanza of the poem—'fortuna, morte e tempo' (I, 1)—but it is also clear that they are linked to the other three forces which have in turn triumphed in the poem. Minerva is associated with Virtú, since Iulio mentions the word twice in his address to her: '[tu] che i valorosi cuori a virtú infiammi, / soccorrimi or, Tritonia, e virtú dammi'

(II, 41). The point of this emphasis is that not only will Amor overcome Morte, and Gloria outlive Tempo, but Minerva or rather Virtú will conquer Fortuna.

However, as well as his views on virtue, Iulio's ideas about love's 'furore' also undergo radical revision in the course of the poem. At the beginning he condemns Love's 'van furor' (I, 13, 21), and he only experiences 'furor' when hunting (I, 35). But the 'Furore' of Love resides in Venus' realm (I, 75); Lorenzo, inspired by Love, fights with 'gran furor' (II, 6) and the 'furor di Bellona' (II, 8); and in the end Iulio prays for Love's 'furor' to fill his thoughts (II, 44), and knows that only love's 'santo furor' can help him overcome fortune (II, 45). This stress on 'furore' is of course linked to Plato's views on the beneficent 'furor' or 'madness' of love, particularly as interpreted by Poliziano's fellow humanist Marsilio Ficino (1433–99). The conclusion of Ficino's most important vernacular work is relevant here. One of the last chapters of *El libro dell'amore*, Ficino's *volgarizzamento* of his 1469 Latin commentary on Plato's *Symposium*, is entitled 'Per quali gradi e furori divini innalzino l'anima'. Here he emphasizes the positive nature of the frenzy of love, the 'furor' dispensed by Venus, stating that it is superior to the other three Platonic 'furores' (the poetic 'furor' of the Muses, the frenzy of Bacchic mystery, and that of Apolline divination), as it is essential for completing the final return of man's soul to God. Ficino's words here have a close correspondence with Poliziano's poem, which was written just a few years later in the same Medicean milieu. Speaking of the gift of the final return of the soul to God, he says: 'Questo gran dono ci dà quella celeste Venere mediante l'amore, cioè mediante el desiderio della bellezza divina e mediante l'ardore del bene' (VII, xiv, 12).[17] Ficino's sentence, from a work almost contemporary with the *Stanze,* suggests that the poem is a poetic illustration of this concept, as Iulio is led to appreciate that love's 'furore' is beneficent and can lead him to both an appreciation of earthly beauty and the pursuit of the good.

Iulio develops in another way in the course of the brief poem. His celebration of the Golden Age as the innocent age before the pangs of love were known (I, 21) is equally misconceived: because that age was a time before war, navigation, and farming existed, as he says (I, 20), then since nature produced everything it must also have been the age before hunting became necessary—indeed Iulio's idyllic evocation of that epoch as one when the earth was covered with the fruit of the trees, and the ears of corn rippled like a sea, is a nostalgic vision which is only realized in Venus' realm. In the course of the poem Iulio learns not to look backwards to a Golden Age but upwards to the realm of Venus. This is confirmed by the fact that the words he uses to describe the animals' Golden Age existence—'veder *cozzar monton*', vacche mughiare' (I, 18)—are the very words used to depict the animals rutting in love in the park around Venus' palace: 'l'un ver l'altro i *montoni* armon le corna,/ l'un l'altro *cozza* [. . .]. E *mughianti* giovenchi a piè del colle/ fan vie piú cruda e dispietata guerra' (I, 85–6, my emphasis). The Golden Age, then, if it exists, does not live in an Arcadian past, as Iulio believed, but in the present and future realm of Love and Venus. Similarly Iulio's idyllic vision of the birds singing ('augei', I, 17) is actualized only when he falls in love: the birds singing are then mentioned three times (I, 44, 55, 60), while in Venus' realm they are also mentioned on three occasions (I, 71, 90, 119); and at the end of Book I Amore himself is described as 'giovene nudo, faretrato augello' (I, 120). The poem as it stands, then, may not be complete, but it does portray a clearly articulated development and reversal both in the protagonist and in the abstract forces that contend for his soul.

Postmodern Elements

If concepts such as *Fortuna* and *Virtú*, and the stages of neoplatonic love are topoi of Renaissance literature, there are, however, also a number of less predictable elements in the poem that share striking similarities with postmodern textual practices. These are apparent in three areas: characterization, narrative method, and the allusive, intertextual style.

Iulio's character at the beginning of the poem is that of the young man who rejects the blandishments of Love and prefers to devote himself to hunting: he is in fact a composite blend of Euripides' Hippolytus, Ovid's Narcissus, and the poet-figura in poem 23 of Petrarch's *Rerum vulgarium fragmenta* (the canzone of metamorphoses). In an analogous fashion, Simonetta is an eclectic fusion of elements drawn from classical and vernacular descriptions of the beautiful woman, from Ovid's Daphne and Claudian's Proserpina to Dante's Matelda and Beatrice, Petrarch's Laura, and Boccaccio's Fiammetta and the Emilia of his *Teseida*.[18] If the two human protagonists are not real characters but simply rewritten textual constructs culled from canonical sources, there is also something that borders on postmodern self-reflexivity in Poliziano's description of the relief at the bottom of

the first door of Venus' palace. There we are told that, having depicted
the birth of Venus from the waves, Vulcan portrayed himself in the
final panel of the door, sweating from his labours in the divine forge
of Mount Etna, but amorous and delighted to have won Venus as
his bride (I, 104). But Vulcan is also in a sense Poliziano, since it is
the poet who has created these verbal sculptures in the labours of
this ekphrastic masterpiece. Thus tucked away in the centre of his
description of the doors, as in a mise-en-abyme, lies a self-portrait of
the artist and poet: the term 'divin fabro' (I, 104, 1) is a Platonic one,
applicable both to Vulcan and to Poliziano.

Perhaps the most paradoxical feature of what is regarded as one of
the first Italian narrative poems of the Renaissance, is its avoidance of
narration, its slippage into description, its refusal to begin. After the
proemio, the text immediately launches into descriptions: the depiction
of Iulio's youthful existence, his passion for hunting, and his rejection
of the blandishments of love (I, 8–12). It is only after describing the
habitual despair with which other lovers greeted Iulio's remarks (I, 22)
that the poem ventures into action with Cupid's decision to have his
revenge on Iulio; the first two genuine instances of the *passato remoto*
are here: 'Né fu Cupido sordo al pio lamento, / e 'ncominciò
crudelmente ridendo' (I, 23–4). This brief burst of activity setting
the poem in motion, however, is instantly followed by an idyllic
description of spring (I, 25), then a brief *passato remoto* of action as
Iulio sets off on the hunt ('prese el cammino', I, 26), but the hunt
itself offers simply more opportunities for description (I, 27), shifting
via similes (I, 28) to a descriptive present tense (I, 29–31). Another
stanza of similes (I, 32) is followed by further present-tense description
of Iulio hunting (I, 33), and only at the end of this stanza does Love
take action again (I, 33–4), creating the beautiful deer which finally
spurs the young man into hot pursuit (I, 34–5). Even here, however,
the action slows down into a *rallentando* present-tense description of
the tantalizing chase (I, 35–6) before finally arriving at the *locus
amoenus* ('pervenne', I, 37, 6), and ending up with the double
contrasting past tenses which mark the first metamorphic climax of
the poem: 'ivi sotto un vel candido li apparve / lieta una ninfa, e via
la fera sparve' (I, 37, 7–8). The doe's disappearance is then swiftly
followed by another shift to the present as first Iulio is described
gazing in wonder and falling victim to love's arrow (I, 38–42), then
Simonetta's beauty is described in a standard *effictio* or top-down

description of the beautiful woman (I, 43–8). Only as she moves to depart is Iulio stirred into activity by speaking, but even her reply contains within it a set-piece description of evening, replete with echoes of similar evocations in Dante and Petrarch (I, 49–54). Her departure (I, 55) is followed by a further description of its effect on the young lover and his reversal of roles from hunter to hunted (I, 56–9). The set-piece depiction of nightfall comes next (I, 60), followed by the present-tense description of Iulio's companions' fears for his safety (I, 61–4), and even their joyful surprise at his return (I, 65–7) contains just one *passato remoto*: 'ognuno allegro alzò le ciglia' (I, 67.1). In the whole of this first section of the poem proper (I, 8–68) there are merely 34 instances of the main narrative tense, the *passato remoto*, an average of just over one every two stanzas, though even the four in I. 10 ('Ah quante ninfe per lui sospirorno! / Ma fu sí altero [. . .] nol piegorno, / mai poté [. . .]') are in fact all descriptive and would normally have been imperfects but for the exigencies of rhyme and metre.

A comparison with Pulci's and Ariosto's poems in the same metre is illuminating: in the same stanzas of his *Giostra* poem (8–68), compared with Poliziano's thirty-four instances, Pulci uses the *passato remoto* eighty times, an average of just over one per stanza (even though much of Pulci's poem up to this point is a description of the participants' clothes and horses); in the same octaves of the *Orlando furioso* (I, 8–68) there are no fewer than eighty-nine uses of the *passato remoto*, an average of almost three instances in each stanza, and more than two and a half times as many as used by Poliziano. This distribution of verb tenses is not the least reason why Ariosto's poem contains more dynamism than Poliziano's.

The main action of the second half of the first book is Cupid's return to Cyprus, but the journey is compressed into two past tenses ('mossesi [. . .] ginne', I, 68, 2–3), before the poem launches into the lengthy description of Venus' garden (I, 69–94) and palace (I, 95–120). In the whole of that ekphrasis, naturally, imperfects and presents abound, and there are only seven instances of the *passato remoto*, mostly relating the mythical deeds sculpted on the doors. In the remaining stanzas of the first book describing Cupid's arrival and his mother's questioning (I, 121–5) there are a more predictable nine instances.

In the second book there is a higher average of the use of this narrative tense (43 in the 46 stanzas), an average of almost one per octave. Nevertheless, many of these are accounted for in the action of the first stanza (4 instances) as Cupid wounds Mars again, and in the burst of activity when Pasitea appears to Morpheus (II, 24–5), these two stanzas alone accounting for thirteen examples. But even in this book, there is still a tendency towards the descriptive mode: once the dream has been dispatched to Iulio, we have a description of the darkness before dawn (II, 27), the dream-vision described in present tense and imperfects (II, 27–34), the reflections on Fortuna and Virtú in the present (II, 35–7), and the description of dawn (II, 38–9, 1–4): in this last section only Iulio's awakening is in the *passato remoto* (II, 39, 5–8); the vision of Glory is in the present (II, 40), as is his final prayer to Amor, Minerva, and Gloria (II, 41–6). Poliziano here thus tends not towards narrative but to beautiful but isolated tableaux of description, and this mode of writing is intimately connected with his distinctive style, as we shall now see.

In terms of theory of style, Poliziano is famous for his intervention in the contemporary debate on literary imitation.[19] In a celebrated exchange of Latin letters with the Ciceronian Paolo Cortesi, Poliziano rejected the whole project of Ciceronian Latin as flawed, particularly in view of the unreliable readings in the manuscript tradition, and championed the cause of those who, like himself, wrote an eclectic Latin that drew on the best styles offered by a range of authors from different centuries, particularly 'Silver Latin' writers such as Quintilian and Statius.

We have seen that each character in the poem is a composite of several other famous personages from classical and vernacular sources, and in this sense Poliziano would agree with today's postmodernists that texts do not refer to anything outside themselves, they simply rewrite other texts: he had already discovered that fashion for rewriting narratives, favoured by today's postmodernists, such as Michel Tournier's rewriting of Robinson Crusoe, or Italo Calvino's rewriting of Ariosto in *Il castello dei destini incrociati*, or of Marco Polo in *Le città invisibili*. The feeling we experience reading Poliziano, that under each line of the *Stanze* there extends a network of echoes of other texts, reminds one of the end of Calvino's *Se una notte d'inverno un viaggiatore*, when the reader discovers that the titles of the ten novels s/he has been trying to read form a perfect opening sentence by themselves: the corollary of this is that each sentence we read in any text may contain ten other texts beneath it, so in the *Stanze* each octave may and often does contain palimpsests of other longer, epic works.

Poliziano's anti-Ciceronianism is paralleled by his rejection of the long, classical epic, for what might be termed the literary equivalent of the soundbite: even at this early stage of his career he had given up translating Homer's *Iliad* into Latin verse, and preferred to translate, again into Latin, the brief, allusive Alexandrian poem by Moschus, *Amor fugitivus* (1473). Nevertheless, since there are countless intertextual echoes of Greek and Latin epic in the *Stanze*, it is clear that Poliziano does not abandon the epic dimension altogether; rather he cultivates a poetics of allusive brevity that at the same time paradoxically hints at the epic vastness of Ovid, Virgil, Dante, and Petrarch. In fact, given Poliziano's poetics of *brevitas*, it is unlikely that even had he completed the poem, *Le stanze* would have run to an epic twelve-book length. As I have suggested elsewhere, in their rejection of the grand style and epic length, in their asymmetrical ekphrasis, and in their intertextual allusivity, the *Stanze* may represent Poliziano's imitation of the epyllion, or mini-epic, imitating the example of Callimachus and Catullus.[20]

The most striking stylistic feature of the poem is the way in which several key passages rehearse standard images from the contemporary debate about literary imitation, and contain self-referential allusions to the intertextual poetics of the *Stanze*: the variety of fauna and flora emphasized throughout the text is emblematic generally of the poet's cult of *docta varietas*, but in particular the image of the bee (I, 25), the harmony of the birds (I, 90), the mosaic description (I, 96) are all echoes of key texts in the imitation debate. A closer analysis of some of these passages illustrates the significance of this aspect of Poliziano's poetics. Let us begin with the set-piece description of the advent of Spring:

1. Zefiro già, di be' fioretti adorni,
2. avea de' monti tolta ogni pruina;
3. avea fatto al suo nido già ritorno
4. la stanca rondinella peregrina;
5. risonava la selva intorno intorno
6. soavemente all'ôra mattutina,
7. e la ingegnosa pecchia al primo albore
8. giva predando ora uno or altro fiore. (I, 25)

If one lists the sources cited by most commentators on the poem, one can observe the poet's eclecticism in practice:

1. Zefiro torna e 'l bel tempo rimena + le rive e i colli di fioretti adorna
    (Petrarch, *RVF* 310, 1 + 9, 6)
2. e quando 'l verno sparge le pruine (Petrarch, *RVF* 72, 13)
3, 5. sí, soprastando al lume intorno intorno [. . .]
    quanto di noi lassú fatto ha ritorno (Dante, *Par.* 30, 112–14)
4. la stanca vecchiarella pellegrina (Petrarch, *RVF* 50, 5)
    la rondinella presso alla mattina (Dante, *Purg.* 9, 14)
5. formosam resonare doces Amaryllida silvas (Virgil, *Ecl.* 1, 5)
6. l'alba vinceva l'ôra mattutina [. . .] soavemente (Dante, *Purg.* 1, 115,
    125)
7–8. We should imitate the bees who fly around selecting the most suitable
    flowers for making honey ('Apes, ut aiunt, debemus imitari quae
    vagantur et flores ad mel faciendum idoneos carpunt', Seneca, *Ep.* 84,
    3); just as bees take from every blossom in the flowery meadows, so
    we should feed on all the best phrases [of other writers] ('Floriferis ut
    apes in saltibus omnia libant,/ omnia nos itidem depascimur aurea
    dicta', Lucretius, *De rerum natura*, 3, 11–12).
    come schiera d'ape che s'infiora (Dante, *Par.* 31, 7)

However, the stanza does not just exemplify the fertile fusion of eclectic
sources. The final image of the bee was invoked by the advocates of
eclectic imitation in Italy from Petrarch onwards, and derived ultimately
from a famous letter of Seneca;[21] however, the wording in the *Stanze*
is clearly closer to the passage in Lucretius, a passage quoted by Poliziano
later in an important, manifesto context, his inaugural lecture to his
first university course in 1480–1, on Quintilian and Statius. There
Lucretius' lines are used to justify the humanist's concentration on
authors whom others consider inferior to—but who, he argues, are
merely different from—Cicero and Virgil.[22] This densely intertextual
octave thus both describes the emblematic bee taking pollen from
many different flowers and inscribes within this description the very
textual strategies the stanza deploys.

A similar role is performed by the other passages. Here is the
description of the birds singing in Venus' paradise garden:

> Li augelletti dipinti tra le foglie
> fanno l'aere addolcir con nuove rime;
> e fra piú voci un'armonia s'accoglie
> di sí beate note e sí sublime [. . .] (I, 90)

The wording here shows that it alludes to another image from the
Seneca letter, that of the harmony of a choir: 'Do you not see how a
choir is made up of many voices, but a unity is produced from the

variety of voices, [. . .] and harmony emerges from different sounds' ('Non vides quam multorum vocibus chorus constet? Unus tamen ex omnibus redditur [. . .] fit concentus ex dissonis', Seneca, *Ep.* 84, 9–10).

The description of the mosaic pavement does not have a specific ancient source, but it does derive from a key passage about classical antiquity by an author of the previous generation, much admired by Poliziano:

> Le mura atorno d'artificio miro
> forma un soave e lucido berillo.
> Passa pel dolce oriental zaffiro
> nell'ampio albergo el dí puro e tranquillo:
> ma il tetto d'oro, in cui l'estremo giro
> si chiude, contra a Febo apre il vessillo:
> per varie pietre el pavimento ameno
> di mirabil pittura adorno il seno.   (I, 96)

At the outset of Book II of Leon Battista Alberti's *Profugiorum ab aerumna libri*, the narrator discusses the impossibility for modern authors of saying anything new without repeating, intentionally or unwittingly, what had already been written by ancient authors:

E veggonsi queste cose litterarie usurpate da tanti, e in tanti loro scritti adoperate e disseminate, che oggi a chi voglia ragionarne resta altro nulla che solo el raccogliere e assortirle e poi accoppiarle insieme con qualche varietà dagli altri e adattezza dell'opera sua, quasi suo instituto sia imitare in questo chi altrove fece el pavimento.[23]

Alberti here parallels the modern author with the ancient craftsman who, according to classical legend, first discovered the art of mosaic ('questo pingere e figurare, come fanno, el pavimento', ibid., II, 160) by putting together the coloured fragments that lay on the floor of the temple of Ephesus: in much the same way, argues Alberti, the modern writer can only seek originality by inserting into his work in a new order various fragments of classical texts. Poliziano was the true inheritor of Alberti's own anti-Ciceronianism, and much admired his individualistic Latin.[24]

Another key feature of Poliziano's style, which may explain the otherwise excessive length of the ekphrasis in Book I, was his cult of asymmetry. He explicitly defends this aesthetic of disproportion ('disparilitas') in the preface to the *Miscellanea* (1489), a preface which is perhaps his most articulate literary manifesto, and which defends his most important Latin work. The models for the *Miscellanea*, a series of 100 chapters discussing major problems of interpretation in classical texts, are the works of Aelian and Aulus Gellius, which are for Poliziano 'books that are more attractive for their variety than for their order' ('libri varietate quam ordine blandiores'), and if these literary models do not constitute sufficient legitimation of his own *varietas*, the humanist claims that this 'disparilitas' is a feature of nature herself, of whom he is 'a disciple in asymmetry' ('disparilitate discipulum').[25] In particular he justifies the structural disproportion of the long and short chapters as well as the work's stylistic variety, surveying as it does a whole range of authors, and describes its style as 'a mosaic-like style, dotted, as it were, with different coloured fragments' ('vermiculata interim dictio, et tessellis pluricoloribus variegata', *Opera*, p. 214). This vivid phrase, which as a description of Poliziano's style was destined to have lengthy critical currency even down to our own time, quickly became a crucial slogan for the humanist's critics and supporters. Shortly after the publication of the *Miscellanea*, his enemy Giorgio Merula derides it as one of Poliziano's 'metaphorae imprudentes':

Likewise, I cannot understand why you defend or want to inflict on us your 'mosaic-like style', except that you would have given all men some precious information if you had explained what 'mosaic-like' means when it is used, I presume, by writers on architecture. (Cur item 'vermiculatam dictionem' vel opponas vel ingeras non plane percipio, nisi quod aliquid gratiae etiam hominibus inibis, si explanaveris quid 'vermiculatam' architecturae scriptores intelligent).[26]

However, around the same time, in a letter of 31 December 1489, one of Poliziano's pupils, Francesco Pucci, openly defends his teacher's style, telling him about the enthusiastic reception in Naples of the *Miscellanea,* and celebrating 'its style which plays with varied and almost mosaic-like intertextual allusions, cultivating all the most elegant Latin words, yet always displaying an authentic and even pure Latinity' ('[oratio] vario quodam, at prope vermiculato intertextu lasciviens, omnesque verborum flosculos captans, candorem tamen ubique Latinitatis, et quasi pudicitiam praefert'; Poliziano, *Opera*, p. 77). Two words here are worth dwelling on: the adjective 'vermiculato' (patterned like a mosaic) and 'intertextu' used as a noun. 'Vermiculatus' became, as we have seen, almost a slogan used by Poliziano, his eclectic followers, and his Ciceronian critics, but it derives from two of the 'new' classical texts discovered at Lodi in 1421, Cicero's *Brutus* and the *Orator*. In the latter Cicero quotes Lucilius' criticism of Albucius Scaevola's style: 'How precisely his phrases are ordered, as though they were all mosaic fragments set artfully and meaningfully in an inlaid floor' ('Quam lepide lexis compostae ut tesserulae omnes / arte pavimento atque emblemate vermiculato') (Cicero, *Orator*, 44, 149; see also Brutus, 274). The mosaic image was thus associated with a style that is criticized by Cicero, therefore it is explicitly anti-Ciceronian. Clearly Poliziano's use of the term polemically echoes Cicero's quotation here, but Pucci's formulation comes instead from the favourite model of the anti-Ciceronians, Quintilian: '[The orator] abandoning weighty content will simply construct "little mosaic fragments", as Lucilius calls them, and will knit together mosaic-like patterns of words' ('Relicto rerum pondere [. . .] "tesserulas", ut ait Lucilius, struet et vermiculate inter se lexis conmittet') (*Institutio oratoria*, IX, 4, 113). But whatever the source, what is clear is that both Poliziano and his pupil reverse the value of 'vermiculatae lexis': what for Cicero and Quintilian (and indeed for Lucilius) had been an excessive attention to individual lexical elements at the expense of content and overall composition of the sentence, is considered as a positive stylistic practice by the two anti-Ciceronian humanists.

As for 'intertextus', since Pucci is clearly echoing Poliziano's own phraseology in his sentence in words such as 'vermiculato', 'flosculos', 'candorem' (Poliziano's 'vermiculata interim dictio, et tessellis pluricoloribus variegata' is inverted by his pupil to become '[oratio] vario quodam, at prope vermiculato intertextu lasciviens'), it is likely that the term 'intertextus' is also one favoured by Poliziano himself. If the mosaic image sends us back via Alberti to the *Stanze*, that word 'intertextu' used by Pucci of Poliziano's style is also emblematic of his new allusive way of writing. 'Intertextus' had only been used literally by classical authors, as a participle, of interweaving in fabrics:

As he left he gave me a gold-embroidered cloak ('Discedens chlamydemque auro dedit intertextam'; Virgil, *Aeneid*, 8, 167)

The outer edge of Arachne's tapestry was bordered by a fine hem containing flowers entwined with creeping ivy ('Ultima pars telae tenui circumdata limbo, / nexilibus flores hederis habet intertextos'; Ovid, *Metamorphoses*, 6, 127–8)

Similarly in the vernacular, in the only occurrence of the word, in Cornazzano's *Vita di Pietro Avogadro bresciano*, it is used as an adjective:

> E taccio i triunfali archi intertexti
> pur di purissimo oro i[n] marmo bianco.[27]

However, in the *Miscellanea* and the texts that surround it, Poliziano and his circle are clearly using the term metaphorically, as a noun, and referring to the interweaving of literary texts, much as we now use the term 'intertextuality': even in the *Stanze* he uses the metaphor of the text as a woven tapestry when he defines himself as a 'testor di carmi' (II, 15).

The *Miscellanea* also show that Poliziano was familiar with classical examples of ekphrasis: in chapter 49 he discusses a Greek poet's description of the statue of Occasio in these terms: 'let us look at Callistratus' elegant ekphrasis describing the same statue' ('sed et Callistrati legimus ecphrasim simulachri eiusdem mire festivam', *Opera*, p. 269), as well as noting in chapter 23 Callimachus' rejection of the epic for the short, learned poem *Hecale* (p. 246). Asymmetry, ekphrasis, allusive intertextuality are then the keynotes of Poliziano's mature Latin works but they are already hallmarks of his style in the *Stanze*.[28]

The image of the scattered fragment, evident already in the early *Stanze*, was to remain with Poliziano throughout his writing in both Latin and the vernacular. In the letter which he penned for Lorenzo to preface the *Raccolta aragonese* (1476), he talks of the Homeric poems being dispersed, then gathered together by the Athenian ruler Pisistratus, thus being restored from death to life:

quasi da morte a sí lunga vita restituto. Imperocché, essendo la sacra opera di questo celebratissimo poeta dopo la sua morte per molti e vari luoghi della Grecia dissipata e quasi dismembrata, Pisistrato, ateniese principe, [. . .] con somma diligenzia ed esamine tutto il corpo del santissimo poeta insieme raccolse.[29]

The *Raccolta* is seen as performing an exercise of cultural *pietas* analogous to that carried out by Pisistratus. Italian or rather Tuscan poetry is then paralleled with classical literature in two ways: first by suggesting that the early Italian poets risked being lost in the 'naufragio' that allowed so many classical texts to perish, and second when Poliziano recycles the (inaccurate) analogy used by Petrarch (*Familiares* 1, 1), when he suggested that Italian poetry—differing from classical verse by its use of rhyme—was in some sense a renaissance of ancient Roman Saturnian metre:

Fu l'uso della rima, secondo che in una latina epistola scrive il Petrarca, ancora presso gli antichi romani assai celebrato; il quale, per molto tempo intermesso, cominciò poi nella Sicilia non molti secoli avanti a rifiorire, e, quindi per la Francia sparto, finalmente in Italia, quasi in un suo ostello, a pervenire.[30]

The motif of the violent scattering of *disiecta membra* resurfaces also in the third important vernacular work by Poliziano, the *Favola di Orfeo* (1480), another brief, fragmentary text which ends with Orpheus being torn limb from limb by the Bacchae. Once again a myth for which there are several intertextual sources proves attractive to Poliziano, and allows his metrically and lexically varied style in the play to echo the theme of dispersal. In fact in the dedicatory letter to Carlo Canale he explicitly alludes to the tearing apart of Orpheus: 'desideravo ancora io che la fabula di Orfeo [. . .] fussi di subito, non altrimenti che esso Orfeo, lacerata: cognoscendo questa mia figliuola essere di qualità da far piú tosto al suo padre vergogna che onore'.[31] The poet's destructive impulse was, he claimed, occasioned by his feeling that the Fabula had been written 'in tempo di dua giorni, intra continui tumulti, in stilo vulgare', though this should probably not be taken too literally.[32] However we interpret his denigration of the *Orfeo*, what is certain is that once again the poet fears for textual fragmentation and dispersal, and this sense of the text as fragment, as vulnerable texture, no doubt derived from his own Herculean labours in reconstituting the correct readings of ancient works. This association of the text with fragmentation and a corresponding obsession with myths of dispersal remained with the humanist until the end of his life. For it is another great myth of *sparagmos* or scattering, the Hippolytus story, that opens the first chapter of the humanist's final great work, the second century of the *Miscellanea*, written in the final year of his life (1493–4):

Cicero's work *De natura deorum* is, in all recent and ancient manuscripts, as mutilated as mythical Hippolytus once was when he was 'torn apart by his enraged horses': his limbs which were scattered everywhere were then, as the myths tell us, collected by famous Aesculapius, put together again, and he was restored to life, though in the end he was killed by a thunderbolt because of the envy of the gods at his return to earthly existence.

But I shall not be deterred by any envy or thunderbolt from attempting to restore to life Cicero, the father of both the Latin language and Latin philosophy, who has been mutilated again in his writings, just as he was beheaded at the end of his life by his enemy Mark Anthony.[33]

Conclusion

Poliziano was extremely conscious of living in post-classical times, and although his age aspired towards a re-naissance of classical texts and values, processes in which he played a major part, nevertheless he was haunted by the fragility and fragmentary nature of the written text. The fragment is both a signifier of the vulnerability of the text, and, as mosaic, part of a newly reconstituted aesthetic work. It is also for this reason that the image of the fragment and the mosaic permeate his works, and it is interesting that critical discourse on Poliziano continues to recycle this imagery of the mosaic or the fragment in characterizing his art.[34] But while the humanist's preservation of the classical canon might seem to inscribe him within that dominant tradition, his cult of the fragment as something that has in itself intrinsic aesthetic value makes him seem closer to our own age: as Ihab Hassan has said, 'Fragmentation—literature as bits and pieces rather than as an integrated totality—is the basic property of postmodernism.'[35] In a similar way, as has been shown by Lecointe, Poliziano's rejection of the hierarchical concept of a Golden Age in literature that is followed by an Age of Silver or decline confirms his fragmentary eclecticism as a radical post-classical alternative.[36] The poet's non-hierarchical attitude to antiquity has important analogies with our own postmodern condition and our approach to the Western literary canon. No doubt this feeling of fragility was exacerbated in the last years of his life, in the final decade of the century, and in the upheaval in Florence between the death of Lorenzo in 1492 and the collapse of the Medici regime two years later. For all these reasons, including that *fin-de-siècle* mood, Poliziano is a Renaissance writer who holds a paradoxically modern appeal for us. The work that best encapsulates these values, despite its early date, is *Le stanze per la giostra*. In its cult of intertextuality and rewriting, in its constant deferring of the action, in its poetics of the fragmentary and discontinuous, the *Stanze per la giostra* seems a strangely modern, even postmodern text. Not surprisingly, the most recent work on Poliziano has drawn attention to the self-reflexive and metatextual constants in his writings in both languages: Bettinzoli speaks of 'la puntigliosa e stratificata autoriflessività di quella scrittura, il suo prender forma sotto i confini di una metatestualità che oscilla tra anatomia critica e ricomposizione delle proprie fonti'; while Bausi defines the humanist's Latin *Silvae* as a 'prodotto essenzialmente metapoetico, [. . .] un brillante esempio di poesia sulla, della e con la poesia'.[37] Calvino said of Borges that the secret of the Argentinian writer's fiction was that it adhered to a strict rhetorical ideal of *brevitas*, which at the same time paradoxically offered glimpses of an epic infinity.[38] As we have seen, neither this terminology nor the textual practices it enshrines would have been foreign to Poliziano.

Notes to Chapter 6

1. Edmund J. Smyth (ed.), *Postmodernism and Contemporary Fiction* (London: Batsford, 1991), 9. A similar list is found in Patricia Waugh (ed.), *Postmodernism: A Reader* (London and New York: Edward Arnold, 1992), 3.

2. Throughout I cite from Angelo Poliziano, *Stanze. Orfeo. Rime*, ed. Davide Puccini (Milan: Garzanti, 1992), 1–141. See now also Angelo Poliziano, *Poesie volgari*, ed. Francesco Bausi, 2 vols. (Rome: Vecchiarelli, 1997), i. 5–42.

3. See the edition of Pulci's *La giostra* in Luigi Pulci, *Opere minori*, ed. Paolo Orvieto (Milan: Mursia, 1986), 53–120. For the links between Pulci's and Poliziano's poems see Mark Davie, '"Questo Agnol [. . .] nato per gloria di Montepulciano": la testimonianza di Luigi Pulci', in Luisa Secchi Tarugi (ed.), *Poliziano nel suo tempo* (Florence: Cesati, 1996), 33–44.

4. Warman Welliver, 'The Subject and Purpose of Poliziano's *Stanze*', *Italica*, 48 (1971), 34–47.

5. For a fuller survey of recent interpretations of the *Stanze* see Emilio Bigi, 'Impegno civile e allegorie neoplatoniche nelle *Stanze*', in Secchi Tarugi, *Poliziano nel suo tempo*, 45–54. For a general survey see Attilio Bettinzoli, 'Rassegna di studi sul Poliziano (1972–86)', *Lettere italiane*, 39 (1987), 53–125; id., 'Rassegna di studi sul Poliziano (1987–93)', *Lettere italiane*, 45 (1993), 592–64.

6. Ida Maier, *Ange Politien: La Formation d'un poète humaniste, 1469–1480* (Geneva: Droz, 1969), 288; Maria Luisa Doglio, 'Metamorfosi, simbolo e favola. Per una lettura delle *Stanze* del Poliziano', *Italianistica*, 12 (1983), 197–216.

7. *The 'Stanze' of Angelo Poliziano*, trans. David Quint (Amherst: University of Massachusetts Press, 1979), pp. xiv–xv.

8. Arnolfo B. Ferruolo, 'A Trend in Renaissance Thought and Art: Poliziano's *Stanze*', *Romanic Review*, 44 (1953), 246–56.

9. Poliziano, *Stanze. Fabula di Orfeo*, ed. Stefano Carrai (Milan: Mursia, 1988), 5–12.

10. S. Berman, 'Neoplatonism in Poliziano's *Stanze*', *Forum Italicum*, 15 (1981), 11–21.

11. R. H. Terpening, 'Poliziano's Treatment of a Classical Topos', *Italian Quarterly*, 17 (1973), 39–71.

12. P. McNair, 'The Bed of Venus', *Italian Studies*, 25 (1970), 40–8.

13. Vittore Branca, 'L'idea trionfale delle *Stanze*', in *Poliziano e l'umanesimo della parola* (Turin: Einaudi, 1983), 44–54.

14. Mario Martelli, 'Le *Stanze per la Giostra*: simbolo e struttura', in his *Angelo Poliziano: storia e metastoria* (Lecce: Conte, 1995), 101–37. The essay originally appeared as a postface to Poliziano, *Stanze cominciate per la giostra di Giuliano de' Medici* (Alpignano: Tallone, 1979), 127–31.

15. Of the following list of animals mentioned in I, 8–68, only those marked by an asterisk have no exact correspondence in the garden or palace doors of Venus: horse (8), beasts (9, 17), birds (17), *goats, sheep, cows (18), sheep, *geese (19), bull (23), tigers, lions, *dragons (24), *swallow, *bees (25), *owl, horse, dogs (26), beasts, dogs (27), beasts (28), dogs, horses, beasts (29), boar, kid, deer, *fox, hares, wolf (30), hounds, deer, greyhound, boar, mastiff, horse (31), centaurs, bear, lion (32), beasts (33), doe, beasts, horse (34), doe, horse (34–8); tiger (39); birds (44), *cricket, *cicada (54), birds (55), beast (59), nightingale (60), prey (61), wolf, bull (66). The range of animals mentioned in this short poem is also no doubt connected to the poetics of *varietas* which the poet cultivated and which is discussed below.

16. For an interpretation that places the entire emphasis on the hunt, see Marina Ricucci, 'Le *stanze*: storia di una caccia', *Lettere italiane*, 47 (1995), 517–48.

17. Marsilio Ficino, *El libro dell'amore*, ed. Sandra Niccoli (Florence: Olschki, 1987), 214.

18. For the many classical and vernacular sources involved, see in particular Sapegno's notes to these passages, in Poliziano, *Rime,* ed. Natalino Sapegno (Rome: Ateneo, 1967); Rossella Bessi's articles: 'Per un nuovo commento alle *Stanze*', *Lettere italiane*, 31 (1979), 309–41; 'Le *Stanze* del Poliziano e la lirica del primo Quattrocento', *Lettere italiane*, 48 (1996), 3–24; and Bausi's commentary in Poliziano, *Poesie volgari*, vol. ii.

19. On the whole question of literary imitation, see Martin L. McLaughlin, *Literary Imitation in the Italian Renaissance: The Theory and Practice of Literary Imitation in Italy from Dante to Bembo* (Oxford: Clarendon Press, 1995), especially 187–227 for Poliziano's interventions.

20. See ibid. 189–90. Although the term epyllion was not invented until the 19th c., Poliziano's enthusiasm for these mini-epics is well documented.

21. See G. W. Pigman III, 'Versions of Imitation in the Renaissance', *Renaissance Quarterly*, 33 (1980), 1–32.

22. *Prosatori latini del Quattrocento*, ed. Eugenio Garin (Milan and Naples: Ricciardi, 1952), 870–80 (esp. 878).

23. Leon Battista Alberti, *Opere*, ed. Cecil Grayson, 3 vols. (Bari: Laterza, 1960–73), ii. 161. For the importance of this 'pagina formidabile' in Alberti, see Roberto Cardini, *Mosaici: Il 'Nemico' dell'Alberti* (Rome: Bulzoni, 1990), 4.

24. For Poliziano's admiration of Alberti, particularly his dedicatory letter to Lorenzo of the 1485 edition of Alberti's *De re aedificatoria*, see McLaughlin, *Literary Imitation*, 198 n. 31.

25. 'Denique si varietas ipsa fastidii expultrix, et lectionis irritatrix in Miscellaneis culpabitur, una opera reprehendi rerum quoque natura poterit, cuius me quidem profiteor tali disparilitate discipulum' (Angelus Politianus, *Opera quae quidem extitere hactenus omnia* (Basle: apud Nicolaum Episcopium iuniorem, 1553), p. 213). Further references to the Latin works are to this edition (henceforth *Opera*) and will be given in the text.

26. Cited from L. Perotto Sali, 'L'opusculo inedito di Giorgio Merula contro *I*

Miscellanea di Angelo Poliziano', *Interpres*, 1 (1978), 146–83 at 161–2. On this exchange see two new important contributions in Vincenzo Fera, Mario Martelli (eds.), *Poliziano: poeta, scrittore, filologo, Atti del Convegno internazionale di studi, Montepulciano, 3–6 novembre 1994* (Florence: Le Lettere, 1998); Silvio Rizzo, 'Il latino del Poliziano' (83–125, esp. 94–100); and Vincenzo Fera, 'Il diabattito umanistico sui *Miscellanea*' (333–64).

27. Antonio Cornazzano, *Vita di Piero Avogadro*, (Brescia, Bibl. Queriniana, MS B.VII.13), c 5ʳ. I am grateful to Diego Zancani for this contemporary vernacular reference—see his article, 'Un recupero quattrocentesco: *La vita di Pietro Avogadro bresciano* di Antonio Cornazzano e il lavoro di un editore del Cinquecento (Remigio Nannini)', in *Libri, tipografi, biblioteche: ricerche dedicate a Luigi Balsamo*, ed. Istituto di Biblioteconomia e Paleografia, Università degli Studi, Parma (Florence: Olschki, 1997), i. 145–67. Interestingly, Alberti uses a similar textual metaphor in his mosaic passage: 'el tessere e connodare in un sieme vari detti e grave sentenze' (*Opere*, ii. 162).

28. On intertextuality in the Latin poems, see Perrine Galand, 'L'Enargeia chez Politien', *Bibliothèque d'Humanisme et Renaissance*, 49 (1987), 25–53.

29. See the *Epistola a Federico d'Aragona*, in Lorenzo de' Medici, *Opere*, ed. Attilio Simioni, 2 vols. (Bari: Laterza, 1913), i. 4.

30. Ibid. 6.

31. Poliziano, *Stanze. Orfeo. Rime,* ed. Puccini, 145–6.

32. Tissoni Benvenuti has shown that this may be a mere topos, based on a similar passage in Statius' *Silvae*, and indeed that Poliziano particularly valued a poetics of sudden inspiration ('subito calore'): see Antonia Tissoni Benvenuti, *L'Orfeo di Poliziano, con il testo critico dell'originale e delle successive forme teatrali* (Padua: Antenore, 1986), 6–10.

33. 'Ciceronis liber de deorum natura non minus lacer in omnibus novis, vetustis etiam exemplaribus reperitur quam olim fuerit Hippolytus turbatis distractus equis; cuius deinde avulsa passim membra, sicuti fabulae ferunt, Aesculapius ille collegit, reposuit, vitae reddidit; qui tamen deinde fulmine ictus ob invidiam deorum narratur. Me vero quaenam deterrebit invidia, quod fulmen, quo minus restituere ipsum sibi coner romanae vel linguae vel philosophiae parentem, nescio equidem a quo rursus Antonio truncatum capite et manibus?' (Angelo Poliziano, *Miscellaneorum Centuria Secunda,* ed. Vittore Branca and Manlio Pastore Stocchi (Florence: Olschki, 1978), 3.)

34. To cite just two examples from many, Ghino Ghinassi, *Il volgare letterario del Quattrocento e le 'Stanze' del Poliziano* (Florence: Le Monnier, 1957) talks of the poet's 'gusto estetico di mosaicista' (p. 85); while Davide Puccini states: 'crediamo che l'arte del Poliziano sia eminentemente arte del particolare se non del frammento' (Poliziano, *Stanze. Orfeo. Rime,* ed. Puccini, p. xlviii).

35. Quoted in Smyth, *Postmodernism and Contemporary Fiction,* 11.

36. J. Lecointe, 'Structures hiérarchiques et théorie critique à la Renaissance', *Bibliothèque d'Humanisme et Renaissance*, 52 (1990), 529–60.

37. Attilio Bettinzoli, *'Daedaleum iter': studi sulla poesia e poetica di Angelo Poliziano* (Florence: Olschki, 1995), 8; Angelo Poliziano, *Silvae,* ed. Francesco Bausi (Florence: Olschki, 1996), p. xvi.

38. Italo Calvino, 'Jorge Luis Borges', in his *Perché leggere i classici* (Milan: Mondadori, 1991), 292–301 (esp. p. 294).

CHAPTER 7

Pico della Mirandola's 1485 Parody of Scholastic 'Barbarians'

Letizia Panizza

Sed nihil est tam incredibile quod non, dicendo, fiat probabile; nihil tam horridum tam incultum quod non splendescat oratione et tamquam excolatur. (But nothing is so difficult to believe that oratory cannot make it acceptable, nothing so coarse and uncultured as not to gain brilliance and refinement from eloquence.)

CICERO, *Paradoxa stoicorum* (Prooemium 3)[1]

Following a dominant line of interpretation, Pico della Mirandola's (1463–94) 1485 long letter addressed to Ermolao Barbaro (1454–93) containing a speech of a medieval Scholastic represents a decisive moment in Quattrocento disputes on the relationship between philosophy and rhetoric. Young Pico, not yet 20 years old and fresh from Scholastic studies, is seen as championing the medievals and their 'barbaric' language. He throws down the gauntlet to generations of humanists going back to Petrarch and including his contemporaries Barbaro and Poliziano, and teaches them a lesson about the dangers of becoming overly preoccupied with philological minutiae, with elegant icing on the cake of truth. The dispute has often been reduced to a simple opposition between philosophy and rhetoric, *res* and *verba*, in which Pico is on one side and Barbaro on the other. In English-speaking countries, this dominant line has been held over many decades by Paul Oskar Kristeller, who put it thus:

Pico praises and defends the medieval philosophers, and insists with great eloquence that what counts in the writings of philosophers is not their words or style, but their thoughts or content. Whereas Ermolao [. . .] despised the scholastic philosophers for their lack of elegance and classical learning, Pico is willing to recognize the solidity of their thought, and to learn from them whatever truth or insight they may have to offer. The line between humanism and scholasticism is clearly drawn as the borderline between rhetoric and philosophy, and Pico, though deeply imbued with humanist learning [. . .] throws his weight on the side of scholasticism.[2]

There are problems about maintaining the above view. In what could be called a counter-current, other scholars have expressed their sense of the complexity, ambiguity, if not irony of Pico's letter, especially regarding the praise of a 'barbaric' style couched, in fact, in an elegance far from Scholastic practice. Hanna Gray was the first to speak of irony; and Brian Vickers has called Pico's piece a mock encomium. Martin McLaughlin and Francesco Bausi have studied Pico's language in this letter, and noted his knowledge of Latin and Greek classics.[3] My own approach would stress the *serio ludere* or 'serious playfulness' of the letter, manifested by all manners of contradictions and absurdities in the speech, and above all, by the parody of classical and early Christian sources—and Quattrocento ones as well. The humour has the purpose of undermining the apparent thesis, showing it to be ridiculous, and drawing attention to a continual double message at work. What Pico and Barbaro 'really' believe is to be found in the hidden and distorted classical sources themselves.

How do we go about finding this out? The first step of my own investigation has been to bring Barbaro much more into account, since the almost exclusive emphasis on Pico's letter has led to Barbaro's long answer, also in the form of a letter-speech, being neglected and even ignored. Barbaro, after all, started the dispute with a letter to Pico of the same year, 1485; and he also closed it. Pico is sandwiched in between, answering Barbaro's first letter, and being answered by Barbaro's second. In an earlier study, I have shown that it was Barbaro who supplied the first comprehensive interpretation of Pico's letter-speech in the introductory section of his reply. There, it was Barbaro who took great pains to spell out the kind of speech Pico had composed—a paradoxical piece, full of learned humour, in which Pico had undermined his apparent praise of Scholastic philosophers and their hatred of style:

You [. . .] defend the barbarians against Barbaro, and consequently pretend
to stand on the enemy's side as if you were your own enemy! [. . .] What I
like most of course is that by feigning a defence you fatally slit the throats of
the ones you defend. Your reasons for doing this are first, the enemies of
eloquence appear unable to protect themselves except by means of eloquent
men—as if they were slaves, women, or dumb animals; and second, if they
are unable to save themselves with you as their champion, advocate, and
protector, still less are they able to engage in combat with you, or, turning
their backs, refuse to do so [. . .] We understand the kind of speech it is and
its double meaning. (*Prosatori latini*, 844)[4]

It was Barbaro who defined the controversy *De genere dicendi philosophorum*, that is, about the appropriate style for philosophical prose
(not, it should be stressed, on the conflict between rhetoric and
philosophy!). And finally, it was Barbaro who made clear that there was
no disagreement between himself and Pico, 'homo lepidissimus,
humanissimus, latinissimus', but rather between the two of them and
the producers of impenetrable Aristotelian Scholastic writings that were
a travesty of Aristotle. Barbaro's invention of an Aristotelian Scholastic
from the University of Padua who praises his own ignorance of the
genuine Aristotle, whose works he has never read and never will,
'numquam lectos, numquam legendos!', he boasts (*Prosatori latini*, 850),
counterpoises Pico's creation. I have also shown that Barbaro's own
voice is encoded in a series of (hitherto neglected) marginal diagrams
of syllogisms, from which the attentive reader can conclude, among
other things, that according to Aristotle rhetoric and dialectic are part
of philosophy, and cannot, therefore, be opposed.[5]

The Biographical and Cultural Context

There are reasons external to the text for questioning the dominant
interpretation.[6] Neither biographical facts nor Barbaro's and Pico's
cultural formation prior to 1485 can sustain the theses of either Pico
despising classical letters and eloquence, or Barbaro despising Aristotle.
On the contrary, in 1485 Barbaro was first and foremost an Aristotelian
philosopher who taught Aristotle, including rhetoric and dialectic, at
the University of Padua, and privately at his home in Venice. In 1478–9,
furthermore, he had translated into Latin not only Aristotle's *Ars
rhetoricae* (a new text for Italian humanists, neglected by Scholastics),
but also late Greek commentaries on Aristotle. In 1482, Pico himself
had praised Barbaro's Latin translation of Themistius, entitled *Libri*

paraphraseos, and he returned to the praise of Themistius in the 1485 letter (*Prosatori latini*, 822).[7] After studying Scholastic philosophy at Ferrara and Paris, Pico, on the other hand, had come to Florence to study Greek and classical literature with Poliziano, and Plato with Ficino. Just before answering Barbaro, Pico had written to Lorenzo de' Medici on the subject of poetry (*Prosatori latini*, 796–805); and contemporaneous with answering Barbaro, Pico was engaged in writing a philosophical commentary in the vernacular on a love poem by Girolamo Benivieni. A recent edition of his own love lyrics demonstrates a more than amateurish acquaintance with the Italian lyric poetry tradition, especially Dante and Petrarch.[8] In a letter to Poliziano, Pico complained of being rejected by philosophers because of his interest in literature, and by humanists because of his interest in Scholastic philosophy and theology. He himself felt penalized for trying to straddle both subjects; the result was that 'I am neither a poet, nor an orator, nor a philosopher (*ut nec poeta, nec rhetor sim, neque philosophus*).[9]

The cultural context, especially the discovery and study of Ciceronian texts on oratory, and through Cicero to the re-evaluation of Aristotle as an excellent stylist as well as an excellent philosopher, is another compelling reason. A key passage in the *De oratore*, for example, presents Crassus, the most outstanding Roman orator according to Cicero, arguing for a parity of merit between the best kind of orator and the best kind of philosopher. Its values inform not only Pico's own oration, but Barbaro's as well—indeed, the passage is a perfect illustration of how so many views expressed in this and other Ciceronian dialogues could be applied with very little modification to Quattrocento conflicts between Scholastics and humanists:

At this stage, I give full leave to anybody who wishes, to apply the title of orator to a philosopher who imparts to us an abundant command of facts and of language, or alternatively I shall raise no obstacle if he prefers to designate as a philosopher the orator whom I on my side am now describing as possessing wisdom combined with eloquence (*sapientiam iunctam* [. . .] *eloquentiae*): only provided it be agreed that neither the tongue-tied silence of the man who knows the facts but cannot explain them in language, nor the ignorance of the person who is deficient in facts but has no lack of words, is deserving of praise. If one has to choose between them, for my part I should prefer wisdom lacking power of expression (*indisertam prudentiam*) to talkative folly (*stultitiam loquacem*); but if we are trying to find the one thing that stands top of the whole list, the prize must go to the orator who possesses learning (*docto oratori palma danda est*).[10]

Note that Crassus is remarkably tolerant towards a person who knows much, but is unable to express himself well. Such a person is not to be praised, but neither is he to be condemned (a position that encouraged humanists in the second half of the Quattrocento not to exclude Scholastics entirely from their studies). Far worse is the loquacious ignoramus who knows little or nothing about what he proposes to discuss (a position that could apply to compulsive talkers on either side). If one had to choose the lesser evil, the tongue-tied man of learning (in Quattrocento terms, the Scholastic) was preferable to the fool talking nonsense.

In Cicero's *Orator*, furthermore, a text known to humanists only after 1421, Aristotle is held up as the model for an orator who wants to unite not only eloquence with philosophy in general, but also rhetoric with dialectic. Cicero translates the opening words of Aristotle's *Ars rhetoricae*—a translation Barbaro follows verbatim in his own rendering of the treatise—as follows: 'Aristoteles principio artis rhetoricae dicit illam artem *quasi ex altera parte* (*antistrophos*) respondere dialecticae' ('At the beginning of his *Ars rhetoricae*, Aristotle says that rhetoric is like the counterpart to dialectic'). However one translates *antistrophos*, it emerges that for Cicero, Aristotle held both rhetoric and dialectic in esteem, and did not treat one as the enemy of the other, like his supposed medieval and Renaissance disciples.[11]

Another fundamental doctrine underlying the Pico–Barbaro exchange concerned the need for both content and clear expression in a prose composition. At the beginning of Book III of his *Ars rhetoricae* (i, 2, 1403b), Aristotle explains that it is no use having good ideas unless one can express them in a suitable way. The principle of *prepon* or *decorum* rules, according to which one chooses the right style for the subject being treated; for prose, lucidity—the Greek *sapheneia*, translated by Barbaro as *perspicuitas*—becomes the most appropriate quality (III, ii, 1–2, 1404b). On the other hand, its opposite, *obscuritas*, becomes an object of scorn. Also relevant for Pico and Barbaro is Aristotle's distinction between the art of rhetoric and sophistry, the latter being the deliberate use of fallacious arguments (I, i, 1355b). Aristotle had composed a whole work, *On Sophistical Refutations*, so that the philosopher could recognize fallacies in an opponent's arguments, and avoid committing them himself. A final point concerns the increasing study and translation in the Quattrocento of Greek rhetoric, in particular by George of Trebizond, whose massive *Rhetoricorum libri V* incorporated all of the Greek rhetorical tradition with the Latin, in which Cicero stood supreme. George of Trebizond, following Hermogenes, also stressed the importance of lucidity as the appropriate quality of prose composition.[12]

The Authorial Frame of Pico's Letter

The parody within Pico's letter itself—I turn now to internal evidence—represents the most conspicuous example he uses of a whole range of strategies that come under the general heading *serio ludere* ('playful seriousness'), admired in antiquity by Horace and Cicero, not to mention Lucian. In the 'frame' parts of Pico's letter, in which he speaks *in propria persona*, Pico provides us with hints about the speech of the invented Scholastic he raises from the dead, and to whom he gives a voice that is not his own (Barbaro's letter-oration follows a similar pattern).[13] Pico indulges in ironic self-deprecation before the speech, and in admissions of paradox and writing a false praise at the very end. Thus, after reading Barbaro's first letter, Pico feels stung. Barbaro's original words need recalling not only because Pico echoes and re-echoes them, but also because they have been almost always taken out of context. Barbaro had been encouraging young Pico to study the best Latin and Greek writers, Christian and pagan, and specifies:

I do not count among Latin authors those Germans and Teutons who were scarcely alive when they lived, and who live on much less now they are dead—or if they do live on, they live to be tormented and despised, since they are commonly called base, unlettered, uncultivated, barbaric (*sordidi, rudes, inculti, barbari*).[14]

To imagine that subject matter was enough was like imagining that an ignorant person could write the *Iliad* or the *Aeneid* simply because he chose the same themes: absurdities that called for making jokes ('Qui enim possum non *iocari* quum scribo *de ridiculis?*' *Epistolae*, p. 86). Barbaro's judgement, often misread as a valuing of style over content, is similar to what Aristotle and Cicero had said in *Ars rhetoricae* and *De oratore* (above), and even closer to Cicero's remarks in the introduction to his *Paradoxa stoicorum* about professional Stoic philosophers of his own age (see the epigraph to this chapter). Cicero condemned the

Stoics for a style termed *horridus* and *incultus*—very much the same adjectives used by Barbaro for the Scholastics. They wrote in such a way, lamented Cicero, that nobody beyond a narrow circle of initiates could understand them, and failed to understand that no matter how difficult a doctrine might be, it could always be made attractive, even resplendent, by being communicated in the right way: 'Nihil tam *horridum* tam *incultum* quod non *splendescat* oratione et tamquam *excolatur.*' Cicero's judgement about the Stoics, and Barbaro's about the Scholastics, was not about placing style above content; on the contrary, it was about fusing the two so that the communication of important doctrines was enhanced. In Barbaro's case, we have seen, this meant making Aristotle clear and pleasant for students and scholars by returning to Greek sources and promoting readable and accurate translations.

There had been no intention to include Pico among the *horridi* and *inculti*. Barbaro knew that Pico was already fluent in Greek, and studying classical literature, including Greek authors, with Poliziano (*Epistolae*, p. 85). Pico's reply is a continuation of the joking. By proposing to defend the 'barbarity' of the Scholastics by raising one of their band from the dead to speak on their behalf as least 'barbarically' as possible, Pico is attempting the impossible. For how could a Scholastic who rejected clear, elegant expression undertake a 'defence'—a rhetorical task requiring elegance—of his own barbarity, indeed, a praise of it? Pico's sham lament, in which he appears to be mortally wounded by Barbaro's pronouncements, is tongue-in-cheek:

I was so disturbed by [your letter], so ashamed and disgusted by my studies— for I have spent six years on these philosophers—that [. . .] in order to console myself I have been wondering whether, if any of these men were brought to life again, they would have any means of defending their cause in some way, for in other respects they were fond of disputation.[15]

After the speech, Pico engages in a palinode, stating unequivocally that he does not share the opinions of the Scholastic he has just raised from the dead: 'I do not myself, of course, agree with their point of view, nor do I think that any educated person of integrity should agree.' Indeed, he has undertaken 'an amusing exercise' ('*exercui me libenter*') on such an ignoble subject matter' ('in hac *materia* tamquam *infami*') to provoke a reply from Barbaro. He has behaved like those who praise a quartan ague, or like Glaucon who praised injustice (Plato's *Republic*, II, 354B–367E) against his own inclination in order to provoke a brilliant refutation from Socrates.[16] 'For if I believed that the barbarians should neglect or ignore eloquence,' further clarifies Pico, 'I would not have almost completely deserted them—as I have recently done—for eloquence and Greek literature and your Themistius.'

Note that Pico identifies his genre for us by using the same words as Aulus Gellius (*Noctes Atticae*, XVII, xii) when he defines paradoxical encomia as amusing exercises 'on unpraiseworthy subject matters' ('de *materiis infamibus* [. . .] *exercendi gratia* disputatis'), undertaken in a playful spirit, but used by philosophers like Plato himself. The definition of Aulus Gellius became the classic one, used by Erasmus to explain his *Praise of Folly*, and by later writers of paradox well into the seventeenth century.[17]

Pico's further admission that he also wanted to strike a blow against grammarians who, 'as soon as they know the sources of a few words [. . .] show off and boast and strut around', imagining that philosophers 'should be considered of no account compared with themselves', does not offer comfort to those who wish Pico to be anti-humanist at heart. If we return to Cicero's ranking, we recall that neither the tongue-tied afflicted with *indiserta prudentia*, nor the fool talking nonsense, *stultitia loquacis*, is worthy of praise—though the latter is worse. In Pico's speech on the appropriate style for the philosopher, neither Scholastic obscurity nor an overly elegant style strewn with poetic tropes is appropriate. But just as Barbaro did not include Pico in attacking inelegant Scholastics, so Pico is not attacking humanists like Barbaro or Poliziano in condemning pedants. Rather, Pico closes his letter with fulsome words of praise for Barbaro that also recall Cicero's description of the perfect orator: he is 'the most eloquent among philosophers, and among the eloquent, to use a Greek phrase, "supremely philosophical"'.[18]

The Comic Scholastic who Speaks out of Character

If Pico had wished his Scholastic to defend a philosophical prose without style and clarity of expression as a 'genuine' Scholastic might have done, his creation would have been very different. He would have used sources available up to the fourteenth century: plenty of references to Aristotle and medieval Aristotelian commentaries and manuals: Peter Lombard, Thomas Aquinas, Albert the Great, Duns Scotus, and those favourite authors of logic manuals at the University of Padua, Peter of Spain and Paul of Venice. He would have referred to the Bible and biblical commentators like Nicholas of Lyra. As it is, the oration is conspicuous for its lack of medieval philosophers and theologians. Aristotle is not mentioned once. There is not a single quotation from the Bible.

In other words, Pico's Scholastic speaks out of character. In praising lack of elegance, he is much more at home with classical pagan Latin and Greek authors—poets, orators, sophists—than with the medievals. Even more bizarre, he is acquainted with fifteenth-century humanist debates; and his 'library' resembles that of a late Quattrocento humanist of the first rank, like a Barbaro or a Poliziano, more than his peers of a century or two earlier. Not all authors are explicitly mentioned. Cicero and Lucretius (the arch-enemy of orthodox Catholic doctrines on the immortality of the soul and divine providence, discovered only in the Quattrocento) are; Aulus Gellius, a favourite author of Poliziano, quoted on several occasions, is not. Horace can be detected; so can Homer. Plato, through the reference to the Silenus of Alcibiades, is present; and so are Plotinus and Synesius; Aristotle, 'the master of those who know', to use Dante's phrase, is not. Through a reference to Apollonius of Tyana, Philostratus, a Greek sophist only recently translated (1473) into Latin by Alamanno Rinuccini, a friend of Poliziano, makes a brief appearance—these are writers a genuine medieval would never have dreamt of in his wildest moments. In further anachronisms, the Scholastic enters into the labyrinthine invectives that took place between Poggio Bracciolini and Lorenzo Valla over the kind of Latin spoken by ancient Romans, whether it should be called 'lingua latina' or 'lingua romana'. Both of these humanists, notoriously Valla, were intransigently opposed to Scholastic learning and linguistic 'barbarity'.[19] The Scholastic also shows some acquaintance with Cristoforo Landino's commentary on Virgil, but is ignorant of Sts Augustine and Jerome. The one early Christian writer mentioned— only to be condemned—is Lactantius; and the one medieval author— on a topic that has nothing to do with the issue under discussion—Duns Scotus. What creates the humour—and the parody—is that our Scholastic never gets anything right, though he thinks he's always right.

Pico's Scholastic is also out of character in not using the weapons of medieval dialectic. Despite continual praise of certain or 'apodictic' knowledge arrived at by syllogistic proof, there is no evidence whatsoever of syllogistic ratiocination. He never even defines his terms, or makes distinctions, and is unable to stick to the point—basic skills of the dialectician. Instead, he pours out metaphors and rhetorical tropes in abundance, typical of a florid or Asiatic prose style more suitable for poetry, the *genus elaboratum* specifically condemned by the same Scholastic: hyperbole, oxymoron, simile, antithesis, parallelism, and repetition of similar-sounding phrases, or homeoteleuton.

A couple of examples will suffice. First, when describing the extreme antagonism he feels towards rhetoric, linguistic adornment, and elegance, he resorts to extreme hyperbole: 'The conflict between the function of the orator on one hand and the philosopher on the other is so great that it would not be possible for them to be more opposed'! There is no hope of reconciliation between the two; but never mind, since 'for eloquence to be divorced from wisdom is perhaps so far from being a fault that their union is a crime'! The Scholastic feels no remorse about obscurity, for 'if, as you say, we are commonly regarded as "sordidi, rudes, inculti", that is a credit to us, not a reproach'. Who would deny that an appropriate linguistic style would make a speech more beautiful (echoes of Aristotle and the epigraph from Cicero)? The Scholastic enthusiastically denies it, and affirms that a speech becomes *less* beautiful. It is preferable to repel and horrify an audience: 'We do not wish [our speech] to be delightful, charming, and witty, but useful, sober, and awesome—in that way, it achieves grandeur out of coarseness rather than gracefulness out of decadence.' Communication is of no importance, for 'we do not wish to appeal to the unlettered masses, but to frighten them away'.[20]

Second, innumerable times throughout the speech our attention is drawn to the contradiction between the Scholastic's adamant rejection of elegance, and his display of an over-refined elegance. Diverse kinds of *serio ludere* are at work here. The Scholastic is like the hypocrite in classical and Renaissance comedy who does not practise what he preaches; indeed, who attacks others for the same faults he is guilty of. The Scholastic would have us believe that medieval philosophical style may be ugly on the outside but is full of gems within (he tries to make a case for Cicero's *indiserta prudentia*); but his own speech, on the contrary, is full of musicality and 'flowers' on the outside, and contains nothing substantial below the surface. It is an example of the *stultitia loquacitas* ranked at the bottom of the list by Cicero. One short passage will serve as example. The Scholastic praises a 'naked' philosophical style, that is, one not clothed with any kind of rhetorical adornment whatsoever—not even a thin veil that might diminish its 'natural' beauty—by reverting not only to metaphors and personification, but also to a series of rhythmical phrases (plus anaphora and alliteration) that are a leading feature of the Asiatic style he says he loathes. At the same time, he warns us that 'we should not play with figures of speech nor indulge in too many words or take liberties with metaphors and other tropes or make bold with artifice in such a serious matter and of such importance, where subtracting, adding or changing anything is a grave offence':

> Quapropter *nec ludendum* tropis
> *nec* [. . .] verbis *luxuriandum*
> *aut* translatis *lasciviendum*
> *aut* factitiis *audendum*
> in re *tam* seria, *tanti* discriminis
> in qua *demere, addere, demutare* aliquid sit flagitium.[21]

Metaphors of Duplicity: Silenus and Binary Oppositions of 'Inner' and 'Outer', 'Surface' and 'Deep'

Parody requires a recognition that the text at hand immediately recalls to the listener or reader another text, the touchstone against which the deformation can be detected. If the listener is not aware of the other text, he or she will not detect the parody, and miss the joke. Pico often has his Scholastic admonish us to look 'within' a speech decorated with elegant adornments, rather then remain 'without'. He also has his Scholastic drop his mask to make an aside to the audience, and to point out a duplicity of meanings. Barbaro understood this perfectly in his own reply (see quotation above, p. 154). Most helpful in deconstructing the speech is Barbaro's report on the reaction of the Scholastics at Padua. They had soon judged it 'the defence of the Scythians and the Teutons, as if it were a eulogy of Typhon and the Furies', that is, a praise of the thoroughly unpraiseworthy, or a paradoxical encomium. Far from being pleased, Barbaro continues, the majority of Scholastics at Padua were extremely annoyed![22]

On his usual tack of recommending the least elegance possible, the Scholastic turns to admonish the unsuspecting reader:

For this reason too we must take care that the ill-read reader (*illectus* [. . .] *lector*) is not seduced by a painted complexion (*cute medicata*) into lingering on the surface without penetrating to the marrow and blood (*ad medullam et sanguinem*) that we so often see infected beneath a whitened face (*cerussato ori*).

The play on *illectus/lector*, drawing our attention to surface elegance just when we are told not to pay attention, should put us on guard. The warning seems sound, until we consider whose 'whitened face' we are being warned against. The Scholastic has one explanation:

We see this, I repeat, in all those whose practice it is to engage the reader's attention with surface appearance by means of varying rhythm and harmony, because there is nothing within but emptiness and illusion (*nihil sit intus non inane et vanum*). If a philosopher behaved thus, Musonius would cry out that we did not hear a philosopher speaking but a flute-player piping (*clamabit Musonius non philosophum loqui sed tibicinem canere*). (*Prosatori latini*, 810)

Two passages from Aulus Gellius (*Noctes Atticae*, XVIII, iv and V, i) reveal that the 'whitened face' is none other than the Scholastic's own.[23] In the first, Apollinaris Sulpicius, the most learned man of his age according to Aulus Gellius, mocks an arrogant pedant who boasts that he cannot only explain the surface complexion (*cutem ac speciem*) of the historian Sallust, but also penetrate within to the very blood and marrow (*sanguinem quoque ac medullam* [. . .] *introspicere penitus*) of the words. Gellius explains that Sulpicius often deflated such pedants with the same kind of irony used by Socrates against the sophists—a remark affording us a perspective on Pico's intentions in creating his Scholastic, and in mocking both Scholastic pedantry and the arrogant Scholastic himself. In the second passage, Gellius reports Musonius (of whom the Scholastic would never have heard) on the need to listen attentively to a philosophical discourse so as not to waste either the philosopher's or the audience's time; otherwise the speech is in vain (*frustra esse*), and they are not hearing a philosopher's lecture, but a flute-player's recital (*neque illi philosophum loqui, sed tibicinem canere*). Pico has replaced the word *frustra* in Gellius with the synonyms *inane et vanum*. The context is reversed: the Scholastic was attacking the supposed emptiness of orators and poets; but it is *his* speech, supposedly philosophical, that sways us with its musicality and rhythms, and is therefore *inane et vanum*.

The most complex self-referential definition of the Scholastic's speech is arguably the comparison of it to the Silenus statuette. The reference takes us immediately to Plato's *Symposium* and the praise of Socrates' irresistible powers of persuasion by Alcibiades (215A–217A). Socrates is compared to the little statues of the satyr Silenus playing his pan-pipes sold at religious festivals: from the outside the satyr looks ugly and shaggy; when opened up, there are found images of the gods.

The comparison, of course, links the speech with Socratic irony and 'pretending', with duplicity and the 'inner' and 'outer', 'surface' and 'deep' meanings of the praise, and also with Pico's (certainly not the Scholastic's!) immediate cultural context. In 1484, the year previous to Pico's letter to Barbaro, Ficino had published his Latin translation of the *Symposium*; and at the time of writing to Barbaro, Pico was studying this dialogue for his vernacular commentary on Girolamo Benivieni's canzone 'Amor dalle cui'.[24] Its contents would have been fresh in his mind. By comparing Pico's words with Plato's in Ficino's Latin translation, the features of the Scholastic's comic desecration stand out. Pico has the Scholastic address Barbaro thus:

> Would you like me to shape for you the *idea* of our style (*ideam sermonis nostri*)? It is exactly the same as the Sileni of Alcibiades! These were statues shaggy, loathsome, and despicable on the surface, but full of jewels and rare and precious ornaments inside. If you thus looked at the exterior, you would see a wild beast (*extrinsecus si aspexeris, feram videas*); if deep within, you would recognize a divinity (*si introspexeris, numen agnoscas*).
>
> 'But', you [i.e. Barbaro] will say, 'my ears cannot bear a manner of writing now rough, now hoarse, and always lacking in harmony; they cannot bear the barbarous words (*barbara nomina*) whose sound alone is almost enough to frighten me. You sybarite! When you mix with philosophers, withdraw from the senses, return to yourself, to your soul's inner sanctuary and your mind's retreat. Listen with the ears of Apollonius of Tyana! When he was outside the body he used to hear not earthly Marsyas but heavenly Apollo playing the music of the spheres in ineffable harmonies on his divine lyre.' (*Prosatori latini*, 812, 814)

For the moment, I call attention to the absence of the name of Socrates (or of Plato) in this passage or anywhere in the speech. Naming him would surely give Pico's game away, but more seriously associate the Scholastic with a sublime figure, to whom he does not deserve in any way to be compared. By substituting the name of Apollonius of Tyana, Pico adds to the grotesque features of the Scholastic's speech, for this first-century miracle-monger, exorcist, and ascetic turned by pagans into a 'better' Christ, and fiercely denounced by the early Church historian Eusebius as a wizard, a charlatan, and master of sophistry, indicates whom the Scholastic really resembles.[25]

Alcibiades praises Socrates to the dinner guests as follows (*Symposium*, 216D–E; Ficino's Latin translation used):

> I shall attempt to praise Socrates by similitudes (*per imagines*). He may surmise that I do this for a comic effect (*ne ad ridiculam sermonem convertam*); the

similitude is made, however, for the sake of truth, not to jest (*imago veri non ridiculi gratia*). I affirm that Socrates is very much like those Silenus figures who [. . .] are fashioned holding pipes or flutes. If the two halves are opened, they are found to hold within an image of the gods (*intus imaginem habere deorum*) [. . .].

Observe that in his outward appearance (*forma exterius*), [Socrates] is also like a Silenus figure. But if you open him up, you will find within amazing sobriety and moral integrity (*intus* [. . .] *mira castimonia et integritas*) [. . .]. He plays the role of the ironist, and never ceases to joke openly about all matters.

I also say that he resembles the satyr Marsyas [. . .]. Are you not a piper? You are a far more excellent one than Marsyas himself [. . .] For he attracted souls by means of his harmony alone [. . .]. You differ from him in this one respect—you produce the same effect by means of your unadorned speech (*nudis verbis*) unaided by instruments.

The text of Plato reinforces the comparison between a sublime Silenus, represented by Socrates, and a 'low', comic one, represented by the Scholastic. Alcibiades chooses Silenus to emphasize Socrates' modesty, and lack of pomposity. As if expecting derision, Alcibiades insists that the similitude is to be taken seriously when applied to Socrates; no such distinction holds for the Scholastic. Like a Silenus, Socrates' outer appearance, ugly and shabby, is in marked contrast with his inner soul, full of extraordinary virtue. Outwardly, he pretends to joke with all, playing his game of irony: his manner of speaking is simple and unaffected, making use of metaphors drawn from everyday life. But once his words are 'opened up', they are found to be superior to anybody else's for their divinely inspired truth.

The metaphor of the pan-pipes, common to all satyrs and therefore to Silenus and Marsyas, and the further comparison with Marsyas, adds to the sublimity of Socrates' teachings. Marsyas used his pan-pipes to move souls, leading them to leave the body, that is, to ecstasy. But for Alcibiades, while Marsyas' music bears some resemblance to the persuasive power of Socrates' words, the latter far surpass (*longe praestantior*) the music of Marsyas in their marvellous effects. Not only: Socrates did not need the music of any instrument to lead his hearers to ecstasy; he was able to move his audience by means of his words alone ('sine ullo instrumento nudis verbis').

On the other hand, by offering Barbaro an *idea* of his speech, the Scholastic immediately falls flat on his face. He appears to want to 'show off' his knowledge of the Platonic ideas to Barbaro, not realizing that one cannot have an *idea* of the style of a speech!

The Platonic ideas are of universals (like beauty, goodness, truth, or justice), not of individuals and still less of artefacts.[26] Rather than talk of ideas, the Scholastic should have followed Alcibiades and spoken of images or metaphors.

There is further equivocation, I believe. Pico has the Scholastic confuse Platonic ideas with the ideas (or forms) of different styles defined by Hermogenes of Tarsias in *De ideis*, the most exhausting manual of style in the Byzantine world, incorporated by George of Trebizond in his rhetoric compilation. Even then, the allusion is self-destructive: the *idea* or 'form' of philosophical prose according to Hermogenes and Trebizond is clarity, 'perspicuitas', as Barbaro translated—which is precisely what the Scholastic's speech is not and does not want to be.

The image of the pan-pipes leads to further misconstruing of the Platonic text. One moment, the Scholastic sarcastically condemns Barbaro for being 'all ears', wanting beautiful sounds rather than the shaggy appearance of Scholastic style, the dangerous seductiveness of a surface rhetoric rather than gems of pure thought. Another, he switches direction, and confesses, perhaps *malgré lui*, that a true philosophical discourse could well lead to ecstasy. Alcibiades compared Marsyas to someone better, the divine Socrates who needed no music. The Scholastic not only advises Barbaro to listen to the harmony of the spheres, to which he himself remains deaf, but then compares Marsyas to Apollonius of Tyana, the anti-model of truth. The Silenus of the Scholastic and that of Socrates involve metaphors of 'outer' and 'inner', 'surface' and 'depth', but whereas the speech of Socrates is attractive and persuasive, drawing an audience in by its very simplicity, that of the Scholastic exults in impenetrability devoid of all charm. He boasts that outside, it is 'shaggy, loathsome, and despicable', and you see 'a wild beast'; inside, it is 'full of precious gems', and you recognize 'a god'.

More probably, there are no images of gods; it is illusory, like Apollonius, and *futile et vanum*, like the flute-player absorbed with his rhythmical cadences (see above, p. 163).

The Praise of the Scholastic's Style as the Praise of Obscurity

The boasts made above of a 'shaggy, loathsome, and despicable' speech for philosophical discourse are carried further by the allied praise of the alleged 'rustic' style of the Bible and early Christian writings in general.

The Scholastic damns an early Christian apologist of the fourth century, Lactantius, in favour of the Greek pagan philosopher-poet Heraclitus, known even in antiquity as 'the obscure' by definition. Addressing the dead Lactantius—another example of raising someone from the dead and creating a fictitious speech—the Scholastic reproaches him for not understanding what kind of style is appropriate for the philosopher, as if Lactantius, greatly admired by other early Christian writers like Jerome and Augustine, and humanists like Lorenzo Valla, were some insignificant contemporary poetaster.[27] 'These are the qualities, Lactantius, that command confidence in a philosopher: that he be a good man, speak the truth, and strive for a style that flows not from the pleasant woods of the Muses but from that dreadful cave (*ex horrendo* [. . .] *antro*) in which Heraclitus said that the truth lay hidden (*dixit Heraclitus latitare veritatem*)'.

The anti-model of clear communication, especially in natural philosophy, Heraclitus plays the role of the main *alter ego* of our Scholastic. Aristotle, Plotinus, and Diogenes Laertius among the Greeks, and Cicero and Lucretius among the Latins had condemned him. According to Diogenes (*Lives of the Philosophers*, IX, 3, 6), he was a misanthrope who wrote in a deliberately obscure manner that nobody understood; even Socrates (ibid., II, 22) thought him obscure. Plotinus (Pico would have Ficino's Latin translation to hand) did not admire him; and what flows from that cave, furthermore, is not the truth. For Platonists, the cave symbolizes those weak shadows of truth, the illusions of the senses. To add to the confusion, the cave in Plotinus is associated with Empedocles, not Heraclitus (*Enneads*, IV, 8, 1). In his dialogue on ethics, very well known to humanists, *De finibus* (II, 15), Cicero reproaches Heraclitus for a deliberately obscure style, reporting that the epithet *ho Skoteinós*—'The Obscure One'—was bestowed on him precisely because he wrote his treatises on natural philosophy 'most obscurely' (*nimis obscure*)!

But it is Lucretius, a pagan poet of natural philosophy anathema to Christians for his Epicurean denial of divine providence and the immortality of the soul, who provides the closest source of the parody. The incomprehensibility of Heraclitus is denounced sarcastically by Lucretius in words that seem tailor-made for the Scholastics and their translations and adaptations of Aristotle's natural philosophy:

> Heraclitus [. . .] *clarus ob obscuram linguam* magis inter *inanis* quamde gravis inter Graios qui vera requirunt.

> Omnia enim stolidi *magis* admirantur amantque
> *inversis* quae sub *verbis latitantia cernunt*
> *vera*que constituunt quae belle tangere possunt
> auris [. . .] (*De rerum natura*, I 638–44)

In a striking oxymoron, Lucretius declares that Heraclitus, 'brilliant because of his obscure style', is not loved by serious scholars searching for truth, but rather by frivolous, foolish people (*stolidi*) dazzled by distorted words (*inversis* [. . .] *verbis*). They love and admire more the truths they discern hidden therein (*latitantia cernunt vera*), and lay down as true whatever pleases their ears, and whatever is overlaid with the sound of attractive speech. Like the foolish followers of Heraclitus, Scholastics err in thinking that within the 'cave' of a horrendous style, they will find the truth lying hidden, *latitare veritatem*. Just as Lucretius scorns Heraclitus as a bogus philosopher, so Pico passes judgement on Scholastics who revel in obscurity mistaken for wisdom. As for the pleasant woods of the Muses, dismissed by the Scholastic as the source of illusion, the opposite of truth, this metaphor brings to mind humanist treatises of the Trecento and Quattrocento. Here, woods and caves are places where truth found in sacred poetry dwells, accessible only to a few (Homer, Virgil, the writers of Scripture). It is a truth higher than philosophy and theology. (For the doctrine, see especially Boccaccio's *De genealogia deorum*, XIV, xx.) The relationship set up by the Scholastic, cave/truth and woods/illusion, is comically reversed.

Lactantius returns in the context of the appropriate style for the Bible and religious writing. It should be recalled that Quattrocento humanists, especially Lorenzo Valla, were in the forefront of the revival of early Latin Church Fathers, masters of rhetoric (Lactantius and Augustine were actually teachers of rhetoric), and hence of moving, persuasive communication. They also realized that the Vulgate New Testament was a translation from the Greek, and began the work of emendation, using Greek manuscripts and commentaries by early Greek Christian writers. Some Scholastics resented a philological approach to what they saw as a divinely inspired Latin, however inelegant, and maintained that the Bible was written for simple people in a crude style—*rustice*—and that it would be inappropriate for the Bible or religious writings to be elegant. Our Scholastic, too, thinks that Christians should have no patience with 'meretricious finery':

For this reason the holy scriptures are read: they are written crudely rather than elegantly (*rustice potius quam eleganter*) because wherever there is a question of knowing the truth, nothing would be more unbecoming and harmful than all that elaborate style of speech (*universum istud dicendi genus elaboratum*) (*Prosatori latini*, 808).

But in Augustine's *De doctrina christiana* we find, on the contrary, the same values expressed as in Cicero's *De oratore*. The best preacher unites wisdom and eloquence. As for whether the writers of the Bible were only wise, or eloquent as well, Augustine insists that 'not only is there nothing wiser [than the Bible], but there is nothing in my opinion more eloquent' (*non solum nihil eis sapientius, verum etiam nihil eloquentius mihi videri potest*, IV, vi, 9–10).[28] Jerome is even more insistent. In a letter-essay on translating Greek religious writings into Latin, widely studied among humanists, he reproaches those who confuse a simple way of life with simple-mindedness: 'What I have always respected is not a garrulous coarseness (*verbosa rusticitas*) but a holy simplicity (*sancta simplicitas*). If anyone says he imitates the Apostles in his manner of speaking, let him first do so in his manner of living [. . .]. It is furthermore absurd (*ridiculum*) for any one of us Christians, among the wealth of Croesus and the refinements of Sardanapalus, to boast only of *rusticitas*' (XII, 5–8).[29]

In a little dialogue with the dead Lactantius, the Scholastic has him assert that the truth is more powerful 'if it is supplied with its own force and adorned with the light of eloquence'—theology united with eloquence. The Scholastic vehemently disagrees, overdoing the subjunctives in a series of hissing alliterative sibilants, combined with anaphora:[30] 'Si fuisses, o Firmiane, tam frequens in sacris litteris, quam *in fictis litibus* fuisti, et hoc non dixisses et *nostra* non minus bene *fortasse confirmasses quam destruxeras aliena*' ('If you had been as assiduous in studying the Scriptures, Firmianus [Lactantius] as you were in conducting imaginary disputes, you would not have said this and would, perhaps, have strengthened our side as well as you destroyed the others')! (*Prosatori latini*, 814, 16).

The Scholastic is parodying famous words of St Jerome, but he has left out a key judgement—the praise of Lactantius as 'the most eloquent man of his age', and 'a torrent of Ciceronian eloquence'—and added one not in Jerome, about conducting imaginary disputes. Jerome had said: 'Utinam tam nostra adfirmare potuisset quam facile aliena destruxit!' ('If only he had been able to affirm our doctrines as easily as he destroyed the enemy's!' (*Epistula* 58). There was nothing imaginary about the disputes—Lactantius was the master of arguing *in utramque partem* against real pagan philosophers of the fourth century. The 'imaginary disputes' are the Scholastic's, who will not accept what the finest philosophers and orators of antiquity, Christian and pagan, have taught; and who, unlike Lactantius, has none of the skills of the dialectician enabling him to argue 'on both sides of an issue'.

Conclusion

To what extent does the evidence presented above (there is much more) afford a new reading of this already celebrated dispute on the relationship of style and rhetoric to philosophical discourse? To a degree probably never surpassed, Pico (and Barbaro, and Poliziano hovering in the background) display the mastery achieved by Italian humanists of the entire tradition of Greek and Latin rhetoric and dialectic, of classical letters and the philosophy of Plato and Aristotle. Cicero's words in the epigraph captures a new confidence of the late Quattrocento about the possibility of disseminating everything knowable, no matter how difficult, provided one had learnt how to speak and write good Latin. Humanists were open to Scholastics, but realized more than they did the need to reform philosophical prose, and reach out to a wider audience. In fact, this dispute shows only too painfully how humanists like Pico and Barbaro had raced ahead of Scholastics, becoming better at their skills than the Scholastics themselves. Most of all, the dispute shows how a new kind of refined, and very learned, humour provided a new weapon to humanists to use against the arrogant and the blindly prejudiced, deflating and demolishing misguided arguments of the adversary. The crisis here lies in the baffling fact that the parody and irony of Pico's letter, and even more so of Barbaro's, were lost on readers within a few decades.

Notes to Chapter 7

1. Latin text, with facing English translation by H. Rackham, in *Cicero*, iv (Loeb Classical Library—henceforth LCL; London and Cambridge, Mass.: W. Heinemann and Harvard University Press, repr. 1968), 254–7.

2. *Eight Philosophers of the Italian Renaissance* (Stanford, Calif.: Stanford University Press, 1964), 58. The literature is immense on this correspondence, and especially on Pico's letter. I shall give only a few landmarks. Kristeller himself returned time and again to the letter, maintaining the same view. See also Eugenio Garin, *Giovanni Pico della Mirandola: vita e dottrina* (Florence: Le Monnier, 1937); Quirinus Breen, 'Three Renaissance Humanists on the Relation of Philosophy and Rhetoric [Pico, Barbaro, Melanchthon]', in *Christianity and Humanism: Studies in the History of Ideas*

(Grand Rapids, Mich.: W. B. Eerdmans, 1968); Henri De Lubac, *Pic de la Mirandole, études et discussions* (Paris: Aubier Montaigne, 1974); William Craven, *Giovanni Pico della Mirandola, Symbol of his Age* (Geneva: Droz, 1981).

3. The counter-current goes back to Hanna Gray, 'Renaissance Humanism: The Pursuit of Eloquence', *Journal of the History of Philosophy*, 24 (1963), 497–514, repr. in P. O. Kristeller and P. P. Wiener (eds.), *Renaissance Essays* (Rochester, NY: Rochester University Press, 1992). See also M. Martelli, 'Il "Libro delle Epistole" di Angelo Poliziano', *Interpres*, 1 (1978), 184–255; B. Vickers, *In Defence of Rhetoric* (Oxford: Clarendon Press, 1988); M. L. McLaughlin, *Literary Imitation in the Italian Renaissance: The Theory and Practice of Literary Imitation in Italy from Dante to Bembo* (Oxford: Clarendon Press, 1995); and F. Bausi, '*Nec rhetor neque philosophus': fonti, lingua e stile nelle prime opere latine di Giovanni Pico della Mirandola, 1484–87* (Città di Castello: L. S. Olschki, 1996).

4. For Barbaro's letters, see the critical edition of Vittore Branca, *Epistolae, Orationes et Carmina*, 2 vols. (Florence: Bibliopolis, 1943). There is no critical edition of Pico's letters, but for the Latin text with facing Italian translation of Pico's letter-speech and Barbaro's corresponding reply, see *Prosatori latini del Quattrocento*, ed. Eugenio Garin (Milan and Naples: Ricciardi, 1952), 804–23 for Pico, and 844–63 for Barbaro. All Latin quotations from these letters are from *Prosatori latini*. English translations are my own, from a forthcoming publication of the letters, with notes and introduction. To save space, I shall insert the Latin only when the words or phrases are of particular significance.

5. My research on Barbaro was first presented in Venice at the 1993 conference marking the 500th centenary of Barbaro's death, and has since been published: 'Ermolao Barbaro e Pico della Mirandola tra retorica e dialettica: il *De genere dicendi philosophorum* del 1485', in *Una famiglia veneziana nella storia: i Barbaro* (Venice: Istituto Veneto di Scienze, Lettere ed Arti, 1996), 277–330.

6. Some of my research on Pico was first presented in Mirandola at the 1994 conference marking the 500th centenary of Pico's death. For Cesare Vasoli's report on all the spoken papers (and for most of the written papers), see 'Giovanni Pico della Mirandola' (*Studi Pichiani*, 5), ed. G. C. Garfagnini, 2 vols. (Florence: Olschki, 1997), ii. 641–95. A fuller version of my own contribution, 'Pico della Mirandola e il *De genere dicendi philosophorum* del 1485: l'encomio paradossale dei "barbari" e la loro parodia', is now in *I Tatti Studies, Essays in the Renaissance* 8 (1999), 69–103. This is the first English article I have written on the dispute; I draw mainly on the latter study, though with different emphases.

7. Barbaro's translation of *Ars rhetoricae* was published only in the next century: 1544 in Lyons and Venice, and Basle a year later. The translation was accompanied by a commentary of Daniele Barbaro, also a philosopher at Padua, using Cicero and Hermogenes, two of Ermolao's favorite authors. I refer to the Basle edition: *Aristotelis rhetoricorum libri tres. Hermolao Barbaro patricio Veneto interprete. Danielis Barbari in eosdem libros commentarii* (Basle: Bartholomaeus Westhemerus, 1545). The Themistius was printed in Treviso (B. Confalonerius & M. Gerardinus) and consists of distillations of minor works of Aristotelian natural philosophy.

8. For poem and Italian commentary, see Pico della Mirandola, *De hominis dignitate, Heptaplus, De ente et uno, e scritti vari*, ed. Eugenio Garin (Florence: Vallecchi, 1942). English translation with notes and study in Sears Jayne, *Commentary on a*

Canzone of Benivieni by Giovanni Pico della Mirandola (New York: Peter Lang, 1984). For his lyric poetry, see *Sonetti*, ed. Giorgio Dilemmi (Turin: Einaudi, 1994). In the letter to Lorenzo, Pico already shows that he knows about *serio ludere*, praising Lorenzo's love poetry for combining the seriousness of philosophers with the playfulness of lovers ('amantium *lusibus* philosophorum *seria* sunt admixta'), *Prosatori latini*, 800.

9. 'Epistolae', in *Opera quae extant omnia* (Basle: S. Henricpetri, 1601), i. 247, letter beginning 'Quod proximis literis tuis', no date.

10. *De oratore*, III, xxxv, 142–3, trans. H. Rackham (LCL, 1968).

11. *Orator*, 113–14. For a survey of the meanings of *antistrophos* in the Renaissance, see L. Green, 'Aristotelian Rhetoric, Dialectic, and the Tradition of Antistrophos', *Rhetorica*, 8 (1990), 5–27. In *Aristotle's Rhetoric I: A Commentary* (New York: Fordham University Press, 1980), W. Grimaldi gives as equivalents of *antistrophos* 'counterpart', 'analogue', and 'correlative'. Cicero had also paraphrased Aristotle's main manual of dialectic, the *Topics*, for Roman use, and expressed great admiration for both Aristotle's exposition of the skills of probabilistic argument and his style, typified by 'its amazing abundance and elegance' (*incredibili quadam cum copia tum etiam suavitate*), *Topics*, I, 3. But Scholastics, who learned dialectic mainly from Boethius' commentaries on Cicero, and from manuals of logic and *sophismata*, did not pay attention to Aristotle and Cicero on the close rapport of dialectic and rhetoric.

12. For an expanded account of this cultural context, see my 'Ermolao Barbaro', 280–5; also, J. Monfasani, *George of Trebizond: A Biography and a Study of his Rhetoric and Logic* (Leiden: Brill, 1976), esp. 248–55 and 261–89. (Trebizond had also translated Aristotle's *Ars rhetoricae* between 1443 and 1446—it is not clear whether Ermolao knew of it); and Monfasani's 'Humanism and Rhetoric', in A. Rabil, Jr. (ed.), *Renaissance Humanism: Foundations, Forms and Legacy*, 3 vols. (Philadelphia: University of Pennsylvania Press, 1988), i. 171–235.

13. The phrase is Cicero's, who pronounces Socrates the most refined example of the genre, especially for his *eironeia* (*De oratore*, II, 269–70; also *Academica*, II, 15). Horace advises the poet to mix humorous and grave material, *ioca et seria*, so as to achieve his task of entertaining and instructing (*Ars poetica*, 333–4, 343–4). In Pico's day, Marsilio Ficino's translation of Plato's dialogues gave greater diffusion to Socratic *serio ludere*; see M. J. B. Allen, *Icastes: Marsilio Ficino's Interpretation of Plato's Sophist* (Berkeley and Los Angeles, University of California Press, 1989), 206–7. For the decisive importance of Lucian, see my article, 'Ermolao Barbaro', 285–90.

14. 'Nec enim inter auctores latinae linguae numero Germanos et Teutonas, qui ne viventes quidem vivebant, nedum ut extincti vivant, aut si vivunt, vivunt in poenam et contumeliam; appellantur enim vulgo *sordidi, rudes, inculti, barbari*' (emphasis mine), *Epistolae*, ed. Branca, i, Letter LXVIII, p. 86 (this letter is not in *Prosatori latini*).

15. *Prosatori latini*, 806. Raising a fictitious person from the dead is a standard rhetorical trope called *prosopopeia* or impersonation. For Cicero (*Topics*, X, 45) and above all Quintilian (III, 8, 51), it is a test of a great orator's virtuosity. Cicero specifies that it allows the orator to use exaggeration (*hyperbole*) and its opposite, understatement, and 'many other wondrous effects' ('multa alia mirabilia').

16. *Prosatori latini*, 822. Gellius claims that both philosophers and Greek sophists used

these kinds of arguments, called in Latin *inopinabiles* ('inconceiveable'), and in Greek '*adoxoi hypotheseis*', that is, paradoxical opinions. Examples given by Gellius are the praise of Thersites, the proverbial fault-finder, and of the quartan ague—mentioned by Pico. Even Plato himself, Gellius says—thus bestowing the maximum authority on the genre—praised the quartan ague. Glaucon is Pico's addition.

17. See my 'Ermolao Barbaro', 289–90. In the Seicento, the learned French libertine François de la Mothe Vayer (1588–1632) includes Pico's praise of the 'barbarians' together with Erasmus, Thomas More, and Girolamo Cardano in a long list of paradoxical encomia that goes back to Greek and Latin antiquity. Gellius supplies the main definition. See my 'Pico della Mirandola' for the full quotation, p. 80.

18. 'Inter philosophos eloquentissimus, inter eloquentes, ut dicam graece, *philosophotatos*', *Prosatori latini*, 822.

19. Aulus Gellius, Lucretius, and Philostratus will be discussed below. For the Poggio–Valla debates on language, see Salvatore Camporeale, *Umanesimo e teologia* (Florence: Istituto Nazionale di Studi sul Rinascimento, 1972); the introduction by Ari Wesseling to his critical edition of Lorenzo Valla, *Antidotum primum* (Assen and Amsterdam: van Gorcum, 1978); and Mirko Tavoni, *Latino, grammatica, volgare* (Padua: Antenore, 1984).

20. 'Tanta est inter oratoris munus et philosophi pugnantia, ut pugnare magis invicem non possint'; and 'tantum fortasse abest a culpa, ut coniunxisse sit nefas', *Prosatori latini*, 808; 'Quodsi vulgo [. . .] habemur *sordidi, rudes, inculti*, hoc nobis ad gloriam est, non ad contumeliam', 812; 'Ego, amice, hoc in plerisque nego, adeo multa sunt quorum splendorem, si quid adiunxeris, elimines et non illustres', 816; 'Nolumus ut delectabilis, venusta et faceta sit, sed ut utilis, gravis et reverenda, ut maiestatem potius ex horrore quam gratiam ex mollitudine consequatur', 810–12; 'Vulgus [. . .] non allectare quaerimus sed absterrere', 814.

21. *Prosatori latini*, 818. For several other examples of rhythmical prose, called *cursus* in the Middle Ages, see my 'Pico della Mirandola', 90–4.

22. *Prosatori latini*, 844. Barbaro associates the speech with Lucian and the 'asinine', other forms of *serio ludere*, in this same introduction. See my 'Ermolao Barbaro', 285–90. On ass literature in the Renaissance, see Nuccio Ordine, *La cabala del asino: asininità e conoscenza in Giordano Bruno* (Naples: Liguori Editore, 1987).

23. For the complete Latin text and facing English translation by John C. Rolfe, see the LCL edn., 3 vols. (1970).

24. The Silenus metaphor has a long history in Renaissance culture, especially from Erasmus' adage, 'Sileni Alcibiadis' to Giordano Bruno. For the Italian significance, see Silvana Seidel Menchi's translation, introduction, and notes: Erasmo da Rotterdam, *Adagia. Sei saggi politici in forma di proverbi* (Turin: Einaudi, 1980). Menchi refers to Pico as probably the first to reintroduce the Silenus metaphor (p. 312 n. 3). For Bruno, see Ordine, *La cabala del asino*, 103–12. For Ficino, *Opera* (Venice and Florence, per Laurentium [da Alopa], no date, but 1484 or 1485). Quotation here, Biponti [Zweibrücken], 1787, vol. X, pp. 256–60.

25. *The Life of Apollonius of Tyana* by Philostratus, together with Eusebius' treatise against him, with Greek and facing English translation by F. C. Coneybeare, are in LCL edn., 2 vols. (1960).

26. I am grateful to Michael Allen for this point. See his article, 'The Absent Angel in Ficino's Philosophy', in *Plato's Third Eye: Studies in Marsilio Ficino's Metaphysics*

and its Sources, Variorum Collected Studies Series CS 483 (Aldershot: Ashgate, 1995), I, 219–40. For Ficino and the Platonic ideas, pp. 234–8.

27. On Lactantius as a model of the Christian orator in the Quattrocento, see my 'Lorenzo Valla's *De vero falsoque bono*, Lactantius and Oratorical Scepticism', *Journal of the Warburg and Courtauld Institutes*, 41 (1978), 76–107.

28. See *Aurelii Augustini Opera, Pars IV, I, De doctrina christiana libri IV, De vera religione*, ed. Joseph Martin (Turnholt: Brepols, 1962), 121–2.

29. *Epistula 57. Liber de optimo genere interpretandi*, ed. G. M. J. Bartelink, *Mnemosyne*, 61 (Bibliotheca Classica Batava; Leiden, 1980), 11–21. On the renewal of biblical studies and patristics in the Quattrocento, see J. Bentley, *Humanists and Holy Writ: New Testament Scholarship in the Renaissance* (Princeton: Princeton University Press, 1983); and E. Rice, 'The Renaissance Idea of Christian Antiquity: Humanist Patristic Scholarship', in A. Rabil, Jr. (ed.), *Renaissance Humanism*, 3 vols. (Philadelphia, Pa.: University of Pennsylvania Press, 1991), i. 17–28.

30. *Prosatori latini*, 814. The Scholastic reports correctly the union of theology and eloquence advanced by Lactantius in a preface well known to humanists of *Institutiones divinae*, III, 1. But the Scholastic sees as a reason for blame what early Christians and humanists, on the contrary, see as a reason for praise.

CHAPTER 8

Boiardo, Panizzi and 'Politics'

Denis V. Reidy

Those of us who have had the pleasure of reading Giovanni Guareschi's charming tales of Don Camillo, or better still, for our present purposes, those of us who have seen the delightful screen versions of the Don Camillo stories starring Fernandel in the title role, admirably supported by Bruno Cervi as Peppone, are in possession of one of the best possible introductions to Sir Anthony Panizzi, to his background, and to his formative years. Let me explain: the screen versions of Guareschi's Don Camillo stories were filmed in Brescello, that quintessentially Emilian town, with its wide central piazza and ample market square, parish church, mayor's office, town hall, and council offices, invariably interconnected by numerous typically Emilian covered walkways or colonnades, 'portici'. It so happens that Brescello's most famous son, Antonio Genesio Maria Panizzi (1797–1879), the bicentenary of whose birth was celebrated in 1997, was born in Brescello on 16 September 1797. If in our mind's eye we endeavour to eliminate the more obvious twentieth-century inventions such as the motor car, electricity pylons, and television aerials from our recollection of those delightful Don Camillo films, we can begin to visualize and recreate fairly accurately what life in Brescello must have been like in Antonio Panizzi's era—a fairly routine, perhaps at times even a dull existence one would expect the son of the local pharmacist to lead, until in 1814 he entered the University of Parma to read Jurisprudence. While at the University of Parma, Panizzi met the University librarian Gaetano Frantuzzi, who was a formative influence on him since it was probably Frantuzzi who instilled in him his initial love of books, particularly of rare books, which was further nurtured through his friendship with Angelo Pezzana (1772–1862), the Director of the Ducal Library in Parma.

We should recall that both Frantuzzi and Pezzana would have been familiar with the works and theories of Lodovico Antonio Muratori (1672–1750) and Gerolamo Tiraboschi (1731–94) and in turn would have certainly imparted their knowledge to the young Panizzi. Clearly Panizzi's bibliographical formative knowledge is certainly firmly rooted in the Italian tradition, and, to a lesser extent, in the French tradition which influenced it.

After graduating in law, Panizzi returned to his native Brescello, where he practised as a lawyer and to all external appearances at least, appeared to be an upright pillar of society. However, Panizzi led a very dangerous double life. At night the respectable lawyer, who had joined a secret society, that of 'I Sublimi Maestri Perfetti' which had links with other patriotic secret societies, the most famous of which being that of the 'Carbonari', worked actively in recruiting and enrolling other similarly-minded patriotic Italians to the society— thereby recruiting new patriots who shared the principal goal of all patriotic Italians during the Risorgimento period—the overthrow of their oppressors from their native Italy and the country's unification. We should recall Metternich's celebrated phrase that Italy was 'a mere geographical expression' and the fact that at the time Brescello was in the Duchy of Modena, ruled by the Habsburg Duke Francis IV who was, in effect, an Austrian puppet ruler. In 1814 the Austrians had gained control from the French of much of northern Italy. The rule of the invader in many parts of northern Italy, and indeed in much of southern Italy, under Bourbon rule, was often very harsh and op- pressive and was consequently bitterly resented by many Italians. Many of the most patriotic Italians at the time joined secret societies whose long-term avowed aim was the eventual overthrow of their oppressors. In 1820, Francis IV, alarmed by the recent revolts against the Bourbon rulers of Naples, decreed the death penalty for any of his subjects found guilty of belonging to a secret society. His police force began a reign of terror and hundreds of patriotic Italians, although palpably innocent, were rounded up and thrown into jail. At nearby Rubiera a young priest became the first of many to be given a travesty of a trial and was summarily executed—indeed the very guil- lotine blade used for executions is preserved to this day in the Museo del Risorgimento at Modena.

Panizzi could not continue to lead his dangerous double life for much longer. Fortunately for posterity he was forewarned of his imminent arrest and was able to flee his beloved native Italy. He was tried in absentia, was sentenced to be executed by hanging, and, although it is unlikely that the customary hanging in effigy was ever carried out in Panizzi's case, all his property was confiscated. Panizzi began his political exile by crossing the Italian border into Switzerland. He stayed in Lugano long enough to write and see his celebrated *Dei processi e delle sentenze contro gli imputati di lesa maestà e di aderenza alle sette proscritte negli Stati di Modena* in print. This work, a blistering attack against Francis IV and his corrupt regime, was published under a false imprint, Torres, Madrid, 1823. The book, incidentally, has now become extremely rare because in later life Panizzi became so embarrassed by this emotional work, regarding it almost as a 'faute de jeunesse', that he set about systematically buying up all the copies he could lay his hands on and subsequently destroyed them. Fortunately, the British Library has the most interesting extant copy, Panizzi's personal copy, complete with manuscript annotations by him (pressmark C.44.d.l.).

Antonio Panizzi arrived in England in May 1823 'with not quite a sovereign in his pocket, knowing no one, nor a word of the language', as he was later to write. At this point I should give some explanation of the title of my essay and what I propose to discuss in it. My title may seem a little puzzling, and so too the relationship between a nineteenth-century scholar of Boiardo and questions of cultural crisis in Italy in the 1490s. To the Boiardo specialist, the inclusion of Panizzi is not at all puzzling because his contribution to Boiardo scholarship is not inconsiderable, indeed it is of fundamental importance. Not unlike a humanist scholar who insisted on an accurate text for his researches, Panizzi argued for a return to the study of Boiardo's original text and not Berni's 'rifacimento'—a very humanistic 'modus operandi'. Panizzi's editions of Boiardo and Ariosto, published with *An Essay on the Romantic Narrative Poetry of the Italians* (1830, BL 2284.d.2.), and especially his edition of Boiardo's *Sonetti e Canzone* (London, 1835) are so important and so well known—and have been so expertly appraised by others including Carlo Dionisotti, Pier Vincenzo Mengaldo, and Neil Harris, to name but a few—that I do not propose to discuss them in great detail, particularly within the confines of this chapter. What I do propose to examine is why Panizzi chose to study Boiardo, and perhaps endeavour to establish his motives for publishing his celebrated editions—not only in terms of his personal career advancement but what may have been some of his goals and wider aims, motives, and ambitions for his scholarship—or in other words, the 'politics' with a small 'p', of his scholarship. Without 'giving the game away' too much at this stage, I also intend to examine whether there were any further benefits produced by Panizzi's scholarship. I intend to quote briefly from the Panizzi papers held in the British Library's Department of Manuscripts (or to be more correct, from Special Collections), some of which are published here for the first time, in order to substantiate and illustrate my points.

Returning briefly to Panizzi's arrival in England in 1823, it is fairly common knowledge that the liberal attitudes of the English, especially regarding political, intellectual and religious tolerance and freedom, so much appreciated by Voltaire in his *Lettres philosophiques* in the eighteenth century, had effectively transformed the English capital into a virtual Mecca for exiles, especially for political exiles, by the nineteenth. Countless political exiles from all over the world—the Venezuelan patriot and statesman Andrés Bello is perhaps one of the most famous—chose to spend the period of their exile in the liberal atmosphere of London, at that period arguably the most powerful and wealthiest capital in the world. The large Italian contingent included Ugo Foscolo, Gabriele Rossetti, the father of Dante Gabriel and Christina Rossetti, Giuseppe Pecchio, Giovanni Arrivabene, Santorre di Santa Rosa, and eventually Giuseppe Mazzini, who was later to edit and launch his celebrated journal *Giovine Italia*, working in the British Museum Library. Indeed there were so many political exiles in London in the 1820s that it was extremely difficult for many to find gainful employment. When Panizzi went to visit Foscolo, who was living with his illegitimate daughter Floriana in Digamma Cottage in Regent's Park, Foscolo advised him not to remain in London but to travel to, and attempt to settle in, Liverpool.

Armed with a letter of introduction (written for him by Foscolo) for William Roscoe, this is precisely what Panizzi did. Roscoe, a wealthy banker by profession and author of the celebrated lives of Lorenzo de' Medici (1796) and of Leo X (1805), introduced Panizzi to many eminent and influential men, including John Ewart Gladstone, the father of the statesman William Ewart Gladstone, George Grote, the historian of Greece, Henry Brougham, the eminent Whig politician, lawyer, and future Lord Chancellor, and last, but by no means least, William Shepherd, the author of *The Life of Poggio Bracciolini* (Liverpool, 1802 and 1837).

Mention of Roscoe and Shepherd prompts me to recall a sentence used by Martin Davies in a recent article: 'Roscoe and Shepherd formed part of a distinct section of cultivated English society which was provincial yet not "provincial", to a large extent self-educated—not, certainly, at Oxford or Cambridge—in literature and history, European in outlook, liberal and even radical in temper.'[1]

This statement, with which I wholeheartedly concur, is, to my mind, important for our appreciation of the cultural and social ambience in which Panizzi found himself during his sojourn in Liverpool. This was the period of the talented 'amateur'—amateur in the best sense of the word—a period during which intellectuals with few, if any, formal qualifications devoted a great proportion of their time to study and the publication of the fruits of their research, which often culminated in substantial monographs, frequently in numerous lengthy tomes.

In order to keep body and soul together, Panizzi was forced to eke out a modest existence by teaching Italian to private students. He supplemented his meagre income by writing reviews and by contributing the occasional article to various periodicals and scholarly journals. Meanwhile his command of the English language had reached such a high level of competence that he soon felt that he was able to accept an invitation to deliver a set of public lectures on any subject of his choice at the celebrated Royal Institution in Liverpool. He opted to give his lectures on the Italian romantic and chivalric poetry of the Quattro and Cinquecento. At first his choice might appear somewhat curious, especially since he had no formal training in literary criticism. Panizzi, we will recall, was a lawyer by profession and he would have had to have undertaken a considerable amount of research into works by Boiardo, Ariosto, Tasso, Pulci, and Fortiguerra, to name but a few authors. Why, we may well ask, should Panizzi have chosen Italian poetry of the Quattrocento and Cinquecento in general and Boiardo's poetry in particular? Apart from wishing to provide posterity with Boiardo's text stripped of Berni's 'rifacimento', it is very likely that nostalgia for his native Brescello, Scandiano, and Parma and a fierce sense of local pride would have influenced his choice—we should recall that Panizzi's political exile had scarcely begun at this period and he probably wondered whether he would ever see his native Brescello, Scandiano, and the Duchy of Modena again, as we learn from an unpublished letter from Panizzi to Thomas Grenville dated British Museum, 17 September 1834:

[. . .] I have taken a liking to Bojardo's poems because they are, in my opinion remarkably fine, because I owe him a great deal (since it is thro' *him* that I have had the honor of becoming acquainted with you more than would have been likely to be the case had he not written the *Innamorato*) and because he was born in my native province; and I, having been in the habit of spending many of my younger days at Scandiano, feel great pleasure in being occupied with the works of a poet whose name is connected in my mind with so many dear recollections [. . .][2]

There can be little doubt that Panizzi held Boiardo's poetry in the highest esteem. Boiardo is one of the first poets Panizzi refers to and quotes from in his first public lecture at the Royal Institution in Liverpool, as we can see from this extract from the manuscript of the text of his lecture:

[. . .] But I must say that if Ariosto's splendid fame has thrown into the shade, more particularly in the estimation of foreigners the names of Bojardo, Berni, Pulci, B. Tasso and Fortiguerra it is however highly unjust to consider them unworthy of notice. Their poems are superior to any poem of this class of which any nation can boast. In justice to Bojardo and Pulci it is to be said that they preceded Ariosto, nor is it to be concealed, to their honor, that he has not disdained to profit by their works [. . .] the idea that from love proceeded poetry and civilization, as well as valorous feats, was expressed by Bojardo in some verses, in which Berni could not find anything to alter, and for which he received the applauses due to his great predecessor, as has been too often the case as I shall point out in its proper place. These verses form the introduction of the fourth Canto of the second book of the *Orlando Innamorato*. Bojardo addresses his lady in the following strain than which nothing better is to be found in any Italian poet. I could not prevail upon myself to give a bad prose translation of this splendid passage and shall therefore proceed at once to read the original

> Luce degli occhi miei, spirto del core
> Per cui cantar solea sì dolcemente
> Rime leggiadre, e be' versi d'amore
> Spirami aiuto alla storia presente [. . .]
> [. . .] Odio crudele e dispietata guerra [. . .]
> Quante nel tempo che d'amor s'accese.[3]

It is certainly true that since Panizzi was born in the same province as Boiardo he was in the enviable position of having a perfect knowledge of the 'dialetto padano' or, more correctly, of the 'koiné padana' indispensable for a scholar wishing to deepen his or her knowledge of Boiardo and a prerequisite for anyone wishing to produce an edition of Boiardo's works. However, I think that there is another reason for Panizzi's choice. We have seen from the reference to Roscoe and Shepherd that at the time there existed a firm tradition, especially in the provinces and among amateur scholars (once again 'amateur' in the best sense of the word), of the production of scholarly monographs. In England at the time it was also fashionable for these scholars to write and publish biographies and to edit humanist texts. In the main these English scholars had tended to concentrate on editing and publishing the *prose* texts of Quattro and Cinquecento humanist authors. The poetry of this period, with some notable exceptions, however, tended not to be studied to the same extent in England. Panizzi identified this 'lacuna' and decided to redresss the balance. Given his nostalgia for his native Brescello, his admiration of Boiardo's poetry, and his knowledge of the 'koiné padana', he was very well qualified to study the works of Boiardo, and indeed the seeds of his future studies and of his celebrated Boiardo editions were sown in this early and fruitful period in Liverpool.

Later on during his stay in Liverpool Panizzi was able to assist Henry Brougham, the eminent Whig politician and lawyer who later became Lord Chancellor. During the celebrated Wakefield abduction trial of 1827, in which Brougham brought about a successful prosecution, Panizzi advised him on Roman and Continental law. Legend has it that Brougham, by now an outstanding public figure and a reformer in education—he was a leader of the movement which firmly established the new University College in London—did not forget Panizzi's assistance to him, and in 1828 persuaded him to apply for the first Chair of Italian at the newly founded University College. Panizzi applied for what was in effect the first Chair of Italian in any English university (the Serena Chairs of Italian were not founded until this century) and was appointed. At that time university professors were paid directly in proportion (pro rata) to the number of students they had to teach. Panizzi's fears that he would have very few students were soon realized. He consequently devoted his time to producing textbooks for his students: *An Elementary Italian Grammar for the use of Students in the London University* (London: John Taylor, 1828, pp. ii, 61); *Extracts from Italian Prose Writers for the Use of Students in the London University* (London: John Taylor, 1828, pp. xi, 558), and *Stories from Italian Writers with a Literal Interlinear Translation* (London: John Taylor, 1830, pp. iv, 103). His salary, however, was barely adequate, so he decided to apply

for other posts in London. He was obviously attracted to the British
Museum, with its large library and good collections of printed books.
The Museum also had the added advantage of being very close to
University College. Panizzi must have also felt that in order to be
appointed to the British Museum, where the senior staff were
encouraged to undertake research and to publish that research—and
Panizzi probably had the intention of making his career at the Museum
and of rising to a high rank in its hierarchy fairly early on in his academic
career and certainly before deciding to relinquish his Chair—he would
have to produce firm evidence of his ability to undertake research and
to publish the same. He therefore decided to turn back to the initial
research he undertook at Liverpool for his public lectures. The fruits
of this early research were soon to be published. His editions of Boiardo
and Ariosto began to see the light of day in the 1830s—his *Orlando
Innamorato di Boiardo. Orlando Furioso di Ariosto: With an Essay on the
Romantic Narrative Poetry of the Italians: Memoirs and Notes by Antonio
Panizzi*, 9 vols. (London: William Pickering, 1830–4) were published
over a period of four years from 1830 to 1834. Since neither his teaching
nor the royalties from his publications produced an adequate salary, he
was obliged to apply for the humble post of Extra Assistant in the
Department of Printed Books at the British Museum. Fortunately for
Panizzi and posterity he was appointed.

Panizzi's vast culture, his love of bibliography and books in general
and of antiquarian books in particular, coupled with his enormous
capacity for work were soon appreciated and he was eventually appointed to the permanent staff of the Museum. The Institution to
which he was appointed had been founded in 1753 and for fifty years
or so it had remained largely undisturbed by change. 'The Old
Curiosity Shop', as it was sometimes disparagingly referred to, had the
reputation of employing elderly gentlemen scholars, many of whom
were in Holy Orders and who in many cases held other part-time
appointments. Panizzi must have been shocked by what he saw and
was determined to drag the somewhat sleepy Department of Printed
Books into the nineteenth century. Nor could he reconcile himself to
the fact that England, arguably the richest and most powerful country
in the world at that time, did not have the equivalent of a National
Library like France's Bibliothèque Nationale—indeed Panizzi's constant war cry was 'Paris must be beaten!'—nor did it have adequate
copyright laws, let alone a proper laid-down catalogue or an adequate
reading room. Panizzi was determined that his country of adoption

should have all these—it is hardly surprising that one of his colleagues was to refer to him as 'an Italian volcano in a Dutch garden'!

Panizzi had realized while still at University College, that is to say even before joining the Museum, that in order to acquire the power to effect significant change he could not remain a humble Extra Assistant for long but had to be promoted and promoted fairly rapidly. Given the great importance the Museum attached to research and publications, he began his researches while still at University College. His 'magnum opus' in nine volumes was begun while he was in academic life—the first volume of which was published as early as 1830. The fact that it took a further four years for his edition of Boiardo and Ariosto to be published and that his edition of Boiardo's *Sonetti e Canzone* was not published until 1835 (London: C. Whittingham) was eventually to stand him in good stead. The idea of continuing his research on Boiardo and Ariosto, which had clearly been well received in his public lectures at Liverpool, was obviously inspired. Panizzi had to find a good printer, and who better than William Pickering, the quality printer of elegant texts who adopted the same printer's device, that of the dolphin and anchor, employed by Aldus Manutius, the printer of textually accurate, elegant, clear, humanist and classical texts in long print-runs of 1,000 to 2,000. The symbolism and the inference to 'festina lente', Manutius' motto also employed by Pickering, was lost neither on Panizzi nor on other cognoscenti.

Panizzi was all too aware that in order to make any progress in his studies, especially since he envisaged preparing a critical edition of Boiardo, he had to consult the rare first editions of Ariosto and Boiardo among others, texts which were so rare that they were not in the collections of the British Museum. Panizzi, however, knew a book collector who did possess all these rare books in his library. He was Thomas Grenville.

Thomas Grenville (1755–1846), the statesman and Whig politician, was appointed First Lord of the Admiralty and later Chief Justice in Eyre south of the Trent, posts he largely regarded as sinecures. These posts were ideal for Grenville because they afforded him the opportunity of dedicating himself to his great passion in life—bibliography and book collecting—and to the expansion of his pride and joy, his private library. Grenville's personal library was no ordinary library—far from it. It was, and remains to this day, one of the richest and most glorious collections of printed books ever assembled by, and in the lifetime of, a single private individual, that is to say by an individual who was neither a member of the aristocracy nor a monarch who could afford to employ and rely on a large staff and a sophisticated network of agents who could acquire books on his behalf. Grenville's library consisted of 20,240 volumes, which at first might not appear to be a very large number. Once we realize that a high proportion of these books consisted of incunabula, the first editions of often rare and essential humanist and classical texts and virtually every first edition of important texts starting with Gutenberg's Bible up to and including the 1550s, we begin to fathom the enormous richness of this great library. Grenville owned a copy of the Gutenberg 42-line Bible, yes, but his copy was one of the much rarer copies printed on vellum, of which there are only twelve copies extant (of the 51 copies known, 39 are on paper and 12 on vellum, of these only 20 copies are perfect—the British Library also has a copy on paper; the value of Grenville's vellum copy alone would be in the region of £9 million at today's commercial price). Grenville's copy of the first book printed in Italy, the Lactantius (Subiaco: Conrad Sweynheym and Arnold Pannartz, 1465), is particularly fine, but he possessed many other treasures—the 'unicum', that is to say a complete copy of Ovid printed by Azzoguidi at Bologna in 1471, the *Sforziada* by Simonetta printed in Milan in 1490 and bound and illuminated for Ludovico il Moro, to cite just a few works from this fabulous library, or rather, this veritable treasure-house of the book.

Needless to say, Grenville owned all the very rare editions Panizzi needed to consult and study, particularly the extremely rare first edition of Boiardo's *Sonetti e Canzone* printed by Francesco Mazal at Reggio Emilia on 19 December 1499. Fortunately, Grenville was a man of considerable means who could freely indulge his costly passion and taste for antiquarian books. He was also a very generous man who encouraged scholarship and consequently welcomed Panizzi with open arms.

The first recorded instance we have of the acquaintance between Panizzi and Grenville dates back to 1829. Grenville unstintingly allowed Panizzi to consult and even borrow a copy of every book he required and over the years the two men became good friends. In order to thank Grenville for his many kindnesses to him, Panizzi had a unique copy of his *Bibliographical Notices of Some Early Editions of the Orlando Innamorato and Furioso* (London: William Pickering, 1831, BL pressmark G.11409) specially printed on vellum for the bibliophile. Similarly, Panizzi had another 'unicum' specially printed for Grenville

—a unique copy of his edition of the *Innamorato* (London: William Pickering, 1830–4, BL pressmark G.11094–11102.) printed on blue paper. We should recall that this last work had been very favourably reviewed and had been very well received by the critics, and Panizzi was beginning to acquire a considerable reputation for himself as a formidable scholar and as an Italianist.

Grenville greatly respected Panizzi's bibliographical expertise and often wrote to him in order to elicit his advice and opinion on his antiquarian books, especially those he was thinking of acquiring for his library. It is very interesting to see how Grenville invariably had Panizzi's letters to him 'tipped in' to the books he acquired, almost as if Panizzi's bibliographical opinions had the function of a certificate of authenticity. An example which I have recently discovered is of yet another unpublished letter from Panizzi dated 2 Gower Street North, 6 May 1835, in which Panizzi informs Grenville how rare his edition of the *Divine Comedy* printed by Francesco del Tuppo (Naples, 1478?, BL pressmark G.11348) really is:

2 Gower St. North
May 6th. 1835

Dear Sir,

The edition of Dante which I beg to return is certainly one of the rarest known, and I never heard of any other copy of it but one in the Library of Stuttgart & another in the Magliabechiana at Florence. Dr. Dibdin says that it has 42 lines in each column, which is not *always* true: in some cases the lines are 45. Nor is it correct to say that it is dedicated to Honofrio Caracciolo: it is dedicated to the *Eletti*/viz. the Magistrates *elected* by the people of the City of Naples. Caracciolo was one of them, but his name is followed by those of four others in Tuppo's address: which address is not in the Neapolitan dialect, but in a kind of bastard Italian somewhat tinged with the writer's dialect. Have you observed that Tuppo says that he has caused several law books to be printed by the Germans (undoubtedly Reusinger)?[4] I have never heard of such publications before. The text also of this edition is very remarkable for its excellent various readings, so that in every respect this is an addition to your collection well worthy of it: and no more can be said in its praise. The arms at the bottom of the first leaf were those of the Ginori of Florence.

With many thanks for having afforded me the opportunity of examining this beautiful volume, I have the honor to be, Dear Sir,

Your very obed. serv.
A Panizzi.

The relationship between Panizzi and Grenville at this period, especially in their correspondence, the majority of which has hitherto remained unpublished, is extremely interesting. Despite the literary conventions and formality of 160 years ago, we can trace the growth of the friendship between the two men. Of greater importance to the Boiardo scholar (not to mention the bibliophile and textual and library historian) is the fascinating information the correspondence contains on Panizzi's edition of the *Sonetti e Canzone*, for it provides us with a considerable insight into the history of Panizzi's text and edition. Note the affection, informality, and generosity which pervade Grenville's letter to Panizzi:

(1) Add. MS. 36714, fo. 340

Thomas Grenville to Anthony Panizzi   Stac[k]pole Court
                                                       30th Aug., 1834

Dear Sir,
    I have this morning received your letter, & do not delay to assure you that it has given me infinite pleasure to have given you the accomodation of any of my books, & that I am persuaded they could not have been so properly placed any where as in your hands towards the perfection of so admirable an edition of Ariosto.
    I write by this post to apprise my servant of your wish to have the two editions of Boiardo Sonetti; but as he may not himself be able to find them, I fear I must trouble you to have the goodness to call in Cleveland Square to take them: you will find them with the Italian books in the book-case nearest to the window; I cannot be quite sure that one or both of them may not be at Lewis the binder's—if so will you be so kind as to tell him that you have my authority to take them from him.
    I go from hence to L[or]d Delamere's Vale Royal Northwhich Cheshire where a line will find me any time in Sept^r, should you want any further information.

                    Ever my dear Sir
                    very truly & faithfully yours
                    Thos. Grenville

To which Panizzi replied thanking Grenville for his generosity. It is also fascinating to see how Panizzi greatly valued Grenville's opinion, the latter being a man of such impeccable taste:

(2) Add. MS. 36714, fo. 341

Panizzi to Thomas Grenville   Brit. Mus.

Sept. 8th [1834]

Dear Sir

I have to apologize for not having sooner acknowledged the honor of your note of the 30th of last month, and thanked you for your kind permission to me of taking from your collection the two editions of Bojardo's lyrical poems, both of which are now in my hands. The reason of my delay has been a wish of submitting to your judgment a specimen of the intended edition of the poems. As you well know the difficulties of hitting upon a satisfactory plan and the time lost in alterations however trifling you can explain to your-self the reason of my delay in writing. I have at last this moment received a specimen that I like and I take the liberty of enclosing a proof; and if not presuming too far on your kindness I should like to hear what you think of it. I mean to print only 50 copies of the volume to be given to my friends. As for the notes, of which also I send a specimen I shall omit them altogether if the book were to become too thick by their insertion.

I have the honor to be with great respect
Yours very truly
A. Panizzi

Grenville's reply is equally fascinating because it clearly demonstrates that he not only had a very good eye for typographical layout, clarity of type, and general design but that he also had a very sensitive ear for poetry—he gave Panizzi some very sound advice:

(3) Add. MS. 36714, fo. 334

Vale Royal Northwich
10th Septr 1834.

Dear Sir

I received last night the proofs which you was so good as to send to me which I do not delay to acknowledge, & which appear to me to take a very agreable shape. Of the Sonetto 1 I perceive that you send me two copies marked in mss. 1/ and 2/. The only difference that I observe between them is in the colour of the ink; that marked 1/ is of a much more dark and & distinct colour, & seems on that account highly preferable to that marked 2/ which certainly is in my eyes too faint & feeble, in it's colour. I hope you will not hesitate to add your notes to the original poems; they will much encrease the value of the publication, & the Sonetti are not numerous enough to make any question of the size of the volume.

I see in your note upon Son: 1. v. 9. you are disposed to question the antithesis which it contains, and perhaps 'amara fede' may in these days appear a little quaint, but I confess I think 'dolci inganni' is a very beautiful expression & very appropriate to a love-song.

I suppose in 'l'approvazione che di quelli che tengono Petrarca per infallibile; che certo e a lui che B[oiardo] deve questo neo' the word che, used 4 times in 2 lines, tho' it has a different sense in each, will strike an English ear as too frequently repeated, but I dare not suggest a criticism on Italian words to an eminent Italian scholar, & therefore mention it only to shew that ignorance of a foreign language may in this instance make an English ear over-fastidious from want of sufficient usage of the language.

I really think you cannot improve the form and shape of your publication always supposing that you adopt the darker ink used in No. 1.

I have not returned your proofs because I presume that you have others; but if you wish for them I will send them to you under a frank of Ld Delamere's.

> Ever my dear Sir
> very truly & faithfully yours
>
> Thos. Grenville

To which Panizzi replied:

(4) Add. MS. 36714, fo. 345

Panizzi to Grenville   Brit. Mus.
                                                Sept. 12th [1834]

Dear Sir

I have the honor to acknowledge your note of the day before yesterday. The difference in the proofs sent is : 1st that one is more spaced than the other, and 2.dly that the *heading* of the one in Italics looks better, I think than in Roman. You are right in your critical remarks on the four *che*; but the few lines which I wrote when sending the sonnets to the printer were merely intended as *something* to set up for the specimen I wanted, not as notes which I intended to print.

My objection to 'amara fede' and '*dolci* inganni' is not to the two epithets each by itself but it is to the antithesis of *amara* in opposition to *dolci*. Had the poet said only '*amara* fede' or only '*dolci* inganni' there could not be, I think, any objection.

I forgot to mention that the ink shall certainly be as dark as that used in No. 1.

As this little publication or rather edition is intended <u>for you</u>, I was anxious to obtain your approbation, well knowing besides that if I were so fortunate as to obtain it I might hope not to be reasonably found fault with by men of taste. To tell you the truth I *fancy* the volume (as I almost see it printed, pressed, and bound) as a very fine one. Do not laugh at my conceit. I never did any thing so much *con amore*. With notes and all it will come to about 300 pages.

> I have the honor to be
> with great respect.
> Yours truly
> A. Panizzi

At the foot of this letter Grenville has annotated: 'answered 15 Sept. draft on Coutts 100 £'. The year 1834 has been added by a different hand, presumably at a later date, in red ink.

Although Grenville was very flattered by Panizzi's wish to dedicate the edition of the *Sonetti e Canzone* to him, he was rather reluctant to grant Panizzi his permission, especially since he knew that the very limited edition of fifty copies Panizzi proposed was not going to be commercially available. Displaying his customary generosity, Grenville sent Panizzi a draft in the magnificent sum of £100 (equivalent to almost six months' salary for Panizzi), accompanied by the following letter:

(5) Add. MS. 36714, fo. 347

Thomas Grenville to Anthony Panizzi   Vale Royal
                                                   15 Septr 1834

Dear Sir,

Now that you have been so good as to point out the grounds on which you prefer the type marked No.2, I entirely concur with your opinion that, being more spread it has a more agreable & more Italian character. Admitting however, as I do, the objections which you make to the antithesis of two epithets such as 'dolci' & 'amari', I am nevertheles more lenient & indulgent on this subject, from it's being an error into which almost all the oldest of the modern poets Italian & English & Spanish will be found to have indulged, & none more so than our own Shakespear, whose authority like that of your Petrarca tho' it does not vindicate the practice, abates the ardour of my critical comments.

Thus far my pen runs on easily, but the latter part of your letter touches upon a subject of more difficulty because of more delicacy. I have always been truly sensible to the kindness with which you have satisfied the occasional literary enquiries with which you have allowed me to trouble you, & with which you have taken so friendly an interest in the details of my small Collection of books & in its gradual improvement; but to permit, if I may use such a word, or to encourage you to incur the expence of printing a work of 300 pages *for me* without any intention of remunerating yourself by the sale of the work, is what upon no consideration I ought or could be brought, as far as I am concerned, to consent to.

At the same time I cannot but be disposed most gratefully to accept your present, & most anxiously to assist in promoting your literary labours, so useful to all readers of taste & so creditable to the distinguished editor. As an humble associate in so laudable an undertaking, I trust you will have the goodness to accept me as such, & have therefore taken the liberty of enclosing a small advance as you will see in the note to Coutts which accompanies this. By your kind concurrence in this indispensible course, you will encrease your claim upon my grateful acknowledgements for your welcome present, & will thus relieve me from difficulties otherwise insuperable.

I cannot but add likewise my earnest wish that you would be induced, after you have indulged your liberality in your presents to your friends, to give the work to the publick, & to derive from it the profit to which you are so justly entitled.

Once more, Dear Sir, accept my grateful thanks for your intended present which will be a most valuable addition to my library.

> Ever very truly & faithfully
> Yours
> Thomas Grenville

(6) Add. MS. 36714, fo. 353

Mess[rs]: Coutts & Co Strand London

Be pleased to answer the Draft of A. Pannizi [*sic*] Esq[r] of the British Museum for One Hundred Pounds on my account.
100 £,   Thomas Grenville
15 Sept[r]: 1834

Grenville's Draft has been scored through by Panizzi, thereby making the Draft null and void.

Panizzi was very moved and flattered by Grenville's very generous offer. He may also have been a little embarrassed by the offer, almost as if he thought he could have given Grenville the impression that that was precisely what he had been 'angling for' all along—the upshot of the matter was that Panizzi replied to Grenville stating that he could not accept his very generous offer:

(7) Add. MS. 36714, fo. 354

Anthony Panizzi to Thomas Grenville

British Mus.
Sept. 17th 1834

Dear Sir

I have just now received the kind note with which you have honored me and I cannot conceal how greatly mortified I am at the *indispensible* condition, as you call it, on which you will do me the honor of allowing me to dedicate to you the edition of Bojardo's lyrical poems. I do assure you that if you insist upon it it will be a very great disappointment to me. I have taken a liking to Bojardo's poems because they are, in my opinion remarkably fine, because I owe him a great deal (since it is thro' *him* that I have had the honor of becoming acquainted with you more than would have been likely to be the case had he not written the Innamorato) and because he was born in my native province; and I, having been in the habit of spending many of my younger days at Scandiano, feel great pleasure in being occupied with the works of a poet whose name is connected in my mind with so many dear recollections. I intend printing a limited number of copies of the lyrical poems because few persons can appreciate them, and still fewer will buy them; whilst the present will be more acceptable if only a few copies of a book not published for sale, be offered to an amateur.

It was this last circumstance which induced me to beg of you to condescend to have the book inscribed to you: for as it would be seen only by those who knew us both, or even either of us, a dedication could not be considered but what it really is intended to be, an expression of gratitude and respect really felt and due. Were I to say that the thought of editing a volume which was to be so inscribed did not render the occupation still more agreable than it would have been, I should not state the fact; but I can truly say that the edition will be proceeded with at all events even should you not allow me to offer it to you—a determination which I hope you will not take. You will see from this that you neither cause, permit or encourage expence, and that consequently I cannot consent to your bearing any.

With many and many thanks for your kindness, and in hope that you will not deprive me of the anticipated pleasure of inscribing my little volume to you, I have the honor to be, with great respect

   Yours very truly
   A Panizzi

Grenville thought that he had offended Panizzi and wrote a prompt reply in which he acceded to his wishes:

(8) Add. MS. 36714, fo. 356

Thomas Grenville to Anthony Panizzi   Vale Royal
                                                  19 Sept^r: 1834

Dear Sir,
I hasten to acknowledge your letter which I have just received. I had hoped
to have overcome the delicacy of your scruples in a matter which appeared
to me likely to press very unreasonably upon you; but your letter expresses
so strong a sense of mortification & disappointment at the earnestness of my
proposal, that I can only say that I will leave the decision upon it entirely to
your own consideration & judgment: & that personally I cannot but be
highly flattered & gratified by the wish that your letter so kindly announces
of dedicating to me your volume of Boiardo's sonnets. Of the more or less
probability that there might be of the volume having an extensive sale, if
given to publication, you are better able to judge than I am, but your doubt
of it's being so is a severe satire upon the taste of the publick, if your doubts
are well founded.

I have only once more to repeat that my former letter had no other object
than that of doing what might be gratifying to you, & that I wish you to do
about it whatever is most agreable to yourself, & that you may be assured that
in all events I shall be highly honoured & gratified by your inscribing the
book to me.

                    I am Dear Sir
                    very truly yours
                    Thomas Grenville

Panizzi did finally dedicate his edition of the *Sonetti e Canzone* to
Grenville and sent him the very first copy off the press. He later had
one of only two copies specially printed on blue paper which he later
presented to Grenville (Milan, 1845; BL pressmark G.11103).

In an unpublished holograph in the Egerton Manuscripts recently
discovered and brought to my attention by Neil Harris, to whom I
am much obliged and whom I wish to thank publicly, Panizzi drew
up a list of friends and a list of the great and the good to whom he
wished to donate a copy of Boiardo's lyrics. The list is important
because firstly it affords us with a rare insight into whom Panizzi may
have been attempting to influence in furthering his career and in his
eventual bid for increased power and influence at the British Museum;
secondly it confirms that Panizzi was still endeavouring to catch the
eye of the influential and was striving to enhance his scholarly
reputation; and thirdly it provides us with an insight into the 'pecking
order' of his friends and the influence he ascribed to them:

Egerton MS. 3677, fo. 469.

Boiardo's lyrics   May 20 1835

1. The King [i.e. William IV]
2. Mr Grenville
3. Lord Brougham
4. The Arch. of Canterbury
5. Lord Lansdown
6. Lord Farnborough
7. Lady Dacre
8. Lord Grey
9. Rogers
10. Lord Auckland
11. Lord Sandon
12. Renouard
13. Mrs Gaskell
14. Mrs Ainsworth
15. Shepherd
16. Roscoe
17. Haywood
18. Ewart
19. My friend [Neil Harris and I have identified this intriguing entry as
    His Royal Highness The Duke d'Aumale]
20. Hallam
21. Brit. Museum
22. Melzi
23. Lord Cawdor
24. Mrs Bilby Thompson
25. Conte d'Agliè
26. Dr Hawtree
27. Mad^{me} Mollier
28. Mrs Ford
29. Courtenay
30. Macaulay
31. Molini
32. Trivulzio
33. Mr Rutherford Lord Advocate
34. Mr Will E. Gladstone
[...]
39. Barnwell
40. Holmes

Incidentally, the list shows to what extent Panizzi's circle of friends had widened by 1835. The list is quite impressive, considering Panizzi had only been in England for precisely twelve years.

As we know, Panizzi's career was meteoric and he was eventually promoted and appointed to the post of Principal Librarian and Director of the entire British Museum in 1856. Some of Panizzi's greatest achievements, apart from his scholarly editions, include the enforcement of the Copyright Act, the creation of the laid-down catalogue, his ninety-one cataloguing rules, and of course, his famous Round Reading Room, opened in 1857 at a cost of £150,000. He received his knighthood in 1869.

Finally 'dulcis in fundo', yet one other great benefit was to be derived from Panizzi's studies of Boiardo. Because of his long friendship with Thomas Grenville, which, as we have seen, started in 1829, and which resulted in Panizzi's studies of Ariosto and especially Boiardo, Panizzi was able to play a very significant part in influencing Grenville to bequeath his fabulous library to the British Museum. Having been treated somewhat shabbily by the Museum's Trustees, Grenville originally had decided to bequeath his library to his nephew, the Duke of Buckingham, who, in all probability, given his financial circumstances, would have sold it off and it would have been dispersed for ever. Panizzi was determined that this tragic scenario should never take place and clearly influenced Grenville into revoking his bequest to his nephew in a codicil. Grenville acceded to Panizzi's wishes and informed him of the contents of his new will, bequeathing his library to the Museum as early as 1845. Grenville had sworn Panizzi to secrecy about the fabulous bequest. Panizzi never betrayed the secret, although knowing Panizzi's temperament, it must have been very difficult for him not to have 'given the game away' when Watts and other members of his staff came to him with offers of rare books advertised in booksellers' catalogues—antiquarian books which the Museum Library did not possess and desperately needed—especially when he had to turn down these offers in the certain knowledge that all these books and many, many more besides, would soon fall into his lap like a ripe plum.

Panizzi did not have to wait long. Thomas Grenville died at Hamilton Place, Piccadilly on 17 December 1846. The British Museum began receiving his exquisite library of 20,240 volumes valued at £50,000, a veritable fortune at the time, early in 1847. The Grenville library is without doubt one of the richest and most important additions to the National Library's collections 'tout court'. Indeed the addition of Grenville's library (coupled with the earlier addition of the Library of

George III in 1837) transformed the British Museum Library from a 'second division' library into one of world-wide importance, virtually overnight—especially with Grenville's superb collection of the works of Homer, Aesop, Ariosto, Boiardo, Dante, Tasso, Pulci, and countless other classical, humanist, and Italian authors too numerous to cite. Suffice it to say that Anthony Panizzi, particularly through his study of Boiardo, and together with his great friendship with Thomas Grenville, ensured that the British Museum, since 1973 the British Library, and indeed posterity, have all inherited a superlative library in general, and a glorious collection of Italian and Italianate fifteenth- and sixteenth-century books in particular, which today forms the very heart and kernel of one of the world's finest collections of printed books.

Indeed it would not be an exaggeration to conclude that had the Grenville Library not been secured for, and bequeathed to, the British Museum, research in London today into the culture of Italy from 1465 to the 1550s in general, and on that of the 1490s in particular, would have been considerably more difficult to undertake—now that certainly would have been a crisis!

Notes to Chapter 8

1. M. Davies, 'Promoting Poggio', *Italian Studies*, 48 (1993), 45.
2. British Library, Add. MS. 36714, fo. 354.
3. British Library, Add. MS. 36714, fo. 398.
4. The German printer is usually referred to as Sixtus Riessinger, of whom little is known except that he was born *c.*1445 and printed in Rome and later in Naples in collaboration with Del Tuppo. He died after 1502.

INDEX